M000114053

THE SACRAMENT OF PENANCE AND RELIGIOUS LIFE

IN GOLDEN AGE SPAIN

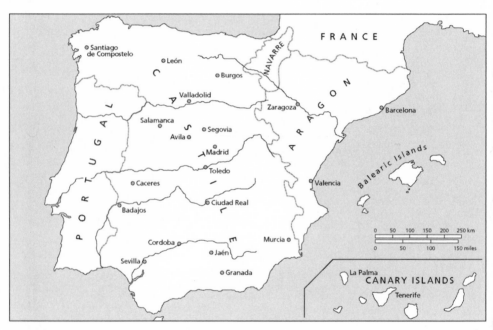

Early modern Spain

M000114053

arly modern Spain

THE SACRAMENT OF PENANCE AND RELIGIOUS LI

IN GOLDEN AGE SPAIN

# THE † SACRAMENT OF PENANCE AND RELIGIOUS LIFE † IN † GOLDEN AGE SPAIN

*Patrick J. O'Banion*

THE PENNSYLVANIA STATE UNIVERSITY PRESS
UNIVERSITY PARK, PENNSYLVANIA

Portions of the text were previously published in
Patrick J. O'Banion, "A Priest Who Appears Good:
Manuals of Confession and the Construction of Clerical
Identities in Early Modern Spain," in *Dutch Review of
Church History*, vol. 85, *The Formation of Clerical and
Confessional Identities in Early Modern Europe*, edited by
Wim Janse and Barbara Pitkin (Leiden: Brill, 2006), 333–48.

Library of Congress Cataloging-in-Publication Data

O'Banion, Patrick J., 1975–
    The sacrament of penance and religious life in golden
    age Spain / Patrick J. O'Banion.
        p.        cm.
Summary: "Explores the role of the sacrament of penance in
the religion and society of early modern Spain. Examines how
secular and ecclesiastical authorities used confession to defend
against heresy and to bring reforms to the Catholic Church"
—Provided by publishers.
Includes bibliographical references (p.        ) and index.
ISBN 978-0-271-05899-3 (cloth : alk. paper)
1. Penance—Spain—History.
2. Catholic Church—Spain—History.
3. Spain—Religious life and customs.
4. Catholic Church—Discipline—History.
5. Church discipline—History.
6. Confession—History.
I. Title.

BX2260.O23 2013
264'.020860946—dc23
2012017709

Copyright © 2012 The Pennsylvania State University
All rights reserved
Printed in the United States of America
Published by The Pennsylvania State University Press,
University Park, PA 16802–1003

The Pennsylvania State University Press is a member of the
Association of American University Presses.

It is the policy of The Pennsylvania State University Press to
use acid-free paper. Publications on uncoated stock satisfy
the minimum requirements of American National Standard
for Information Sciences—Permanence of Paper for Printed
Library Material, ANSI Z39.48–1992.

This book is printed on Nature's Natural, which contains
30% post-consumer waste.

FOR *Rachel*

# CONTENTS

## ACKNOWLEDGMENTS

After being so long at work on a project about sin and its forgiveness, it's difficult not to feel a strong sense of the debts I owe and the mercies I have received, for they are many. Like a good confessor, Hal Parker has served as a mentor for many years, always encouraging and available, both trustworthy and probing, and patiently willing to listen and instruct. I am honored to have received his attention as a doctoral student and continue to be grateful for his friendship. Over the years, Christine Caldwell Ames, Jodi Bilinkoff, Wietse de Boer, John Edwards, Phil Gavitt, Jim Hitchcock, Tom Madden, Nick Paul, Carla Rahn Philips, Richard Pym, Erin Rowe, Damian Smith, and too many others to name have offered helpful suggestions, read drafts, and given prudent criticism.

Throughout the course of this project, I was fortunate to receive funding from a number of institutions. Without their support I would not have been able to work in the libraries and archives of Spain or to spend time analyzing and writing about what I found there. I offer special thanks to the Fulbright Foundation, the American Historical Association, the ACLS, the Andrew W. Mellon Foundation, and the Program for Cultural Cooperation Between Spain's Ministry of Culture and United States Universities. My time abroad was the richer for having met and learned from James Amelang, Ray Ball, Nick Bomba, Mercedes García-Arenal, Bill Goldman, Mayte Green-Mercado, J Melvin, and María Tausiet.

Closer to home, the generosity and encouragement of many people have sped this book toward completion. Jason and Camden Chang, Chris and Jessica Chong, Walker and Kirsten Cosgrove, Lloyd and Heather Jackson, Brian Lee, Max and Chrissy Seraj, and Jay and Jen Simmons have opened their hearts and homes in unforgettable ways. An ever-growing number of Beneses, O'Banions, Azars, Vander Meulens, and Westenbroeks have provided the support that only family can offer. At Lindenwood University, Jeff and Kris Smith have helped me negotiate the demands of teachings and writing. By right, my most heartfelt expression of thanks goes to my wife, Rachel. She has not only patiently endured the time it has taken to complete this project; she has rejoiced with me in my vocation along the way. This book is for her.

# ABBREVIATIONS AND CONVENTIONS

| ADC | Archivo Diocesano de Cuenca |
| AGS | Archivo General de Simancas |
| CCC | Consejo y Comisaría de Cruzada |
| PRCD | Patronato Real, Concilios y Disciplina Eclésiastica |
| PRCS | Patronato Real, Cruzada y Subsidio |
| AHN | Archivo Histórico Nacional de España (Madrid) |
| BAV | Biblioteca Apostolica Vaticana (Rome) |
| BNM | Biblioteca Nacional de España (Madrid) |
| doc. | documento |
| exp. | expediente (record) |
| Inq. | Inquisición |
| leg. | legajo (file) |
| MHSI | Monumenta Historica Societatis Iesu |
| p.a. | primera audiencia (first audience) |

For unfoliated inquisitorial manuscripts, the date of the testimony or a description of where in the trial documents the citation occurs (e.g., *primera audiencia*) has been provided. If a manuscript comprises a single folio, no folio number is given.

Modern accents have been added to proper names, but original spelling has been retained as it appears in the source documents unless a standard English equivalent exists: Ysabel Martínez, but Teresa of Avila. A similar convention has been used with place-names.

# INTRODUCTION

There is a corresponding increase both in the priest's power . . . and of his knowledge. . . . The power and knowledge of the priest and church are caught up in a mechanism that forms around confession as the central element of penance.
—MICHEL FOUCAULT

During the summer of 1581, the inhabitants of Los Sauces on the island of La Palma in the Canaries alerted the Inquisition that one Pantaleón de Casanova had, for some years, shirked his annual duty to confess.[1] The witnesses were sworn to secrecy, but perhaps Casanova got wind of trouble; on 10 September he tried to remedy the situation by confessing to a Franciscan friar on Tenerife Island. "How long has it been since you last confessed?" the friar asked. "Well," responded the layman, "I didn't make my annual confession this year, but usually I do, just like the Holy Mother Church commands." Casanova described how an episcopal representative had threatened him with excommunication unless he separated from the woman with whom he was living. "Since I didn't want to throw her out," he told the friar, "I didn't confess. Instead, I left Los Sauces." Now he was trying to "leave for Spain and get off this island."[2]

Casanova found the Holy Office as unimpressed by his attempts to avoid prosecution as it was unhappy about his repeated failures to confess. It considered him "suspect of heresy for having remained aloof from the sacraments of penance and the Eucharist for so long."[3] Many of his neighbors testified against Casanova. Not even his parish priest (*cura*) could offer protection; he had never confessed the defendant.

The sacrament of penance, one of the seven sacraments of the Roman Catholic Church, which served as conduits of grace between God and the faithful,

The epigraph to this chapter is drawn from Foucault, *Abnormal*, 176.

had its roots in sinful humanity's need to be reconciled with a holy deity. That need for forgiveness went beyond merely addressing the actual sins that people committed on a daily basis, for everyone was born separated from God as a consequence of Adam's rebellion. This state of original sin necessitated the cleansing waters of baptism, which infused grace and made the recipient a beneficiary of Christ's meritorious sacrifice on the cross. Baptism cleansed sinners of the guilt (*culpa*) they incurred from original sin and satisfied the punishment (*poena*) they deserved. It also removed the stain of guilt and paid the penalty for any actual sins committed before baptism. It granted entry to the church and made the recipient a child and friend of God. But the temptations of the world, the flesh, and the devil frequently lured Christians from the righteous path. Sins committed after baptism not only incurred new guilt but demanded additional punishment.

Yet, according to the Roman church, not all sins were equal. Some were venial and could be expiated simply by confessing them to God and making restitution. They did not demand priestly intercession in the sacrament of penance. But more serious sins, which killed the grace infused at baptism, were mortal; those who committed them became "children of wrath and enemies of God."[4] The *culpa* for such offenses could only be remitted sacramentally. While the early church had allowed penance only once in a lifetime, during the Middle Ages it became possible to receive the sacrament multiple times. Indeed, in the famous decree *Omnis utriusque sexus* the Fourth Lateran Council (1215) had obliged all Christians who had reached the age of accountability (about age seven) to confess their mortal sins to their own priest (*proprio sacerdoti*, typically understood to mean their parish priest) at least once a year before receiving the Eucharist.[5] When they did so, penitents needed more than just a desire to avoid suffering eternal punishment, or *attrition*. While fear of hellfire might draw the sinner toward confession, the sacrament itself was necessary to transform attrition into *contrition*, sorrow for having offended God combined with the intention of not persisting in the sin.[6]

In most cases, the priest subsequently either absolved the sinner of guilt or pronounced the confessant excommunicate, but some serious offenses, known as reserved sins, were passed on to higher ecclesiastical officials. The judicial power by which priests declared the forgiveness or condemnation of sinners was rooted in the power of binding and loosing given by Jesus to Peter in Matthew 16:19, according to the Roman church's reading of that passage. As Peter's successor, the pope wielded authority on earth to bind and loose spiritually by absolving or excommunicating. He delegated this power to bishops

*Fig. 1*   Confession and communion. From Luis de Granada, *A Memoriall of a Christian Life* (Rouen [London], 1599), 215. Courtesy of Saint Louis University Libraries, Special Collections.

and priests, who meted out God's justice and mercy in the forum of confession in the name of the Father, Son, and Holy Spirit.

While *culpa* could be absolved, sinful actions still required restitution in the form of *poena*. Although offenses committed against a supremely exalted and holy God deserved eternal punishment, the atoning sacrifice of Christ had satisfied divine justice on their behalf. Yet the damages caused by both mortal and venial sins had to be set right in the here and now as well as in eternity, and this meant addressing the demands of temporal punishment. It was for this reason that confessors assigned penances or acts of satisfaction (*opera satisfactionis*). These might be horizontal communal acts, like restoring stolen goods or reconciling with a neighbor. They might be directed vertically through the saying of prayers such as the Our Father and Hail Mary or in the completion of pilgrimages and fasts. Or they might combine the horizontal and the vertical by, for example, obliging the sinner to attend public masses while holding lighted tapers or wearing penitential garb. Through these *opera satisfactionis* sinners endured punishment for their sins.

Yet it often happened that believers, whose sins had been absolved in confession, died before making full restitution of the temporal punishments those sins demanded, by failing to complete acts of satisfaction or completing them imperfectly. Thus the church came to understand the need for a doctrine of purgatory. Sinners who had been restored to good fellowship with God but who had not yet been completely purged of the remnants of sin spent time in this antechamber to heaven. Only Christians entered purgatory, and everyone in purgatory eventually went to heaven, but only after making full restitution for sins and undergoing a process of refinement.

In premodern Europe, the boundaries between the here and the hereafter were often permeable, and so it was possible for those living on earth to aid their loved ones in purgatory, just as it was possible for the heavenly host to assist earthly or purgatorial pilgrims. By endowing masses, praying for the intercession of saints, and gaining indulgences for the dead, friends and relatives could speed the souls of beloved sinners on their way to heaven. Those who did so hoped that, when they died, others would act in a similar fashion on their behalf.

We can speak, then, not merely of a sacrament of penance, which was necessary for getting into heaven, but of a great penitential economy that suffused culture and was foundational to religious life. This system underwent dramatic challenges during the early modern period, especially from Martin Luther's rapidly spreading reform movement, which denied the confession's sacramental character, viewed acts of satisfaction as works righteousness, and attacked the doctrines of indulgences and purgatory.[7] But as the story of Pantaleón de Casanova suggests, even in stoutly Roman Catholic Spain, people had variegated experiences with the sacrament of penance.

To be sure, Casanova made a mess of his confessional obligations, but his story emphasizes the complex reality of the sacrament in an early modern context; it could put confessants in a real bind. In Casanova's case, in order to receive absolution, he would have had to put his mistress out. Failure to do so meant excommunication, spiritual (and often social) separation from the community of believers. The sacrament thus engendered moral reform by exposing sinful activity—here, illicit sexuality and interaction with a potential heretic, for his lover was a descendant of converted Muslims, a *morisca*. Community life also exerted strong influence upon the confessional experience. Family, friends, and neighbors often provided ill-treated penitents with invaluable support, but here the inhabitants of Los Sauces turned against one of their own. Finally, the episode gestures at the defendant's (unsuccessful) attempt to circumvent the system of penitential regulation by confessing outside his parish and trying to get "off this island."

In early modern Spain, the sacrament proved trying in other ways as well. Many felt conflicted about revealing deeply guarded secrets to fallible confessors, particularly when they played an active role in a community's social life. Although priests were bound to confidentiality by the seal of confession, a priest might (maliciously or inadvertently) let slip a few words that could damage a penitent's reputation. Especially for women, confession entailed the possibility of sexual solicitation and subsequent public scandal. To heretics and even to the misinformed, the sacrament posed a threat because confessors used the encounter to determine parishioners' orthodoxy. Many early modern churchmen came to view confession as the linchpin in a program to reform the religious lives of laypeople, since priests used the encounter to examine, catechize, and correct. Ecclesiastical superiors ordered confessors to deny absolution to penitents who could not recite the appropriate prayers or who had not sufficiently scoured their conscience in preparation for the sacrament. For the numerous reserved sins, among them heresy, public blasphemy, and sexual solicitation in the confessional, the church obliged priests to remit penitents to the pope, the bishop, or the Holy Office.

Confessants had their own agendas, of course. Most saw confession as a necessary stop on the road to salvation and so they participated in it. Some formed deep spiritual friendships with confessors. As the early modern church pressed penitents to meet their confessional obligations and ratcheted up expectations about what constituted a complete and fruitful sacramental encounter, most laypeople in Spain responded by meeting those expectations. They did a better job of completing their mandatory annual confession and often participated in the sacrament at other times during the year as well. Most memorized the prayers of the church and the Ten Commandments and learned how to make the sign of the cross properly, when to kneel, and how to demonstrate proper humility in the confessional. This did not mean, however, that confessants became merely passive participants in the encounter. Laypeople knew what scandals could arise from confessing embarrassing sins or sins that demanded public penance. They valued their good standing in the community and vigorously guarded their honor. If they rarely refused outright to engage in the sacrament, they often took part warily. Some deceived their priests, leaving embarrassing or entangling sins undisclosed, but confessants knew that doing so tempted the justice and mercy of God.

Such inconveniences make it all the more remarkable that during the early modern period the sacrament of penance became more attractive to laypeople. In fifteenth- and early sixteenth-century Spain, the sacrament lacked both rigor and force. While the idea of penitence was deeply embedded in religious culture, auricular confession was a marginal component of religious life.[8] Yet in the decades that followed it moved to the center, becoming a prominent component of lay devotion. In terms of popularity, proliferation, emphasis, and theological, material, and liturgical development, Spain's *siglo de oro* proved to be a golden age for confession.

This gold, however, contained a certain quantity of dross, for during this period Spanish confessional practice, while in theory well regulated, rarely adhered to the letter of the law. After the Council of Trent (1545–63), the kings of Spain urged bishops and archbishops across the Iberian Peninsula to convene provincial councils and episcopal synods, which formulated intricate programs for enforcing penitential compliance at the parish level. All baptized Christians were to confess annually to their parish priest, normally at Lent before receiving the Eucharist—the Easter duty. If the number of penitents proved overwhelming, the *cura* could draft other episcopally licensed confessors to meet the demand. *Curas* were to keep registers (*matrículas* or *padrónes*) in which they recorded which parishioners had fulfilled their paschal obligations. The names of those who failed to do so were read aloud at Mass and posted in their church for all to see. Parish priests were to pronounce the obstinate excommunicate and annually forward *matrículas* to the bishop. This would make apparent whether the local minister had been shepherding his flock conscientiously and open the way for bishops to pursue recalcitrant sheep with more severe measures. Prolonged refusal to confess would result in a denunciation to the Holy Office on charges of heresy (for obstinately disobeying the precepts of the church), an inquisitorial trial, and, at least theoretically, relaxation to the secular arm and death.

This system was clear and rigid. It recalls Keith Thomas's description of the sacrament: "The personal confession and interrogation of every single layman was potentially an altogether more comprehensive system of social discipline than the isolated prosecution of relatively notorious offenders."[9] Likewise, confession's dependence upon the communication of information to authority figures conjures Michel Foucault's depiction of the relationship between knowledge and power.[10] Foucault suggests that confessors and their ecclesiastical superiors wielded power because they had knowledge; this conjunction of knowledge and power facilitated social discipline. Thomas Tentler has similarly argued, "Knowledge supports the authority of the priest. He is in control because he has the requisite information to conduct the confession with confidence."[11]

The confessional may have had great disciplinary potential, and sometimes it afforded a Foucauldian combination of knowledge and power that enabled authorities to exercise control over confessants. The parish reality, however, rarely allowed confession such a robust function. This conclusion runs counter to expectations, particularly since Spain has so often been viewed as the acme of oppressive religiosity, rife with inquisitors, their lay cronies (*familiares*), seminary-trained priests, and the powerful arm of the secular state using religion to perpetuate entrenched authority. Nevertheless, the ramshackle settlements that grew up at the local level bore only a passing resemblance to the plans devised in the corridors of power. Priests rarely refused to comply with the demands of their superiors, and laypeople rarely viewed themselves as religious renegades, but the parish proved rather untidy and far too complex a context for synodal decrees to address adequately.

Still, Foucault was right to say that knowledge implied power, and the early modern confessional was a rich fount of knowledge.[12] The power that flowed from it, however, did not flow in one direction, for the sacrament was as much a system of inclusion as of exclusion, as much an affair of the laity as of the clergy, as much a means by which laypeople were empowered as a method by which the powerful remained in control. In confession, power was negotiated, not forfeited.

This notion of *negotiation* has proved to be a handy tool for focusing attention on the dialogical nature of sacramental encounters. Priests never simply imposed Tridentine norms on confession at the local level, because no clear, authoritative Tridentine voice existed to tell a confessor how to interact with the bewildering diversity of penitents with whom he came into contact. This was not for lack of trying; theologians formulated a vast array of instructions, guidebooks, and practical advice for confessing early modern Spaniards. Ultimately, however, too broad a range of (often contradictory) decrees and advice existed. In the midst of this ambiguity, the confessor and, significantly, his confessants found it expedient to interpret and apply those prescriptions according to their best judgment. This flexibility in the relationship between dominant (clerical) and subordinate (lay) groups allowed confession to maintain popular legitimacy into the modern era.

There is another sense in which *negotiation* is a useful concept for studying penitential activity. Confessants negotiated the sacrament by navigating, often with practiced skill, the loopholes and gray areas in the system of confessional regulation formulated at the episcopal level. Rather than alienating people, this bureaucratization actually enabled them to engage that sacrament in new and creative ways. It became easier to circumvent specific priests, avoid entanglements with high ecclesiastical authorities, fulfill sacramental obligations, and redress grievances.

Councils could decree and bishops could legislate; kings and queens could demand obedience to church and state, but when a sinner knelt before a confessor in the confessional, they entered into a dialogue. The personalities, theological leanings, and social status of the priest and penitent, their feelings toward each other, their lineage, gender, ethnicity, and reputation, their familiarity with each other—all of these variables affected that conversation, but none of them fully determined its course. In most cases, the possibility existed that, if both parties played their parts well, the end would be a mutually satisfying process of reconciliation in which sins were confessed and absolution granted.

## Historians and the History of Confession

Historians find themselves on much firmer ground for studying these complicated interactions than they were even a generation ago. A bumper crop of research on Roman Catholic Europe and its non-European mission fields has grown up alongside studies on Protestant and Orthodox regions and cross-confessional analyses.[13] In meeting the challenge posed by John Bossy in 1975 to infuse real life into a "bloodless universe" of penitential *summae* and theological debate, scholars have focused the historical lens on how individuals, especially laypeople, experienced the sacrament in relatively delimited times and places.[14]

Rather than read prescriptive treatises and decrees alone, historians have turned up new sources for the study of confession—saints' lives, visitation reports, trial transcripts, parish records, written confessions, marginalia, wills, and such artifacts of material culture as confessionals, religious art, and church architecture. This has revealed an incredibly intricate world. The tortuous theological debates about sin and the forgiveness of sin became heated during the early modern period, but those who sought forgiveness in confession and those who administered the sacrament found themselves embroiled in controversies and debates every bit as intense, and often much more personal. While confession rarely led to bloodshed, it frequently raised blood pressures.

We have also come to realize confession's intimate connection to other historical themes. Roman Catholic confession, for example, required that at least one of the parties involved be an ordained priest. But who were these priests, and how did they differ (or not) from their medieval predecessors? What about their relationships with the faithful whose souls they tended? These questions have led historians of confession to the topic of clerical formation, since the Council of Trent placed local clergy on the front lines of the reforming program; they became both its main targets and its chosen tools for effecting grassroots change.[15] As the church's local representatives, parish clergy needed a behavioral and educational reformation of their own before they could effectively reform their flocks.

Many members of the ecclesiastical hierarchy pursued this goal, even mandated its implementation, with seminary training as the preferred path to success. Did improvements actually occur? Some historians have argued that local priests underwent a process of professionalization during the early modern era. As a result, they became the unwanted purveyors—unwanted by the laity, at least—of an alien system of baroque Tridentine morality among marginally Christianized European laypeople.[16] This suggests that while priests may have labored to implement reforms, the laity did not necessarily approve of their efforts. Andrew Barnes put it this way: "In the end, the reform of the parochial clergy pushed the rural laity further away from the church."[17]

Other historians have questioned this model of clerical professionalization, emphasizing that laypeople often held on to customs and traditions in spite of reforming programs, or that they actually sought better-trained clergy, becoming an impetus for reform in their own right. Marc Forster and Allyson Poska, among others, have emphasized the laity's ability to arrive at compromised religious settlements with local priests and, sometimes, to resist the implementation of reform altogether.[18] Unfortunately, historians of early modern Europe still know very little about the secular clergy, and in Spain this lacuna is particularly acute.[19] Nevertheless, to judge from the example of northern Italy, there is every reason to question the effectiveness of seminaries in forming priests along a Tridentine model until the eighteenth century.[20]

Historians often focus on the role played by local clergy as enforcers of ecclesiastical reforming programs at the parish level, an emphasis that stems from historiographical debates about the relationship between religion, social discipline, civilizing processes, and state formation.[21] Here, clerics become the purveyors of top-down programs, and confession itself becomes the locus wherein the church regulated moral order and enforced social discipline, a veritable instrument for the onset of modernity. Yet the compromised nature of local religious settlements and the incomplete character of early modern clerical formation bid one take great care in claiming confession as a mechanism for modernization. In fact, the local implementation of reforming programs for sacramental confession indicates that bottom-up initiatives affected practice as much as did top-down decrees.

As this suggests, another important historiographical axis for confession is the role of lay agency. Concepts of social discipline, confessionalization, and Christianization are distinct in many regards.[22] However, historians tend to view early modern reforming programs as implemented from on high upon a passive and oppressed laity. Tentler, for example, sees the fact that "hierarchical and priestly authorities are in command" of the sacrament as an "almost truistic observation," and he argues that medieval *summae* were "designed to present a coherent system in which [those authorities] can order, threaten, persuade, control."[23] From this vantage point, the power relations at play appear truly lopsided.

Michel Foucault, who emphasized the dialogical nature of confession, was still drawn to a top-down model. Even as states built institutions that allowed them to exercise control over subjects' bodies, the church developed "an immense apparatus of discourse and examination, of analysis and control," wherein "all, or almost all, of an individual's life, thought, and action" passed through the confessional to be seen and heard by the priest.[24] To be sure, Foucault hardly imagined these interactions between laypeople and clerics occurring in a vacuum. They happened in a hierarchically ordered society in which religious authority entailed power that could be wielded in various ways. Confession, then, became "a ritual that unfolds within a power relationship." The recipient of the confession, Foucault explained, became more than a simple interlocutor; he became "the authority who requires the confession, prescribes and appreciates it, and intervenes in order to judge, punish, forgive, console, and reconcile."[25]

This insight, certainly an important part of the larger picture, deserves careful reflection. Foucault tied these developments to the program advanced at Trent and modeled for implementation by Archbishop Carlo Borromeo in Milan (r. 1564–84).[26] However, many scholars have emphasized that reforming programs promulgated at the highest levels always became negotiated phenomena when brought into contact with local communities.[27] In France, for example, while a rhetoric of rigorous reform dominated discourse about clerical behavior, the parish reality failed to correspond: "Once they were left alone with their flocks, the clergy naturally responded with a series of makeshift compromises."[28] Likewise, the power relations at work between confessors and confessants demand cautious and patient analysis. Confessants, particularly devout ones, exercised real influence, and priests often needed the penitential exchange as much as those they confessed.[29] All of this suggests that perhaps confessors were not the only ones judging, punishing, forgiving, consoling, and reconciling.

Spaniards participated in the sacrament of penance from their youth. They discussed it in church, on the streets, and at home. They understood, with a perspective born of experience and necessity, the ins and outs of confession. They knew how to use the elaborate top-down system of confessional regulation formulated at the episcopal level to their advantage. To be sure, sacramental confession typically operated in the midst of a hierarchical structure, with the priest exercising authority over the penitent. At times, confessants experienced that structure as oppressive or wrong. However, this did not mitigate the vast array of loopholes and tricks that laypeople used, before, during, and after the encounter, to minimize potential dangers and disadvantages.

The oppressive use of religious power tended (as it still does) to fall most heavily upon weak and marginalized members of society. Just as nobles seldom faced the inquisitorial tribunal for blasphemy, so well-born women rarely became targets for priests who sexually solicited their penitents.[30] Confession thus intersects the field of gender and minority studies and questions about how the early modern reformations affected these groups. Certainly, on the issue of women, opinions have been divided in recent decades.[31] Of late, however, a number of authors who have considered the religious and confessional lives of women have fashioned answers that tease out the subtle interplay of religious power dynamics in early modern society.[32] Increasingly, historians have come to recognize that, even when disenfranchised from official avenues of power, early modern women knew how to assert themselves and found their own ways of exercising influence.[33] The same held true for their penitential activities. In fact, many women found confession an important part of their identity.

This is not to say that discrimination, gender-based or otherwise, did not exist. For example, Old Christians (i.e., Spaniards who could claim to be free of Jewish or Muslim blood) often treated the marginalized differently from how they treated one another. Converted Jews (*judeoconversos*), gypsies, and *moriscos* frequently experienced prejudicial treatment and harsh punishments for misdeeds, both real and perceived. However, these groups also found ways to subvert and overcome their marginalization by colluding with local priests and seigneurs, burying their pasts, using penitential bureaucracy to their advantage, and shunning the confines of the parish.[34] Although they did not always succeed, the marginalized deployed strategies and wielded power in the search for a modus vivendi.

Debates about insiders and outsiders highlight the communal nature of early modern society. Did confession support or erode that communalism? Some have taken the increasing prominence of confession as emblematic of a more interiorized and individualistic (read: modern) religiosity. In the 1980s John Bossy argued that early modern Roman Catholicism saw confession transformed from a highly communal practice focused on rooting out social discord into an institution focused on penitents' offenses against God.[35] In Jean Delumeau's opinion, this interiorization of moral rigor produced "the most powerful mass imposition of guilt in history."[36] The turn toward self-discipline and introspection thus heralded the modern self. In a similar vein, the literary critic Peter Brooks has suggested that "what we are today—the entire conception of the self, its relation to its interiority and to others—is largely tributary of the [Lenten] confessional requirement."[37]

Focusing on Roman Catholic Bavaria, David Myers has reconsidered this model. Myers agrees that alterations in setting, ritual, and performance made the sacrament "more conducive to private counsel and interior discipline."[38] However, rather than a guilt complex, the result was "chronic uncertainty" about the sinfulness of actions. This in turn led increasingly scrupulous confessants to listen with ever-greater fervor to the authoritative voices of the church. Clerical counsel became more, not less, important.

Wietse de Boer offers a more direct attack against the interiority thesis in his study of Borromeo's Counter-Reformation Milan by emphasizing the on-going communal nature of confession. Both Foucault and the literary critic Matthew Senior saw Borromeo's development of the confessional box as especially expressive of the modern individualistic self.[39] It resulted in what Senior has called "'ghostly' conversation" and established a barrier between "the Imaginary, face-to-face encounter between priest and penitent and reduced the encounter to the Symbolic."[40] Instead of confessing intimate details to a real person, penitents confessed to a disembodied ear devoid of personality or identity.[41] However, de Boer suggests that Milanese reform of confession did not disrupt the sacrament's communal nature. Borromeo developed the confessional not to afford confessants privacy but to separate male priests from female penitents. Furthermore, once imposed, the laity were often slow to accept the use of confessionals.[42] Borromeo's focus on imposing moral order *through* the confessional apparatus meant that the sacrament held striking communal and public implications.

Likewise, Jodi Bilinkoff's study of devout female confessants, and the ways in which their confessional lives became a matter of public record, challenges the notion that early modern confessional behavior served as a conduit for or an expression of a modern, individualistic religious ethos.[43] The seal of confession forbade priests to disclose secrets while the penitent lived, but after the death of holy confessants spiritual directors often published *vitae,* which described confessional encounters in detail. These works circulated widely and became important models for early modern Roman Catholic readers, thus drawing the private encounter into the public sphere.

In Spain, confessional practice also continued to exhibit strong communal elements. The enclosed confessional did not become an important piece of architecture in most churches until well into the seventeenth century. Moreover, as in Milan, when it gained ground, the confessional's main purpose was to impose a physical barrier between female penitents and their priests and to do so in a publicly visible way. Although confession was private in certain regards, that privacy belies a series of communal interactions that affected how priests and penitents engaged one another. Family ties, social connections, and patronage networks had deep and sometimes determinative consequences for confessional behavior. However, some developments ran contrary to this ongoing communalism. The rising population and availability of regular priests gave laypeople easier access to confessors whom they did not know and who did not know them. This trend did more to increase expectations about anonymity than the imposition of the confessional. It is ultimately more indicative of modern individualism in the early modern period than is scrupulosity among confessants.


## Scope, Sources, and Methodology

The chronological scope of this study spans the two centuries between 1500 and 1700. While such round numbers are admittedly somewhat arbitrary, they represent meaningful boundaries. Archival documents and early printed books that prove useful in studying early modern Spanish confessional practice multiplied around the mid-sixteenth century. After 1700, however, while printed sources remained abundant, inquisitorial activities and the archival records they produced tapered off. The two centuries that we focus on here thus provide a rare, detailed glimpse of confessional practice.

Moreover, much evidence suggests that from the mid-sixteenth century confession became more important for many Roman Catholics. In 1500 it constituted an infrequent and marginal component of devotional life, which most people performed no more than annually. By the late seventeenth century it had become a remarkably popular aspect of lay piety among Spaniards, with deep ties to communal life and religious identity. During those two centuries, Spanish presses flooded the market with vernacular confessional manuals, the Jesuits took up residence in Spain and popularized frequent confession, parish churches introduced confessionals, and bishops developed elaborate schemes for regulating sacramental behavior. Between 1500 and 1700, early modern confessional practice did more than just develop; it underwent a process of maturation.

It is precisely at this point, however, that historians find themselves prone to commit the sin of despair. For despite confession's importance during this period, the secrecy that surrounded the encounter makes it notoriously difficult to study. Consequently, historians often rely upon prescriptive sources that describe confession from an official point of view. These works—confessional manuals, ecclesiastical decrees, devotional works, even hagiographical lives—illustrate what the church wanted confession to look like.[44] But if the goal is to describe confessional practice, then the descriptions they offer are highly problematic. Relying primarily upon prescriptive literature assumes too much about the correspondence between the ideal and the local reality. They were not the same.

This is not to say that prescriptive literature has nothing to offer. On the contrary, it is indispensable for understanding confession, since it describes how the church sought to use the sacrament as a reforming apparatus.[45] Close readings can also highlight the variety of distinct, and often contradictory, approaches to confessional practice. Ironically, as we shall see, this abundance of advice undermined episcopal attempts to use confession, especially the mandatory Lenten confession, as a means of regulating and reforming laypeople.

Fortunately, sources of a more descriptive nature also exist. For Spain, rich inquisitorial archives offer up precious glimpses of confessional life, but at a cost. Trial records (*procesos*) are challenging sources. Some historians have cast doubt upon the reliability of statements made under torture and suggested that educated, legally minded inquisitors and scribes often imposed their worldview on the proceedings.[46] William Christian has suggested that "building a picture of rural Catholicism from [the inquisitorial] archives would be like trying to get a sense of everyday American political life from FBI files."[47]

While these criticisms have some merit, *procesos* offer a great deal of useful information. Proceedings against lesser offenses (blasphemy, scandalous words, and lewdness) and against priests who made sexual advances toward their penitents (cases of sexual solicitation in the confessional), neither of which entailed torture, have proved particularly useful for this study. Certainly, inquisitors had expectations about the nature of heresy and led their witnesses. Our concern, however, is not the relationship between inquisitorial justice and the reality of guilt but rather aspects of confessional behavior in which the judicial proceedings were relatively uninterested.

The key to using *procesos* to study sacramental practice lies in seeing that inquisitorial scribes recorded a great deal more than just confessions and verdicts. They also preserved rich supplementary descriptions of daily life. Although the flotsam and jetsam of courtroom testimony are, to be sure, mediated through inquisitorial authorities, they nevertheless communicate a remarkably gritty sense of the material world in which confessions happened and sometimes provide insight into the emotional or mental world of participants as well. Occasionally, scribes recorded penitential behavior because it had a direct bearing upon the trial, but usually such descriptions come as offhand remarks and incidental details of little direct significance to the judicial proceedings—where a confessional was located, what it looked like, what sins were confessed, the order of the ritual, the identity of the officiating priest, and so forth.

Furthermore, by the mid-sixteenth century, procedure obliged inquisitors to question all defendants about their sacramental activities, even when this had no bearing on the trial. Did they confess and commune? When? Where? And with whom? In turn, witnesses and neighbors who could speak about the religious activities or reputation of the accused might confirm or contradict the original report. Even if evidence could be twisted or misremembered, such details still express early modern Spaniards' assumptions about good and bad penitential behavior.

To put it another way, the verdicts pronounced by inquisitors are often less useful than the descriptions of penitential activities, opinions of confessants and confessors, and expectations about the sacrament that witnesses provided. In a case of sexual solicitation, for example, the most interesting bits (for our purposes, at least) often have less to do with the solicitation than the description offered of the encounter. Where was the sacrament administered? How did the confessant choose her confessor? What did she expect to happen? What did she do when matters took a turn for the worse? Did she continue confessing with the priest in spite of the offense? Such information proves invaluable for studying confessional practice. Few early modern people left autobiographical accounts or otherwise indicated what they thought about the religious activities in which they engaged; historians must look elsewhere if they want to catch sight of the elusive common folk in the confessional box.

*Procesos* are complicated sources, to be read carefully, but the rich insights they offer into early modern religious life validate the effort. The sheer number of documents available—thousands upon thousands of folio pages—provides a remarkably robust picture of confessional practice. A careful balance of the insights and limitations offered by descriptive and prescriptive sources illuminates the process of religious transformation during the era of the reformations and brings into sharp relief the complexities faced by ecclesiastical leaders who sought to implement reforming programs at the local level.

In the pages that follow, we turn in chapter 1 to the realm of prescriptive literature and ask how ecclesiastical authorities and theological discourse attempted to construct confession and the role of the confessor, and how those ideas were communicated to priests and laypeople. Here we focus on printed manuals of confession. These works often exhibited a remarkable pastoral emphasis and played an important role in the church's attempt to reform the religious lives of the people. Yet authorship often skewed prescriptive discourse about the sacrament. Members of religious orders, bishops, and local priests offered differing assessments of proper confessional practice, constructing it in ways that supported their own vision of reform.

Moving from prescription to description, chapter 2 explores the sacramental experience. The changing face of the early modern ritual of confession exposes laypeople exerting influence over the sacrament. During this era, as many laypeople began to confess multiple times each year, the church focused more intensely on properly forming and imposing meaning upon sacred space. Consequently, the confessional often became contested territory where priests and penitents sparred, making judicious use of tactics, gambits, and loopholes. Usually, a declaration of absolution brought the process of reconciliation to an end, but that outcome frequently depended less upon a strict implementation of episcopally mandated norms than upon a subtle interplay of negotiation that ameliorated rigid confessional legislation.

Chapter 3 explores that interplay and the institutions that made it possible. While Spanish bishops and synods established rigorous bureaucratic systems of confessional regulation, translating them to the parish proved difficult. Episcopal decrees imposed a very particular mode of penitential behavior, but parochial enforcement was uneven. Yet the laity of Spain did not simply refuse to obey ecclesiastical pronouncements. Instead, most Old Christians used loopholes, contradictory decrees, and theological disagreements to facilitate their confessional practice. This approach allowed them to maneuver within the system and, even for the highly bureaucratized Easter duty, to assert ownership over the experience.

In chapter 4 we pursue this theme by examining the tools used by laypeople to circumvent the episcopal system meant to regulate confessional behavior, especially the *bula de la cruzada,* a remarkably popular indulgence. Among other benefits, it allowed bearers to confess to the cleric of their choice at Lent, whether or not he was their parish priest. It also gave confessors the power to absolve penitents of nearly all sins, even those reserved sins that would otherwise have fallen under episcopal, papal, or inquisitorial jurisdiction. The episcopal hierarchy, the religious orders, the Inquisition, and the Spanish state frequently worked at cross-purposes because they had different priorities and goals. As a consequence, institutions such as the *cruzada* facilitated surprising freedom in penitential practice.

Yet institutional structures were not the sole influence on confessional experience. Thus, in chapter 5, we turn to social class, economic status, and gender. Often, the wealthy and powerful received preferment, but particularly devout confessants and devoted confessors sometimes shifted that dynamic in surprising directions. Under the right circumstances, a poor, illiterate woman could wield as much influence as a king in her relationship to a spiritual director. Gift giving and personal connections mattered as well. Support networks formed by families, neighbors, and groups of women often provided important lines of defense for the redress of grievances when the confessional encounter went wrong—when a priest broke the seal of confession or in cases of sexual solicitation. However, when those networks broke down, the results could be disastrous for the individual.

The final chapter explores what happened when the dynamic of confessional negotiation that most people experienced collapsed. This occurred most frequently for marginal ethnic and religious groups. Many Spaniards believed that *judeoconversos,* gypsies, and *moriscos* abused confession. In practice, the members of these groups tended to take distinct approaches to the sacrament: most Jews ultimately embraced the sacrament, assimilating into Old Christian society over a period of generations, changing their surnames, relocating, and burying their past. Gypsies fled from confession, withdrawing from parish structures and forming itinerant societies, which successfully evaded ecclesiastical oversight and secular persecution. The case of the *moriscos* represents the most dramatic failure of confessional negotiation. Perceived as a military threat and obstinate in the face of Christianizing programs, some three hundred thousand baptized *moriscos* were expelled from Spain between 1609 and 1614.

Early modern Spain witnessed a dramatic uptick in attempts to regulate lay confessional practice. The church hierarchy did this because it believed that it knew what its sheep needed and that it could do a better job of caring for the flock of Christ than it had in the past. As was the case elsewhere in the post-Tridentine Roman Catholic world, confession became central to caring for people and disciplining them when necessary. In fact, confessional piety did increase among the laity—dramatically so—but that new confessional piety tended to pull Spaniards away from the parish and into the arms of regular orders. Different people, of course, participated in the sacrament in different ways, but many proved reluctant to confess to their parish priest for a variety of reasons, among them social status, honor, personality, devotion, gender, and ethnicity. Yet, rather than heralding a crisis between a disobedient laity and an unyielding church, the various agendas of bishops, *curas,* mendicants, Jesuits, monarchs, nobles, laymen, and laywomen coalesced into a ramshackle system of confessional practice. It was unwieldy, to say the least, but it proved resilient and, for many, surprisingly attractive.

I

# HOW TO BE A COUNTER-REFORMATION CONFESSOR

I have always been attracted to learning, though half-educated confessors have done my
soul great harm, and I have never found any with as much of it as I should have liked.
—TERESA OF AVILA

In 1590, a group of Spanish novices in the Society of Jesus sent a letter to the
Holy Office of the Inquisition. In that letter, later forwarded to Pope Sixtus V,
the novices complained that their superiors had ordered them to confess every
six months to the rector of their college and then to repeat those confessions
to other officials when they made their rounds. This was done so that the
superiors would know how "to govern [the novices] outside" the confessional.
Those superiors used the confessions, which the authors felt ought to have
remained secret, to determine advancement in the Society, and thereby "the
holy sacrament was made pernicious."[1]

By way of response, the novices embarked upon a risky plan: they left
potentially thorny sins unconfessed and went over the heads of their superiors,
making the controversy known to authorities outside the order. Exactly why
they felt justified in adopting this course of action and chose to expose their
actions to the Holy Office is not self-evident. After all, their incomplete confessions were, at least potentially, incompatible with the church's theology of
salvation and their own order's understanding of the obedience that novices
owed their superiors.

This vignette appropriately muddies the waters of our expectations about
confession in post-Tridentine Roman Catholic culture. Although many scholars
have envisioned the sacrament as an almost unilateral imposition of institutional
authority upon the disempowered, recent historiography has complicated this

The epigraph to this chapter is from Teresa of Avila, *Life of Saint Teresa*, 40.

depiction. LuAnn Homza, for example, has argued that clerical formation trained priests to "promote an inclusive enterprise based on mutual respect" rather than to promote a highly bellicose clerical supremacy.[2]

In a 1984 essay, Peter Burke encouraged historians to consider the process of negotiation between ordinary people and the saints of the Counter-Reformation in order to understand why the latter came to be set apart as holy by members of their own society.[3] In this chapter, we take Burke's approach in a slightly different direction by considering what it took for the church and the people to view confessors as effective. For early modern Spain, prescriptive sources that laid out normative penitential practice indicate that authorities did not simply implement a clear Tridentine program from the top down. Rather, they came to allow a limited but very real process of power sharing and negotiation between confessors and confessants, even if they sometimes did so unwittingly.

In order to understand how this could be the case, we turn to early modern clerical formation and the dissemination of moral theology. One of the most important avenues by which this dissemination occurred was the remarkable proliferation of confessional manuals, which became an important means of communicating to confessors how to conduct their duties properly. But manuals also provided laypeople with powerful tools for understanding the inner workings of the sacrament. This reminds us that penitents did not necessarily have the same objectives as their church and that local confessors were forced to mediate between institution and individual. An analysis of prescriptive sources will enable us to begin to see how Spaniards, both lay and priestly, learned to engage the sacrament and one another.

## Describing the Good Confessor

Prescriptive confessional literature helped set the agenda for sacramental practice in early modern Spain and became an important component in the formation of clerical identity. To judge from Henry Lea's influential *History of Auricular Confession and Indulgences in the Latin Church* (1896), one would expect prescriptive sources to be, at the root, tools of clerical oppression. After all, early modern moral theologians believed that the church's ministers were obliged to police and regulate the behavior of its lay members. Their learning, training, and ordained status set them apart. Yet prescriptive confessional literature does not describe a program of unhindered clerical will to power.

In fact, the strikingly pastoral emphasis of these prescriptive works often goes unnoticed. Their authors, especially authors of confessional guidebooks, envisioned the penitential experience as a complicated series of negotiations and dialogues between priests and penitents. Confessional literature did not exist simply to help the church accrue power for its own sake; it sought the creation of a confessional environment in which laypeople responded submissively to priestly authority. Instead of reading prescriptive literature as though its authors intended confessors to control the masses via the sacrament, coming to a contextualized understanding of early modern religious life requires that allowances be made for a much more subtle interplay between piety and power.

Of course, the sacrament of penance could hardly be described as egalitarian; it remained, both conceptually and in practice, a profoundly hierarchical ritual. Yet Spanish efforts at clerical formation sought to create the type of priest who was responsive to laypeople's needs. Indeed, in order for confession, the centerpiece of the Tridentine program of religious reform and reeducation, to be successful, the priests working on the front lines—in parish churches, monasteries, and on missions—had to conform to specific modes of behavior and conspicuously exhibit that morality to their parishioners and spiritual directees. One way of describing the behavior expected of confessors is to consider three of the key concepts used in confessional manuals to construct the early modern doctor of souls: legitimacy, knowledge, and prudence.[4]

A legitimate confessor operated within the ecclesiastical hierarchy and did not seek to overreach his authority. He was an ordained priest, not a spiritual renegade. One needed permission to confess, but that authority could come in various ways. Parish priests held jurisdiction over their own parishioners immediately, by virtue of their office. Other confessors—members of the religious orders, chaplains, ordained sacristans, or unaffiliated priests—were expected to stand for an episcopal examination before receiving a license to perform the sacrament in a given diocese.[5] Good confessors refrained from absolving sins reserved to ecclesiastical superiors.[6] The specific number and types of reserved sins, and which were reserved to the bishop, which to the pope, and which to the Holy Office, changed over time; keeping track of them was another part of the job. The legitimate confessor also confessed penitents in a manner that reflected Roman Catholic uniformity in ritual by relying on customary lists of sins to guide the encounter, adhering to the opinions of church doctors, and using the standardized sacramental formula of absolution.[7]

Such well-ordered legitimacy assumed a spiritual hierarchy that placed con-fessants below their confessors and encouraged lay humility toward priests. Authors advised priests to remind penitents that they were confessing not simply to a man but to God's representative.[8] Like many other dioceses, Bar-bastro required the penitent to exhibit a submissive bearing in confession. He "should be on his knees, without a sword or any other arms; and the women with modest habit and head covering; and everyone with hands joined to-gether, and eyes downcast, showing in the modesty on his [or her] face internal feeling and pain." This posture both demonstrated repentance and reinforced the authority of the confessor.[9]

Concerns about lay humility were often associated with concerns about jurisdictional encroachment, which had become a pressing issue. While post-Tridentine reform efforts relied upon secular priests and bishops to carry out pastoral ministry, they also encouraged regulars to act as missionaries and spiritual advisors. Many laypeople preferred confessing, even at Lent, to mem-bers of religious orders instead of their *cura*. Regulars hardly apologized for stealing the parish priest's sheep; they elaborated upon the many reasons why, and the various situations in which, confessants might legitimately turn to them. A constant jockeying took place among the regular and secular clerical hierarchies, as each asserted its authority at the expense of the other. As we shall see, outside theological polemics and griping, these conflicts played them-selves out in actual communities.

In addition to being legitimate, confessors were expected to be learned. This did not, however, mean learning for learning's sake, but practical knowledge of the confessors' craft.[10] One authority noted that for a confessor to be per-fect in knowledge, he would need to internalize "theology, canons, laws, and even the synodal constitutions of the land." Since, however, this ideal was unlikely, a confessor had minimally to be literate and capable of distinguish-ing which sins were common among different people, which were mortal and which venial, under what circumstances excommunication was necessary, and which offenses were reserved to ecclesiastical superiors.[11]

Teresa of Avila brought the tension between the ideal and the reality to life when she described one of her early confessors as being "of very good birth and understanding" and as having "some learning, though only a little." She had initially turned to the priest because she "had always been attracted by learn-ing." But he turned out to be only half-educated. She "supposed [him] to pos-sess knowledge" and assumed that her "whole obligation was simply to accept what [he] said." In fact, he called mortal sins venial and dismissed venial sins altogether. Truly learned confessors, Teresa assured her readers, have "never led me astray," but she admitted that she had "never found any with half as much [education]" as she would have liked.[12]

Moral theological training was meant to enable priests to effect a "complete and fruitful" confession, but without being too suggestive. Learning about previously unknown sins might tempt a penitent to perform those very offenses. Thus a confessor should not "ask about every sin that might be committed but only about those which were common" to the sort of person being confessed.[13] This type of moral theological profiling encouraged the confessor to frame questions with consideration to his confessant's estate (*estado*), office, occupation, and the time since his or her last confession.[14]

The emphasis on legitimacy and knowledge bore fruit in the virtue of prudence. Prudence emphasized the pastoral nature of the sacrament by urging priests to create a confessing environment that prospective penitents would recognize as safe. Martín de Azpilcueta, author of an influential confessional manual, explicitly described conspicuous priestly morality as a means of achieving this goal, for it was safer and better to entrust the administration of sacraments "to a priest who appears good than to one who appears to be bad."[15] Although some laypeople may have embraced some form of Donatism—the belief that an immoral or lackadaisical priest fundamentally marred the efficacy of the sacrament—Azpilcueta did not emphasize conspicuous morality because of this theological concern; the church understood that sacraments functioned *ex opere operato,* by the working of the sacrament, and not because the priest himself was inherently good. Rather, a priest exhibited holiness so that laypeople would be drawn to him. Holy priests offered better prayers and demonstrated greater devotion, thereby producing better results.[16] For confessors, being noticeably meek, modest, and humble in speech, not smiling too much or making profane jokes, and living an exemplary life would earn the laity's respect.[17] A priest who behaved improperly, or whom the people *believed* to behave improperly, would never be trusted. Even the aura of misconduct could ruin a confessor's reputation. As one author put it, "It is not enough to be chaste without appearing so."[18]

So prudent priests endeavored to earn their confessants' trust. They kept penitents from gossiping about other people's sins and limited the details of a confession when appropriate. They tactfully prompted confessants about forgotten or hidden sins, especially carnal ones, lest the shepherd inadvertently teach his flock new ways to offend God. They confessed only one penitent at a time and assigned acts of satisfaction that could be performed in private, lest gossips speculate about the sins committed by their neighbors.[19] And they maintained the secrecy of confession, since "if the priest does not keep [the encounter] secret, the sacrament is destroyed, for no one will want to confess."[20]

In order to elicit good confessions, priests were urged to "persuade and admonish" penitents by admitting that they themselves were sinners, thereby encouraging confessants to share openly without fear of offending their priest.[21] One author forbade clerics from showing indignation or anger during a confession, lest penitents become disinclined to admit embarrassing or serious offenses.[22] Good confessors listened with great tenderness, because in so doing they created a safe space in which even the most heinous sins could be disclosed.[23] They received the sinner "with joyful gravity" and throughout the entire process showed themselves to be "sweet and affable, prudent, discreet, gentle, pious, harmless, and eager to uncover [confessants'] wounds and desirous of their health."[24] After hearing a confession, the priest was "to look at [the penitent] discreetly" to see if he bore the proper contrition.[25] Such precise behavioral advice, discreet glances, and careful scrutiny of expressions suggest that authors of prescriptive literature had given serious thought about how best to convince penitents to bare their souls. They understood that achieving a complete and fruitful confession depended as much on the behavior of priests as on that of confessants.

Many feared that a confessor whom laypeople believed had behaved inappropriately, whether outside or, especially, during the sacrament, would find himself unable to fulfill his office well because confessants were not stupid. If a priest betrayed the confidence committed to him once, he probably would not receive it again. He would elicit only rote lists of sins and would fail to persuade penitents to trust him with their heaviest burdens. A priest known to behave in a sexually inappropriate manner would find his penitents unwilling to reveal carnal sins. Many authorities advised that if confessants anticipated danger from confessing a particular sin to a particular priest, whether for fear of sexual solicitation, vengeance, or because he was known to reveal confessions, they could make an incomplete confession, omitting the troublesome offense.[26] Others suggested that in such cases the confession should be postponed until a better opportunity presented itself.[27] For the Dominican theologian Domingo de Soto, even fear of marring one's reputation justified an incomplete confession.[28]

## Forming the Good Confessor

Priests learned about these expectations, and along with them the assorted procedures and rules for sacramental practice, in various ways. The most important, at least for the secular clergy, may ultimately have been the establishment of seminaries, but in many areas they were a long time coming. Few dioceses were as precocious as Cuenca, where even parish priests were quite well educated in the early modern period.[29] Clerics in the north, for example, experienced little educational reform.[30] Spain saw twenty seminaries founded in the second half of the sixteenth century, mostly in Castile, but several subsequently closed for lack of funds. The seventeenth century saw the establishment of only eight new seminaries.[31] The clerical elite continued to be trained in universities, and in the mid-sixteenth century none of these offered courses in which students read cases of conscience, as the casuistic approach to moral theology was known.[32]

As this suggests, many confessors received only limited practical instruction. Yet some religious orders provided opportunities for continuing education. Some Jesuits offered public lectures on moral theology, open to both priests and laypeople.[33] According to his biographer, Saint Simón de Rojas (1555–1624), an influential Trinitarian and popular spiritual advisor, "knew of the many souls whom confessors have started on the road to heaven," but because of the "inadequacy of some [confessors], other souls were in danger of going to hell and dragging many with them." For this reason, the saint established a course of lectures for the confessors in his monastery.[34]

Regular priests were not the only ones who received this type of training. In the 1560s the Jesuits of Avila established a series of lectures on cases of conscience at the *colegio* of San Gil to help local clergy become more effective confessors. Jerónimo de Ripalda offered the lectures, which proved successful, for about three years. Luis Muñoz succeeded Ripalda and continued his lectures for twelve more years before retiring to devote his attention entirely to the confessional.[35] In the Catalonian diocese of Solsona, Dr. Anselmo Valenti Capiscol lectured local confessors during Lent at the cathedral church in 1598.[36]

Those who had not been called to be parish priests underwent a formal process of examination and episcopal licensing before they could confess. Preparation for the tests entailed a period of study to ensure that candidates understood the theological contours and practice of confession. Some manuals of confession, like the one written by Alonso Gómez, were written specifically for priests who were preparing to sit for licensing examinations. And Gómez's advice was not insignificant; he served as an examiner for the Archdiocese of Toledo, the peninsula's largest and most prestigious see.[37]

Once a confessor found himself on the front lines, however, he invariably faced difficult confessional conundrums. Several authorities, among them Archbishop Pedro Guerrero of Granada (r. 1546–76), advocated a twofold remedy for this problem. Guerrero encouraged priests to seek the counsel of more learned and experienced confessors and to turn to the wisdom enshrined in penitential literature.[38] Ephemeral by nature, face-to-face conversations between novice priests and their veteran counterparts have left little evidence, but they probably occurred with some frequency. In 1550, for example, Salvadora Pérez of Lorca confessed to Judaizing and perjuring herself before the Inquisition. When her confessor at the Monastery of San Francisco in Murcia found the case too complex to manage on his own, he asked Salvadora's permission to consult with the monastery's preacher before deciding how to proceed.[39] This approach appears to have been typical for priests who faced difficult pastoral issues.

## Manuals of Confession: Varieties, Contents, and Contexts

A bit more can be said about manuals of confession, which were something of a cottage industry in early modern Spain. Throughout the Catholic world, moral theology evolved into a distinct pedagogical discipline, and the proliferation of moral theological treatises kept pace with this change.[40] While morality always maintained ties with dogmatic theology, beginning in the late Middle Ages and with increasing frequency in subsequent centuries, writers found it convenient to treat the subject in a separate context. Where, by and large, moral theological discussions had previously appeared in the context of the Scholastic *summa,* authors increasingly wrote treatises, manuals, and handbooks devoted specifically to moral casuistry, penitential practice, and pastoral theology.[41]

In Spain, the genre's writers, editors, and publishers proved remarkably energetic. Between 1550 and 1700 more than one hundred advice manuals were written for confessors and penitents, and the vast majority of these underwent multiple printings or editions. Hundreds of cheap copies lined bookstores' shelves, and they were often reproduced in pirated versions.[42] The Dominican Bartolomé de Medina's *Breve instrucción de como se ha de administrar el sacramento de la penitencia* was printed at least fifteen times between 1579 and 1626.[43] Beginning in 1625, the Franciscan Enrique de Villalobos's *Manual de confessores* underwent at least eleven printings.[44] The Jesuit Antonio Escobar y Mendoza's *Examen de confessores y práctica de penitentes* went through fifty-three editions by 1665, and the Capuchin Jaime de Corella's *Practica del confesionario,* first published in 1686, was reissued at least twenty-eight times over the next eighty years.

Perhaps the genre's most successful work during this period, and certainly one of its most influential, was the Augustinian Martín de Azpilcueta's *Manual de confessores y penitentes.* Part of Azpilcueta's success arose from his manual's early influence on Jesuit confessors and its inclusion in the curricula of many fledgling Tridentine seminaries.[45] Furthermore, between 1552 and 1650, Azpilcueta's manual was printed in Castilian at least eighty-one times; it was revised, abridged, and translated into Latin, Portuguese, French, and Italian another ninety-two times.[46] Latin editions were printed north of the Alps, in the Low Countries, and in the Holy Roman Empire. Azpilcueta was one of the principal authorities at the Douai-Rheims seminary for future English priests.[47] And his influence extended to the New World: a 1576 purchasing order from Mexico City to Seville for 1,190 volumes requested more copies of Azpilcueta's *Manual* than any other book.[48] Sales were good in Peru as well.[49] Seminary libraries invariably held copies, but priests with little formal education also knew the *Manual;* it was the most frequently owned example of the genre among the priests of early modern Avila.[50] Azpilcueta became "part of the cultural baggage of the day."[51]

Members of the regular orders wrote nearly all of these advice books, because many of the orders saw confession as part of their vocation and because they were free from the daily responsibilities that consumed the time of *curas.* Yet many saw manuals as an invaluable component in the formation of secular priests as well. As early as 1565 Archbishop Guerrero mandated that, since confession was such a difficult and weighty matter, confessors should possess manuals and study them carefully.[52] Far to the north, a synod in the archbishopric of Santiago de Compostela issued a similar decree in 1576, obliging confessors to study the Bible, devotional works, and cases of conscience. Among others, Azpilcueta, the *Summa Sylvestrina* (1516), the *summula peccatorum* (1525) of Cajeton, and Francisco de Vitoria's *Confessionario util y provechoso* (1562) were specifically recommended.[53] In 1605 the bishop of Avila explained that *curas* needed to know how to confess different types of people. Thus he required that every parish priest possess a few *sumas de casos de conciencia* and imposed penalties upon those who could not present the books during episcopal visitations.[54] Other dioceses levied similar fines.[55]

Around the oval frame:

DOCTOR NAVARRVS MARTINVS AB AZPILCVETA CANONICVS REGVLARIS ORDINIS SANCTI AVGVSTINI

In the cartouche below:

*Insignis forma doctrina insignior vnus.*
*At superat summi cultus vtrumque Dei.*

*Fig. 2*    Martín de Azpilcueta (1492–1586). From Martín de Azpilcueta, *D. Martini Azpilcueta Navarri I.U.D. celeberrimi. . . .* (Cremona, 1591). Courtesy of Pitts Theology Library, Candler School of Theology, Emory University.

Either these episcopal proclamations proved effective or the confessors themselves came to rely upon manuals to help resolve challenging confessional dilemmas. Certainly, many priests, even those with limited education, owned them. Gerónimo González, the *cura* of Valmayor (Toledo), noted in 1582 that he had "never studied," did not know Latin, and had never "opened a Latin book in his life." Yet he owned multiple vernacular cases of conscience.[56] Similarly, in 1594 Juan de la Olmeda, a Franciscan living at the convent at Torrijos who had "only books in the vernacular because he just studied grammar," possessed Bartolomé de Medina's *Breve instrucción,* Juan de Pedraza's *Summa de casos de conciencia,* and Azpilcueta's *Manual.*[57] Bernardo de Amor, a confessor in Mondéjar, owned fifteen different manuals in 1650.[58] And, as early as 1563, a Sardinian Franciscan living in Spain, who had "not studied theology but only a little bit of grammar in [his] youth," blamed his misunderstanding of basic moral theology on Azpilcueta by claiming that the *Manual de confessores* taught that fornication was not a mortal sin.[59]

The works that I am describing as confessional manuals actually constitute a rather diverse lot. Most authors wrote in the vernacular, although some—especially the Dominican of Salamanca—continued producing Latin treatises. Some works, like Pedro Martír Coma's brief *Directorium curatorum* (1577), which despite its Latin title was written in Castilian, were published as cheap, easily transportable duodecimo editions for parish priests. They aimed to communicate the most necessary bits of information. Others, like Juan Machado de Chávez's massive *Perfecto confesor y cura de almas* (1641), which appeared in two folio volumes, sought to address every detail and debate.

The most characteristic examples of the genre were general works that provided information about the broad theological and practical contours of confession for a wide audience, such as Azpilcueta's *Manual.* However, some authors composed their works with a more specific readership in mind. Francisco de Luque Fajardo's *Fiel desengaño contra la ociosidad y los juegos* (1605) trained priests to confess addicted gamblers. Hernando de Camargo y Salgado's *Luz clara de la noche obscura* (1650) helped spiritual directors to distinguish confessants' true revelations and prophecies from false ones. Francisco de Carrasco's *Manual de escrupulosos y de los confesores que los goviernan* (1686) was written for priests working with especially scrupulous penitents. Even among the more general manuals, one encounters a wide range of styles, emphases, and components. All authors showed respect for the masters who had preceded them, but members of religious orders tended to favor their own authorities. José

Gavarri, a rather unusual character, frequently relied on personal anecdotes and his years of experience as a Franciscan missionary confessor.[60]

In terms of content, these works typically offered explications of standard lists such as the Ten Commandments, the seven deadly sins, and the commandments of the church. They offered definitions of key theological and administrative concepts: contrition and attrition, mortal and venial sins, jurisdiction and reserved sins. They resolved difficult cases of conscience and discussed appropriate confessional behavior for both priests and penitents. Manuals sometimes provided sample confessional dialogues and frequently contained long sections, usually organized along social and professional lines, that described the specific sins that the various *estados* were prone to commit.

To be sure, a consensus existed among the authors on many issues, but given the number of treatises published and the intricacy of the subject matter, differences of opinion invariably surfaced. For example, how frequently devout confessants could confess became a hotly disputed issue in the mid-seventeenth century.[61] Perhaps the most salient point, for the moment, about these often complex disagreements is simply the theological climate in which they occurred. That climate was conditioned by a school of moral theology known as Probabilism, which arose and flourished in Spain between the late sixteenth and early seventeenth centuries. As an explicitly formulated system of morality, Probabilism erupted in the late 1570s in the writings of the Dominican Bartolomé de Medina (1527–1581), professor of theology at Salamanca, but the movement found its clearest early modern proponent in the Jesuit Francisco Suárez (1548–1617).[62]

Probabilism gained ground at the expense of an older approach, usually called Tutiorism, which had been advocated by medieval theologians such as Alexander of Hales, Bonaventure, Albert the Great, and Thomas Aquinas.[63] A straightforward common-sense approach, Tutiorism viewed the moral law as an external standard, a clear set of rules to be broken or obeyed. Probabilism, by contrast, saw morality as less starkly black and white by emphasizing *intent,* since seemingly sinful acts were sometimes committed innocently. It embraced freedom of conscience, teaching that when confronted with moral uncertainty, the Christian could appropriately follow his or her internal sense of right and wrong. In order to keep the specter of antinomianism at bay, however, Probabilists still demanded that a theological authority be marshaled to legitimize a moral decision. Once invoked, however, a single weighty authority sufficed, even if he contravened other more probable opinions. As Medina explained, "If an opinion is probable, it may be followed, even though the opposite opinion be more probable."[64]

In fact, a wide spectrum of positions developed among moral theologians, from those of a more rigorous Tutiorist bent to the laxer approach of theologians who argued that however unsafe a moral course might appear, it could be safely pursued as long as a single authority condoned it. But the most rigorous and lax approaches were condemned in the second half of the seventeenth century. And in spite of the popularity of Probabilism, it eventually became a more marginal position, eclipsed by Probabil*ior*ism. Positioned between Tutiorism and Probabilism on the moral theological spectrum, Probabiliorism suggested that when confronted with two probable opinions, one could safely pursue only the more plausible course as morally acceptable.

The historian Arturo Morgado García has suggested that the rise of Probabilism and its variants, particularly the laxer versions, paved the way for the "discrediting of moral theology."[65] Generations of bad press for Probabilism have bolstered this conclusion. In the 1650s, for instance, Blaise Pascal lampooned Probabilists in his *Provincial Letters*. For Pascal, the "moral elbow-room" and "liberty of conscience" they provided was inherently unsafe. His fictional Jesuit interlocutor in the *Provincial Letters* explained that confessors could absolve sins "just as we please; or rather, I should say, just as it may please those who ask our advice." But those who sought certainty in forgiveness saw Probabilism as a dangerous path to tread, a source of cheap grace that bound confessors to absolve penitents in almost any situation. Indeed, Pascal's Jesuit explained, "to refuse absolution to a penitent who acts according to a probable opinion, is a sin which is in its nature mortal."[66] The confessor, not the penitent, found himself upon the rack!

Yet the notion that Probabilism discredited moral theology is somewhat overstated. Some theological opponents, particularly Protestants and members of the theological sect known as Jansenism, considered such moral casuistry to be highly problematic and directed polemical fire against the movement. If, however, one is speaking of the laity in early modern Spain, it is not clear that any discrediting occurred. In fact, Probabilism grew, at least in part, out of a pastoral need to respond to excessively scrupulous confessants who agonized over the moral implications of every decision.[67] It enabled the confessor to assuage burdened consciences by assuring them of God's expansive grace. For Robert Maryks, Probabilism did not gain purchase among the Jesuits because it sanctioned sloppy confessional practice. Rather, that sophisticated ethical system, rooted in the classical rhetorical tradition, infiltrated the Society of Jesus when, in the late sixteenth century, it began to focus on educating the young.[68]

This theological wrangling meant that most manual writers operated within a theological climate that allowed for a certain degree of moral messiness. By its very nature, Probabilism did not demand strict adherence to a single authoritative mode of behavior. To be sure, manuals often dealt with established points of dogma. There were always seven sacraments, always ten commandments, and Protestantism was always a heresy. However, one encounters a great diversity of advice—even contradictory advice—from authors, especially on procedural issues, such as what questions to ask confessants, whether to hear the confession of ill-prepared penitents, whom priests were allowed to confess, and so forth. So too, one finds a surprising diversity in the guidelines offered to confessors for interacting with penitents. This flexibility created an environment in which both penitent and priest had a hand in shaping the confessional experience.

## Jurisdictional Conflicts in Confession

One important area in which we can see this diversity of opinion playing out is the jurisdictional conflicts that arose over determining who could confess with whom. Portions of this debate were engendered by the proliferation of the *bula de la cruzada,* a popular indulgence that allowed bearers to confess, even at Lent, to a priest other than their *cura.* But determining precisely *which* priests were acceptable became a hotly disputed issue. The regular clergy who authored confessional manuals typically favored expansive interpretations. The Dominican Probabilists de Soto and Ledesma proved particularly lenient, arguing that any ordained minister who was not suspended or excommunicated was acceptable, even if he lacked an episcopal license. And once confessed, penitents needed not confess again with their parish priest.

Furthermore, each religious order had its *mare magnum*—its great ocean— of papal privileges, and in the early modern period none more so than the Jesuits. Pope Paul III (r. 1543–49), for example, blurred jurisdictional boundaries for confession in 1545 by granting the Society authority to hear confessions without sitting for an episcopal license.[69] In 1552 Julius III (r. 1550–55) gave Jesuits permission to absolve confessants of heresy.[70] At Trent, the bishops fought back. The twenty-third session confirmed that regular priests could hear confessions only with the approval of the local bishop. Yet the pope again stirred confusion in the wake of the council by permitting mendicants to confess without being examined. This prompted a succession of Spanish bishops to send scathing reports to Philip II in 1567 and 1568 about the inconveniences that had resulted.[71] Popes reiterated the need for episcopal oversight of all confessors in their diocese throughout the seventeenth century. Regulars, however, seem rather to have been selectively deaf, as each order held fast to its *mare magnum*.[72] But secular clergy could play these games as well.

In 1568 the bishop of Córdoba, Cristóbal de Bernardo de Rojas y Sandoval (r. 1562–71), came into conflict with mendicant confessors in his diocese. He complained to the king that "although some [regulars] come to be examined, they are few, but those who hear confessions are many."[73] The bishop therefore moved to revoke all previously granted licenses for confessors in order to bring the regulars into line.[74] Alvaro de Villegas, the co-administrator of the archbishopric of Toledo, employed this stratagem against regular confessors in his archdiocese in 1620. He planned to force them to reapply for licenses so that he could reexamine them, weed out those he found disagreeable, and assert episcopal authority over confession. The regulars mounted an elaborate defense, and the Franciscan provincial Fray Diego de Barrasa drew the king of Spain into the affair. The religious orders called Villegas's bluff and closed their churches to penitents. The ploy worked; on 6 August 1621 the papal nuncio suspended the administrator's order.[75]

In 1622 Spanish bishops secured from Gregory XV (r. 1621–23) a *motu proprio* that they hoped would cement their authority over regular confessors. But the religious orders fought back and persuaded Philip IV (r. 1621–65) to request a revocation of the order from Gregory's successor, Urban VIII (r. 1623–44). Urban eventually rescinded his predecessor's *motu proprio* and, in 1625, confirmed a series of decisions in favor of the regulars.[76] According to this latest pronouncement, a bishop could not force a reexamination of a previously examined confessor, nor could a license be rescinded without cause. Furthermore, licenses could not be revoked en masse except in consultation with Rome. Bishops, however, retained the right to reexamine individual confessors whom their predecessors had licensed.[77] In the late 1620s, when Bishop Cristóbal Lobera y Torres of Córdoba (r. 1625–30) complained to Urban VIII about the number of regulars confessing without licenses issued in the diocese, the pope responded with a letter favoring episcopal efforts.[78]

These controversies demonstrate the lively and convoluted nature of the debates surrounding jurisdiction and some of the ways in which they played out, as each party lobbied ferociously to secure its privileges. Repeated pronouncements and the need to appeal for papal and royal support suggest just how contentious and porous jurisdictional enforcement remained in early modern Spain. Determining who could confess to whom must have been a thorny issue, even for those priests who tried to follow the decrees of the church. It is no surprise, then, that in the midst of ongoing debate, regular authors of confessional manuals affirmed more lenient positions on jurisdictional matters, while episcopal synods proved less permissive.

## Moral Theology and the Laity

We might well wonder whether, in the midst of these tortuous debates, priests actually attempted to follow the direction of prescriptive literature. We know for certain that they did not do so all the time. Inquisitorial trials against priests who sexually solicited penitents during confession, for example, reveal that some clerics ignored prudent counsel on matters of great consequence. Yet we cannot know precisely how confessors carried out their duties on a day-to-day basis; they kept no records of the exchanges and, under normal circumstances, the confessional seal bound them to secrecy. Inquisition archives provide valuable information about confessional practice for some trials, but these represent only a small fraction of the confessions made in early modern Spain. The vast majority left no paper trail, and this is as much proof as we are likely to find that most confessions played out more or less satisfactorily to the parties involved.

Yet this does not mean that laypeople understood or viewed the sacrament exactly as the church wished. Many Spaniards, for instance, remained rather misguided—at least as the church saw it—about moral theological matters.[79] In practice, popular opinion carried as much weight as the words of Aquinas or Azpilcueta. The hundreds of *procesos* conducted against Old Christians suggest that lay sensibilities did not necessarily conform to the views expressed in prescriptive treatises. Inquisitors, for example, frequently found it difficult to convince laypeople that fornication was a mortal sin. Nevertheless, laypersons do appear to have at least operated out of the proper theological categories. After all, except in rare instances, disagreements about fornication centered on whether it was a mortal or venial sin, not whether sin existed at all or whether penitents were obliged to confess serious offenses. How, then, did the masses appropriate their basic Christian moral worldview, and what impact did it have on their confessional activities?

Catechesis formed one important locus of instruction. In his study of New Castile, Jean Pierre Dedieu emphasized the precocity of Spanish bishops, who began printing catechisms and emphasizing catechesis at episcopal visitations a hundred years before the French.[80] As early as 1566, for example, Toledo ordered its priests to catechize on Sundays and on other feast days after High Mass.[81] But the effects of such programs remain ambiguous. The work of Dedieu and Sara Nalle indicates that by the end of the sixteenth century, the vast majority of people tried by the Holy Office in Toledo and Cuenca had learned the basic prayers of the church, were able to recite the Ten Commandments, and could make the sign of the cross properly.[82] Yet the degree to which the catechized moved beyond rote memorization of the Ten Commandments to reflection on moral issues is more difficult to quantify. Kathleen Comerford, working mostly in an Italian context, has suggested that catechesis remained fairly uneven in the sixteenth and seventeenth centuries. While laypeople received some doctrinal instruction from individuals and religious orders, many parishes did not even own copies of the Roman Catechism. What emerges is "not exactly a picture of failure," but the lack of centralization and standardization produced "almost accidental" success when it succeeded at all.[83] Spain started its catechetical program early, and while we await further research, we can expect that the impact was more substantial there, even if it was far from a total success.

Yet other avenues existed for training the laity. In addition to catechesis, Trent encouraged preachers to use sermons to teach churchgoers what was necessary for salvation, what vices to avoid, and what virtues to pursue so that they might "escape everlasting punishment, and obtain the glory of heaven."[84] Most parish priests were expected to preach at least once a week, during High Mass on Sunday, but some Spaniards had additional opportunities to attend sermons. In urban areas the conjunction of regular communities, well-trained secular priests, and endowed preaching benefices generated an abundance of stirring and learned homilies. Thus, to take one early example, Mari Díaz, a holy woman born in the village of Vita, moved to Avila in the 1530s "because she had heard it said that there were sermons" there.[85]

Missionaries visited smaller towns and villages in the countryside, which proved to be an especially difficult field of labor owing to the lack of well-trained priests. In parishes where the *cura* was not up to the task, bringing in a regular cleric to preach the daily (or at minimum thrice-weekly) sermons during Advent and Lent became common practice.[86] In 1558, for example, Francisco de Mendoza y Bobadilla, cardinal bishop of Burgos, requested "eight or more" Jesuits to "preach and teach Christian doctrine and hear confessions."[87] The sermons preached during missionary visits (often lasting a week, and sometimes two or three) and Lent focused on sin and salvation. In addition to their intended purpose of stirring up repentance, these seasons provided an opportunity for laypeople to take stock of their lives and reflect upon moral issues.

Even the sacrament of penance itself afforded a teaching opportunity. Diocesan authorities admonished priests to correct penitents who failed to perform the necessary prayers and rituals or who had an inadequate grasp of doctrine. As a confessor and confessant came to know each other over time, particularly in the case of a long-term relationship between a spiritual director and directee, the priest might offer more advanced lessons. For example, in Oropesa, the Jesuit Francisco López taught a group of *morisca* confessants the doctrines of the church so well that no one would have guessed they were New Christians.[88] In the 1620s Gerónima de Noriega, a thirty-six-year-old *madrileña* widow who worked as a laborer, learned from her Carmelite confessor the complex vocabulary of mystical theology.[89]

The relationship between confessor and confessant sometimes spilled over into more practical advice for negotiating the penitential encounter. Fray Francisco de Atocha, a Franciscan in late sixteenth-century Baeza (Córdoba), advised doña Luisa de Salazar not to confess to Jesuits "because they were very scrupulous" and prone to make something out of nothing.[90] The suggestion came in the wake of his having sexually solicited doña Luisa, but the advice is precisely the sort of counsel that passed between neighbors, kin, and the members of parish communities. For a quick confession, they might visit a certain priest. Particular orders or confessors were popularly identified as hard on some sin or other. Readers advised their illiterate friends about the finer points of confessional behavior, and devout neighbors urged others to make a general confession with a Jesuit for the good of their souls.

Morality intersected with the arts as well. Hilaire Kallendorf has demonstrated the degree to which moral theological matters informed and became incorporated into early modern Spanish theatrical productions as a result of Jesuit influence. While members of the Society sometimes performed *moralidades,* sophisticated versions of the medieval morality play, Jesuits also trained a remarkable number of students (by 1700 the Jesuit *colegios* enrolled fifteen to twenty-five thousand students)[91], among them a host of influential playwrights. As students, they learned cases of conscience and later went on to explore moral decision making in their own works, particularly through the oft-repeated theatrical question "¿Qué he de hacer?" (What must I do?). Audiences saw difficult moral conundrums, frequently drawn directly from the pages of confessional manuals, enacted on stage.[92] In similar fashion, popular devotional music combined doctrinal and moral instruction with aesthetic appeal in order to persuade.[93] This may not have made lay Spaniards rigorous casuists, but it suggests that the people engaged with moral theology in unexpected ways.

Early modern Spaniards also became more conversant with auricular confession because of its connection to the other rituals. The church required that people confess before receiving other sacraments. For instance, the 1605 Synod of Barbastro ordered affianced couples to make confessions before they married so that the grace effected by the sacrament of matrimony would not be obstructed by the sinful disposition of the parties involved. The synod called upon parish clergy to enforce this rule by refusing to marry anyone who had not complied.[94] Serious illnesses that demanded extreme unction also required confessions. Many dioceses admonished doctors to urge their patients to be reconciled to the church lest they perish in a state of mortal sin. Some ordered physicians not to treat patients who refused the sacrament.[95] Penance was similarly connected to confirmation and holy orders, but the Eucharist always maintained a particularly close affinity to sacramental confession.

In early modern Spain, participation in the sacrament of the altar became an increasingly important component of lay religious life. In this it mirrored confession. The seventeenth century saw the eruption of a grand controversy over the propriety of very frequent, particularly daily, communion.[96] Although few Spaniards participated anywhere near that frequently, most authorities felt that even weekly recourse to the sacrament was safe so long as a reliable spiritual director exercised oversight. For some, this development augured a crisis in the relationship between the laity and clergy. Since the Fourth Lateran Council, receiving the Eucharist had been tied directly to sacramental confession, because penitents who had committed mortal sins could not commune without being absolved. Thus, as people communed more frequently, they were drawn into the confessional as well. However, not everyone found this close connection between the two sacraments obvious. During the late Middle Ages some writers had argued that confessing directly to God was as effective as confessing to an ordained priest.[97]

By the sixteenth century, the annual obligation of reconciling with one's *cura* had centuries of authority behind it. But was that obligation merely an ecclesiastical mandate for a particular historical context (i.e., in order to combat heresy, particularly thirteenth-century Catharism)? Or was it a universal *de iure divino* command for all times?[98] In the wake of the Protestant controversy, the Council of Trent affirmed decisively that confession according to the Lateran mandate was a perpetual and universal divine command.[99] In order to receive the Eucharist and complete the Easter duty, all Christians above the age of discernment were obliged to confess their mortal sins to their parish priest annually. At least at the level of episcopal legislation, on this point as on many others, the Spanish church fell into line with Trent.

Those who failed to make their Lenten confession or who, for whatever reason, had not confessed by the first Sunday following Easter (Quasimodo Sunday) had their names recorded by the *cura,* visibly posted in the church, and read aloud at Mass. They were refused the Eucharist, pronounced excommunicate, and reported to the bishop.[100] If more than a year passed between confessions, they were regarded as suspected of heresy and therefore liable to the scrutiny of the Holy Office.[101] This is precisely what happened to Francisco García of Damiel (Ciudad Real). Francisco was a notorious sot who drank away his property and was publicly cudgeled in a community-sponsored effort to beat some sense into the ne'er-do-well. Among his missteps, Francisco avoided confession and failed to fulfill his Easter duty, for which he was fined four *reales*.[102] Eventually, the Inquisition charged him with being a *luterano* in 1573, and several neighbors testified against him.

Legislation of this sort has resulted in confession being described as a form of "social control," a term that seems to indicate that the sacrament fulfilled a social function by reminding people how they ought to behave and establishing a system of oversight and discipline to deal with troublemakers.[103] This is obvious enough. However, discussions of social control have a tendency to downplay the religious or devotional weight of experiences. Confession becomes *merely* a means of "giving to the Church control over the conscience of every man."[104]

This approach fails to do full justice to the variety of lay interaction with confession. Although it is difficult to document quantitatively, a raft of anecdotal evidence suggests that many people, especially women, confessed much more often than the church demanded. Angelina Mullet, twenty years old, married, and living in the parish of Santa Cruz in Mallorca, told the Holy Office that by mid-December 1679 she had already made fifteen confessions to her *cura* that year. Her neighbor Catalina had confessed every Friday during the second half of the same year.[105] Beginning around 1607, the unmarried Catalina Reus had confessed "for two years more or less and she was accustomed to confess every week on Friday."[106] Indeed, the deep, intimate, and sometimes risky relationships formed between spiritual directors and their confessional daughters became an important component of female spirituality in the early modern Catholic world.[107]

Nor were women the only ones who confessed more often than required. Jesuit missionaries in Spain announced surges in sacramental participation among males.[108] In mid-sixteenth-century Córdoba, one member of the Society noted that "boys, youths, and old men sought confession very sincerely, disregarding the petty rumors of certain people, which not only fail to keep them from this holy exercise once it is started, but rather kindle and enflame them all the more."[109] In 1639 Pedro Manuel, a day laborer in Alcázar de Consuegra, reported that, when possible, he confessed every month.[110] Likewise, early in the seventeenth century, the Jesuits of Madrid convinced Juan Antonio, a Sevillano businessman, that he should confess and commune on a daily basis.[111]

Whether confession itself attracted devotees or the appeal lay in its close ties to the Eucharist, a longing for spiritual friendship, a desire to avoid ecclesiastical prosecution, or some other reason, the evidence suggests that the sacrament became more popular than ever before. It frequently figured as a subject for the great artists of the age. While images of sacramental confession are rare, painters such as El Greco and José de Ribera frequently painted their subjects "in penance." Confession played a profound role in the lives of the model saints of the Counter-Reformation, such as Teresa de Avila, John of the Cross, John Nepomuk, Francis de Sales, Simón de Rojas, Carlo Borromeo, and many others. More writers paid closer attention to confession and spilled more ink over the subject than in any previous epoch. Aided by the printing press, their works found their way into the hands of many.

Yet even if moral theology penetrated deeply into lay consciousness, did laypeople have space in their lives for something like a manual of confession? An initial skepticism seems appropriate. After all, manuals had their literary roots in the theological and penitential *summae* of the Middle Ages. Such Scholastic treatises of moral theology would have been impenetrable to all but the most learned of laypeople. By the middle of the sixteenth century, however, vernacular works in the genre were not only proliferating; many were clearly marketed to laypeople as devotional tools. Many of them gestured at an intended lay audience in their titles: Azpilcueta's *Manual de confessores y penitentes*, Fernández de Córdoba's *Instrucion de confessores . . . y de los penitentes*, Benito Remigio Noydens's *Practica de curas, y confessores y doctrina para penitentes*, and Felipe de la Cruz's *Norte de confesores y penitentes*, to cite only a handful of examples.

The rise of vernacular penitential manuals was obviously a consequence of the printing press and rising literacy in Spain, but it also dovetailed with the growing trend of early modern how-to literature into which these authors placed their work.[112] Significant as well is the fact that the sacrament of penance became the centerpiece of post-Tridentine reforming programs, the linchpin that held everything else in place.[113] As the bishop of Córdoba told King Philip II in the wake of Trent, "I do not consider all of the council's other reforming decrees combined to be as important as this one [on the proper examination and training of confessors]."[114] Reforming the people demanded godly and learned confessors, and manuals seemed a means of bringing that goal within reach. They provided a flexible opportunity for education and a ready reference work for local priests without demanding their attendance at a university or seminary lecture hall. Manuals that detailed the process of making a successful confession, therefore, became a necessity. They multiplied as confession became more popular among laypeople.

For laypeople, this literary productivity created two distinct advantages. Manuals served both as practical tools that taught them how to make good confessions and as a standard by which penitents could evaluate the behavior of their confessors by comparing them with the ideal clerics of religious literature.[115] Publication of confessional manuals in cheap vernacular editions made them available to the literate lay population of Spain. An unbound copy of Pedro de Ciruelo's *Arte de bien confesar* sold for just ten *maravedíes* in mid-sixteenth century Toledo, which would have made it affordable for just about anyone who wanted a copy.[116]

The degree to which manual ownership and readership penetrated the lay estate is difficult to assess; we dare not expect widespread consumption of such texts. Yet anecdotal evidence occasionally surfaces showing that members of the middling and even lower social and economic groups had access to or owned practical treatises of devotion, including manuals of confession.[117] Juan Jiménez, for example, had lived for forty-odd years in Santa Cruz before taking a position as a servant at the monastery in Guadalupe. Whether the book came into his possession before or after he arrived at the monastery is unknown, but within five years of being there he owned a confessional manual.[118]

More important than the number of manuals owned by literate lay Spaniards of the middling and lower sorts is the fact that the ideas within those books could be communicated and disseminated among a community. Those who could read to those around them who could not. These literate communities provided laypeople with a mechanism for questioning how they were being confessed. They familiarized laypeople with proper confessional behavior, which enabled them to make more fruitful and complete use of the sacrament, but the dissemination of manuals also gave laypeople access to the inner workings of a previously mysterious process. While they could not become confessors, they could understand the rationale by which a priest was supposed to conduct and assess confessions and use that knowledge to audit his conduct. This type of behavior has led Homza to describe Spanish laypeople as "rational sheep."[119]

The manuals themselves sometimes offer glimpses of being used in this way. Azpilcueta, for example, addressed the problem of penitents who argued with their priests about how to conduct a confession properly. If a confessant disagreed with the confessor's opinion, the priest should try to convince the layperson to change his or her mind; ultimately, the priest needed to refuse absolution if the confessant was clearly wrong. However, "if the confessor does not have such a clear and indisputable argument and only holds his position as a result of probabilities or if [the confessor] has doubts or sees that the penitent alleges the opinion of a notable doctor with some reason," then the latter should be left to his opinion and absolved.[120] This sort of advice is all the more striking when we consider that Azpilcueta wrote in the decades *before* vernacular manuals flooded the market or Probabilism developed into a coherent system.

Examples of similar behavior appear in the work of other writers as well. The Dominican Pedro de Ledesma noted that a priest with limited experience or knowledge might still perform a confession if the penitent was sufficiently well informed to "supply the defect of knowledge in the confessor."[121] Likewise, the Jesuit Fernández de Córdoba suggested that if a parish priest was inaccessible, then his parishioners could confess to another priest, as long as they were learned, virtuous, communed frequently, and understood the gravity of their sins.[122]

Laypeople also used to their advantage the jurisdictional conflicts between regular and secular priests that played out in manuals and clerical debates. The Franciscan Felipe Diaz, writing at the end of the sixteenth century, lamented how easily confessants could circumvent the prescribed system of confessional jurisdiction. "It is a very great pity," he wrote, "that there is no sinner, regardless of how ill prepared he might be when coming to confess, that cannot find someone somewhere who will absolve him, and that there is no contract so illicit that someone will not vouch for it."[123] Or, in the less refined language of the layman Bartholome de Funes: "if one confessor doesn't absolve me, I just go to another."[124]

## Conclusions

The picture that emerges is a complex one. A limited but significant measure of recourse existed for laypeople dissatisfied with the care they received from their normal confessors. Penitents exercised a degree of influence over their confessors by challenging them with the theological authority of manuals, taking *cruzada* indulgences, withholding some sins from certain priests, or making only incomplete confessions. For their part, priests learned from prescriptive literature to maintain an overarching position of authority in the dialogue of confession by responding conscientiously to such challenges. They were taught to exhibit their authority with care and to limit its exercise when appropriate in order to draw penitents into a mutually satisfying sacramental experience.

Early modern Spanish manuals of confession sought to train priests to negotiate with the laity. A priest's inappropriate behavior or failure to treat penitents respectfully jeopardized not just sacramental confession but devotional practice, ecclesiastical jurisdiction, the hierarchy's authority over the laity, and even the salvation of Christ's sheep. Manual authors worked to teach priests how to increase the influence of the church in people's lives, even if they sometimes disagreed about how that should happen. An aspect of social control was at work in the administrative and bureaucratic developments in confessional jurisdiction, and ultimately the framework within which confession occurred proved to be both stable and hierarchical. While it might have been possible to exploit the system's loopholes or shop around for an obliging confessor, even the proudest and wiliest of penitents still had to kneel submissively, admit his or her sins, and beg for forgiveness.

Nor should we forget that some priests ignored the damage they inflicted upon the sacrament by behaving lackadaisically or inappropriately. This burden fell most heavily upon marginal members of the community who lacked robust support networks. Even when priests followed the advice of the prescriptive literature, the latitude for negotiation granted to confessants was limited. Yet, however limited, those negotiations were real. The Tridentine program for reform and reeducation of the masses, particularly because much of the responsibility for implementing that program fell on the shoulders of *curas* and other confessors at the local level, minimally required the willing compliance of the laity. Especially in Spain, where many penitents could find ways of avoiding bad or inadequate priests, confessors often found it expedient to limit the exercise of their power in order to conduct the sacrament more effectively.

# 2

## HOW TO BEHAVE IN CONFESSION

A confesión de castañeta,
absolución de zapateta.
—SPANISH PROVERB

From an ecclesiastical perspective, the sacrament of penance constituted a struggle of unparalleled dimensions for the heart, mind, and soul of the Spanish populace. In confession, penitents not only revealed their own particular sins; they laid bare their worldview and theological presuppositions. They found themselves corrected, admonished, instructed, encouraged, reprimanded, and judged. So fundamental was this second plank of salvation for the shipwrecked sinner (to borrow the arresting language of the church fathers) that without it there could be little hope of salvation.[1] Those who avoided the sacrament separated themselves from the community, becoming religious and social outcasts. The Roman church used the encounter to instill and reemphasize the institutional uniformity so important to post-Tridentine Christianity. In confessionalized early modern Europe, where many viewed heresy as political dissent, secular rulers found sacramental observance a useful test of their subjects' loyalty.

That, at least, was the plan. As priests working on the front lines quickly learned, however, persuading confessants to play their role was easier said than done. Reforming religious life at the local level proved to be no easy task. Fundamental problems frustrated the implementation of programs laid out at councils and synods, with all of their religious and social implications. A lack of manpower; poorly trained, overworked, or untrustworthy priests; unruly, apathetic, and disobedient laypeople; sexually licentious confessors and manipulative confessants—all of these retarded progress. Leaders with vision and charisma to match Carlo Borromeo or Teresa of Avila were never thick on the ground. Even the energetic archbishop Juan de Ribera of Valencia (r. 1568–1611), whose long tenure provided ample time to implement systematic reform, met with as much failure as success.[2]

Aware of these complexities, manual authors and ecclesiastical synods emphasized the pastoral role of the clergy and offered practical advice to the priests whom the church called to navigate these treacherous waters. Yet there is limited value in parsing prescriptive literature in order to reveal the model for reforming confession. Millions of laypeople confessed sacramentally in early modern Spain every year, and although most encounters followed a loose script, each one was unique. Prescriptive literature has proved illuminating thus far, but we must now enter the confessional itself and consider the relationship between the regulatory script and the reality of penitential practice.

Although no transcripts of early modern confessions exist, a variety of sources record memories of confessions. Whether these come from priests, penitents, or the pen of a notary, they are both valuable and dangerous. Some memories survive in *vitae,* whose authors often idealized the encounter in order to establish the credentials of a potential saint or her spiritual director. Others are culled from inquisitorial trials, which frequently recorded testimonies about sacramental confession. Here, however, one finds fading memories, leading questions, contradictory reports, and complex agendas. The same is true of the occasional letter or missionary report. We cannot in every case know how faithfully an author recorded events.

Even the records that do exist merely describe individual encounters with the sacrament. They do not necessarily reflect either the norm or the range of experiences available. Indeed, this diversity of experience makes studying the sacrament of penance as an aspect of religious life a great deal more frustrating. The proverbial silver lining, however, is the sheer number of extant sources. Their abundance allows abnormal experiences to be distinguished from typical ones. The aggregate picture that emerges from this sifting of information allows for a certain confidence in drawing a faithful likeness of confession in early modern Spain.

This chapter explores the ritual of confession as those individuals experienced it and describes the temporal and spatial aspects of the experience—where, when, and how often early modern Spaniards participated in the sacrament. It also examines the arsenal of tactics and tricks that priests and laypeople relied upon to facilitate a mutually satisfying confessional experience. We shall discover that although early modern synods and bishops formulated strict procedural norms for confession, their decrees met with mixed success at the local level. Yet, while confessional strategies often flouted the letter of the episcopal law, they rarely represented a wholesale revolt against the sacrament.

## The Increasing Frequency of Confession

The rhythms of the church calendar beat at the heart of the ritual of confession, tying it to significant life events, one's community, and places of worship. The faithful received the body of Christ at Easter, with the approach of spring, and in order to avoid doing so while burdened with mortal sins, most made confessions toward the end of Lent. Failure to do so could be viewed as scandalous and irreverent even if one had, remarkably, committed no mortal sins since last confessing.[3] Early modern Spaniards also made confessions before receiving first communion, when they married, before undertaking dangerous voyages or going off to war, and, from their sickbed, during periods of protracted illness or grave injury. Increased missionary activity, the spread of Probabilism, the popularity of communion, a renewed sense of Catholic identity, ecclesiastical emphasis on the sacrament, the spread of devotional treatises and penitential guidebooks, and even the decline of certain medieval forms of piety caused some Spaniards to begin to confess more often than in previous generations. Consequently, confession became more than just a Lenten phenomenon.

While Easter remained the year's principal penitential moment, many people saw particular feast days as appropriate as well. At the end of the seventeenth century, for example, Vicenta Morales of Játiva, from at least the age of eighteen, expressed a special devotion to la Virgen del Carmen and to the local Carmelite monastery by making an annual confession there to commemorate the visitation of the Blessed Virgin in July.[4] Others confessed on the feast days of the Holy Trinity, the Virgin, Pedro de Alcantara, Saint John, on New Year's Day, and at Christmas.[5] In Granada, the layman Pedro de la Cruz, who served as porter at the Jesuit house, mixed work with piety, gaining a "reputation for wheedling those who had called on other business" into making a confession as well.[6]

Those devoted to the practice of frequent confession, frequent communion, or both found themselves in the confessional once a week or once every other week, practices known respectively as *ocho a ocho* or *quince a quince*. For instance, the young single woman (*doncella*) Barbara de Santa Teresa from Alcázar de San

Juan (Toledo) confessed weekly for at least a year and a half.[7] Some people, apparently, were even more zealous. Toward the end of the seventeenth century, Gerónima de la Cruz claimed that she customarily confessed three days in every seven.[8] Such behavior could, however, be viewed as a sign of peculiarity. Padre Juan Ballasteros of Villarobles seemed equally concerned about the amount of time that Catalina Almagro, another *doncella*, spent in the confessional and about her claims of having received visions of the Virgin. The two became uncomfortably linked in Ballasteros's mind.[9]

Many Spaniards, even those who do not appear to have been remarkably devout otherwise, made an extra confession or two per year when offered the right inducement. In 1568, for instance, Pedro Diaz, a shepherd from Polan (Toledo), suggested that visiting a prostitute was not a mortal sin as long as she received payment. When summoned by the Inquisition, Diaz mentioned that he confessed at Lent and that recently he had also confessed in order to gain an indulgence.[10] He seemed to have no qualms about frequenting brothels or bragging about it to his neighbors, but that did not mean that he would spurn an opportunity for an indulgence. Martín de Gamboa, a weaver, confessed twice during the Lenten season of 1561, once for Easter and once for an indulgence.[11] Indeed, after the Easter duty, gaining a *jubileo* became the most commonly cited reason for participating in the sacrament.

Many made pilgrimages and gained the spiritual benefits associated with particular churches and shrines, but these generally required pilgrims to be shriven before they could receive the indulgences. The great centers of pilgrimage in Spain—Santiago de Compostela, Monserrate in Barcelona, and the Virgin's shrine at Guadalupe—were augmented by a vast array of holy sites that boasted merely regional or local reputations.

Many Spaniards also took the Portiuncula indulgence, so called after Saint Francis's little church outside Assisi.[12] Anyone who visited it on the feast day of Saint Peter *ad vincula* in early August, having confessed and communed, received a plenary indulgence, which remitted all temporal punishments owed for past sins. The benefits could be applied to another person, even to a soul in purgatory. By the end of the fourteenth century, churches outside Assisi also began receiving permission to grant it.[13] *Madrileños* frequently mentioned receiving "el jubileo de San Francisco" at local churches in the seventeenth century. In 1623 Manuel Pinto Periera, a Portuguese residing in Madrid, gained it at the local monastery of the Discalced Carmelites.[14] The following year, Francisco Gutierrez, a bricklayer, gained it at the parish church of San Sebastian.[15] Juan de Medina, a soldier of the guard, confessed for the indulgence of the Portiuncula at the Hospital de la Corte and then communed at San Gil in 1644.[16]

Confessing for an indulgence became a common enough practice, even by the mid-sixteenth century, that failure to participate could raise suspicions. A companion who had taken the Portiuncula in 1560 pointedly asked one Bartolomé, a Frenchman working as a servant in Toledo, why he had not yet confessed and communed for the indulgence. The Frenchman supposedly responded that he confessed directly to God and considered the sacrament of penance merely a way for priests to make money. Later, when the Inquisition tried him for heresy, Bartolomé assured the Holy Office that he had been joking and in fact confessed biannually.[17]

To be sure, there was a great difference between confessing a few times a year—at Lent, for an indulgence, on special holy days—and the practice of weekly or even daily confession advocated by some religious orders, especially the Jesuits. Nevertheless, exceeding the yearly confession demanded by the church became typical of religious life in early modern Spain. Writing in 1568, the Franciscan Francisco de Alcozer saw frequent confession as part of a package of devotional practices in which laypeople ought to engage. He suggested that they should "hear mass every day, recite the Hours of Our Lady and the Penitential Psalms, fast on Fridays and on other days when it is not obliged, visit hospitals and the sick and make their beds, confess and commune every week or two, and set some time aside to contemplate the passion of Christ our Redeemer or some other good and holy thing."[18] Fray Francisco advocated a robust devotional regimen. And while his expectations were hardly met by most Spaniards, one has a strong sense from anecdotal evidence that a large portion of the population exceeded the minimal once-per-year requirement that the church demanded.

This general interest in the sacrament was matched by an intensification of clerical attention. Writers produced a slew of works on the subject. Episcopal and inquisitorial apparatuses confronted the practice of sexual solicitation in the confessional. Jesuits preached the benefits of spiritual direction and taught their novices and anyone else who listened the ins and outs of moral casuistry. As individuals from all walks of life—not only religious virtuosi but normal people, especially women—confessed more frequently, they formed deep, meaningful, and sometimes problematic relationships with confessors. Indeed, both laypeople and clerics gave sustained, serious, and deliberate consideration to the significance of the confessional encounter, what they wanted out of it, and how they could attain their goals.

## Preparing for Confession

Following the lead of late medieval moral theologians, authors of early modern prescriptive and devotional literature urged Spanish Christians to prepare themselves for a good confession long before they confessed. For the layperson, preparation began with a period of self-examination to bring past sins to mind, sins of which the confessant might initially have been unaware, let alone repentant. Bishops, synods, and manual authors obliged confessors to remind laypeople to examine themselves before confessing and sometimes sent confessants home unconfessed when they had not prepared themselves sufficiently.[19] Popular devotional works geared toward helping confessants make good confessions frequently touted the importance of preparing for the sacrament.[20] And manuals of confession often served a similar function, particularly those written in the vernacular for both laypeople and clergy. Many manuals included fictional dialogues between priests or otherwise addressed penitents "who want to know how to examine their consciences to confess themselves well," which served to prepare assiduous penitents.[21]

Authorities disagreed about what constituted a sufficient examination of the conscience. Francisco de Vitoria encouraged attentive Christians to devote a little time each night to rehearsing the sins committed during the day, reproaching themselves, and memorizing the offenses in order to recall them at the next confession.[22] The most common bit of wisdom suggested that penitents should give as much forethought to the sacramental encounter as to an important business transaction.[23] Nevertheless, some contested even that rule of thumb. Antonio Fernández de Córdoba, concerned about overly scrupulous confessants, granted the importance of serious self-examination but refused to impose a set standard.[24]

Confessors, by contrast, prepared themselves by determining whether they had the appropriate knowledge, prudence, and jurisdiction to officiate at the sacrament in an appropriate and effective manner. Guidebooks also offered more immediate and practical spiritual advice. Pedro Martír Coma, the Dominican bishop of Elne, explained that because of the importance of the task ahead of him, the confessor needed first of all to set aside time for prayer.[25] Martín de Azpilcueta also recommended prayer as the first step and offered a model based on Psalm 51.[26]

It is difficult to say whether confessors and confessants carried these preparations out. Some overly scrupulous penitents spent too much time scouring their consciences beforehand and rehearsing their peccadilloes in the confessional.[27]

Inquisitorial records shed little light on this practice, but vernacular devotional works that prepared confessants and confessors to think about sacramental preparation became undeniably popular. Furthermore, *procesos* indicate that people thought about confession and discussed it with family members and neighbors, especially around the Lenten season. Manuals readied confessors to expect divergent levels of preparation from penitents, which indicates that, while laypeople may not have been uniformly conscientious about preparing themselves, many at least gave some attention to the task.

Spiritual biographies offer examples of preconfessional preparations. Take the case of Saint Baltasar Álvarez (1533–1580), an early member of the Society of Jesus. His biographer, Luis de la Puente (1554–1624), recounts how as a young man, long before entering the priesthood, Álvarez began examining his conscience twice a day.[28] As a spiritual director, Álvarez later persuaded worldly men to set aside time, for the good of their souls, to pray and meditate.[29] If, however, it took a saint to persuade such people to reflect on the state of their souls, perhaps we should not expect too much from the less heroically virtuous.

No doubt, the seriousness with which individuals prepared for the sacramental encounter varied. Since laypeople tended to participate in very frequent confession only for a period of time and rarely for their entire lives, the role of the sacrament and the attention paid to it shifted, depending upon a confessant's phase of life. Some penitents must have made the sacrament a central part of their weekly schedule. Others saw it merely as an annual inconvenience. Whatever their level of preparation or sincere interest, most early modern Spaniards at least completed their Easter duty. This meant that priest and penitent would inevitably meet in the confessional space.

The eminent Jesuit Probabilist Antonio Escobar y Mendoza urged priests to ask penitents important jurisdictional questions before any confession of sins occurred. Was the confessant a member of the confessor's parish? If not, was she allowed to confess to someone other than her *cura*? Above all, did the confessor have the authority to absolve her? Additionally, the priest needed to know if the penitent had sufficiently scoured his conscience beforehand, was excommunicated, and had completed the penance from his last confession.[30]

The Aragonese Franciscan José Gavarri, an experienced and, by his own testimony, very successful missionary in Spain, urged priests to ask seven preliminary questions: How long since your last confession? Do you have unfulfilled vows? Have you paid your tithe? Have you failed to complete other religious obligations? Have you been ordered by a confessor to reconcile with a neighbor but failed to do so? Have you completed all of your penances? And, asked with great delicacy, have you committed bestiality (which Gavarri believed was a hidden plague, especially in rural areas)? Failure to heed this advice, Gavarri warned, would be disastrous: "If you don't ask [these questions], pretty much all of the rest of the work you do in hearing confessions will be in vain." Indeed, the confessor was better off not having confessed anyone![31]

Gavarri's interest in the more bizarre aspects of his penitents' sex lives strikes one as more than a bit peculiar, but in general his advice reflects the norm. Even episcopal synods encouraged such preparatory questions. To cite but one example, the 1583 synod convened in Salamanca under Bishop Jerónimo Manrique Figueroa (r. 1579–93) exhorted priests not to hear any confessions without first knowing the quality and *estado* of the penitents, the time since their last confession, and whether they had undertaken a sufficiently rigorous self-examination.[32] Advocating a procedure, however, was one thing; seeing it successfully carried out was quite another.

Penitents sometimes used the initial encounter to audit priests in a similar fashion. Being shriven by someone who lacked ordination, jurisdiction, or episcopal approbation, or who was constrained from confessing certain people (e.g., priests under the age of thirty-five could not confess women) could lead to undesirable complications for laypeople. María Gutierrez, from the *pueblo* of Retuerta, experienced this firsthand. In July 1667, an out-of-town visitor, Fray Francisco de Bustos, appeared at her house in the mountains outside Toledo looking for lodgings. Their conversation soon turned to the sacrament of penance, and María asked the young Trinitarian if he had been approved to confess (*si era de confesión*); she wanted to be shriven. The mendicant responded, falsely as it turned out, that he was *de confesión,* and María "knelt before him, and he confessed her in just the same way as the parish priest or any other confessor" who had received episcopal approbation.[33]

Soon thereafter, however, María's parish priest, concerned that she might commune based on her confession to the young friar, summoned her. Believing that the false priest had absolved her of her mortal sins, María would have defiled the body of Christ by receiving it, potentially, in a state of condemnation, thereby heaping damnation upon her soul. When María answered his summons, she admitted that she had confessed with de Bustos, but her *cura* "advised her that she was not able to commune because her confession was invalid [*nula*]." The Trinitarian not only lacked an episcopal license and was too young (to confess women, presumably); he had never even taken holy orders![34]

María had taken advantage of a serendipitous situation: a confessor at her doorstep. Perhaps she disliked her parish priest or felt uncomfortable disclosing a particular offense to him. Perhaps she was busy and had not found time to visit the parish church. Perhaps she was merely struck by the opportunity of confessing to a young, seemingly holy friar. Whatever her motives, María soon found herself rehearsing her sins once again, this time to her *cura,* standing at the center of a religious controversy, and explaining her actions before the Holy Office.[35]

## The Confessional Space

It is somewhat surprising that María failed to recognize the sequence of events that put her in this situation as extraordinary—Fray Francisco had confessed her "in just the same way as the parish priest or any other confessor." Here was an adult woman, even if one who lived in a backwater rural community. She knew about confessional jurisdiction and the episcopal licensing of confessors, and she understood how such things affected her. Yet episcopal authorities would surely have been disappointed to learn that anyone in mid-seventeenth century Castile viewed their own home as an appropriate venue for the sacrament. For more than a century the threat of soliciting confessors had loomed large, and both the Inquisition and the episcopal hierarchy of Spain had waged a war aimed at keeping confessions, especially those of women, out of private, confined, and dark spaces.

The primary impediment used to discourage priests and penitents from engaging in or planning illicit liaisons during confession was the confessional box, but it took time to appear in parish churches. In the Archdiocese of Granada, for example, the Provincial Council of 1565 merely pronounced that priests should not hear confessions outside a church except in cases of necessity.[36] In late January 1582, however, Archbishop Juan Mendez de Salvatierra (r. 1577–88) circulated a brief document among his priests in which he ordered all churches in his archdiocese, including those belonging to religious orders, to erect "wooden confessionals" within two months for the administering of the sacrament to women. Only when the press of confessants became especially heavy could women be confessed outside them.[37] In 1576 Santiago de Compostela's synod forbade confessing anyone in private homes and ordained in particular that all women, regardless of status, should be confessed inside a church and in a publicly visible confessional.[38] In 1602, under Bishop Andrés Pacheco

(r. 1601–22), the Diocese of Cuenca followed suit, ordering confessionals to be placed in the most visible and public parts of churches so that the confessors and penitents could be seen. Women were not to be shriven outside them.[39]

What precisely these documents meant when they spoke of *confesionarios* changed over time. During the later Middle Ages, the typical apparatus was a simple chair upon which the priest sat and before which penitents knelt. Women may have worn veils, and the confessor sometimes covered his face with a cowl to create a sense of distance. After Trent, new types of confessionals were developed. In 1582 the Archdiocese of Toledo, for example, ordered the construction of "open" confessionals, which interposed "a sheet of wrought iron or a small lattice" between the parties.[40] This probably meant no more than the addition of a screen to the traditional medieval confessional chair, which allowed confessor and penitent to remain clearly visible to those around them.[41]

By the end of the seventeenth century, however, the language had changed considerably. The 1682 Toledan synod placed confessionals in the most public areas of churches and described them as "closed on all sides and with a little door in the front about one *vara* [i.e., 2.8 feet] high, where the confessors can enter and be seen by the people." As before, a "grate or lattice" separated priest from penitent.[42] The synod forbade face-to-face confessions and the use of benches or chairs so long as an enclosed confessional was available. As Wietse de Boer has argued, the publicly visible nature of these spaces became an important means of protecting one's reputation.[43] Passersby and confessants waiting their turn might not have been able to hear every word spoken, but they could at least monitor body language and physical interaction.

These synodal constitutions, however, did not legislate an altogether new apparatus. While the Archdiocese of Toledo began requiring confessionals in parishes only in the 1580s, cloisters in the region had used them for some time.[44] The confessional of the Discalced Carmelites in late sixteenth-century Toledo must already have been enclosed, since Fray Diego de la Trinidad had to open the door to steal a look at one of his confessants.[45] In 1602 Beatriz de la Hindad, cloistered at the Jeronomite Monasterio de la Concepción in Madrid, described her convent's confessional as separating the priest from the nun not just by a wooden partition but by the very walls of the monastery. In order to confess, Beatriz "knelt down in a confessional on the part inside the monastery and [her confessor] sat down on the part outside where a little window is located with a metal grill and on it some small holes through which one could not stick a hand nor even a finger, which is the ordinary confessional where everyone is confessed."[46]

While parish churches did not adopt this sort of monastic apparatus, they did bring confessionals to bear upon lay confessants, although slowly. Anecdotal references to confessionals in parish churches become more frequent the later one proceeds into the seventeenth century. The town of Miguelturra, south of Ciudad Real, had a confessional in 1605.[47] Escariche, east of Madrid, had two built in 1610 at the request of an episcopal *visitador*.[48] San Gines in Madrid had at least two by 1625.[49] Santa Quiteria in Alcázar de San Juan had a *confesionario* in 1659 near the altar of Nuestra Señora del Carmen and another in the Chapel of San Juan.[50]

In other words, by the time María Gutierrez confessed her sins to Fray Francisco de Bustos in 1667, her diocese had been working to restrict the location and space of confession for more than eight decades. As the 1601 synod explained, "In order for the holy Sacrament of penance to be administered with greater reverence," confessionals were to be placed in every church, and women in particular were not to be confessed in chapels, hermitages, or their own houses unless ill or because some other legitimate impediment kept them from church.[51] Nevertheless, despite these decrees, one continues to find healthy laypeople confessing outside the prescribed locations.

During Lent of 1588, for example, an itinerant Franciscan confessor from Guadalajara confessed many people, both men and women, not in the local church but behind closed doors in the home of Sevastian Serrano, who lodged visiting friars.[52] In July 1599 an unlicensed priest in the Catalonian parish of Llorenç Savall was disciplined for hearing the confessions of men and women both in the parish church and "in the house of Jaume Busqueta in the bedroom, a place more suitable for sleeping than for administering this sacrament."[53] Likewise, many parishes implemented synodal mandates slowly and had to be urged toward obedience by episcopal *visitadores*. Whether out of nefarious intentions or sincere pastoral motives, missionaries continued to confess peasants in the fields as they worked, *curas* confessed women at night and in dark corners of churches without partitions, and mendicants shrived laypeople of all sorts in their cells.[54]

## Kneeling, Crossing, and Praying

The physical environment of the confessional, in all of its various forms, spoke powerfully of the relative statuses of confessor and confessant. The penitent knelt submissively, "in demonstration of his humility and recognition of his guilt," with head bowed and hands folded.[55] Regardless of rank, gender, religious caste, or social status, inside this court of the conscience all confessants were sinners in need of grace. Francisco de Roys y Mendoza (r. 1667–72), bishop of Badajoz, emphasized the leveling effect of confession when he commanded "both priests and laypeople that they who come to the Sacrament of Penance must kneel with the humility that is demanded by that worthy act." There was, he decreed, "no reason" why defendants "in that sacred Tribunal should be in any other position before that one who looks on as Judge."[56]

The priest, robed in clerical garb and crowned with the authority of the church, sat quite literally as judge, acting in God's place and foreshadowing the heavenly justice to be visited at the Day of Judgment.[57] As the 1607 Synod of Osma explained, confessors must "always be seated like judges, which, in that act, is what they are."[58] The 1583 Salamancan diocesan synod explained that, "in their habit, in their face, and in their movements," priests should "show the penitent the gravity and authority" of the sacrament. They were to wear specific vestments: if a secular priest, a surplice (if they could lay hold of one conveniently); if a regular, the habit that they wore in the choir.[59]

Confessants recognized and performed specific postures and actions as part of the penitential experience. They frequently mentioned kneeling and associated it with confession. However, while proper procedure required a penitent to bend the knee, laypeople recognized that kneeling occurred in preparation for confession, not as part of the sacrament per se. Some witnesses, for example, demonstrated confusion as to whether or not a priest could be charged with having sexually solicited them in confession if they had knelt but proceeded no further. In 1589 or 1590 Lucía Hernández of Piedra Buena (Toledo) knelt before Don Gabriel de Osca "in order to begin to confess." But then Lucía's testimony became hesitant; she could not remember whether she had made the sign of the cross, intoned the ritual language, and thereby initiated the confession proper.[60]

Both confessors and penitents experienced genuflection as a transitional moment between regular life and the sacrament. The Franciscan friar Gregorio de Tapia, charged in 1582 with sexual solicitation, defended himself by claiming that *technically* the offense had not occurred during confession. Mariana de Tapia, related to the friar on her father's side, described the encounter in the following manner: she "knelt at [the priest's] feet in order to confess, and as she began to cross herself Fray Gregorio said that he didn't want to confess her because of his scrupulous conscience." He alleged that since she "looked good" to him and he felt very bad about the death of her father, he wanted to be of some service to her. Uncomfortable with the situation, Mariana decided to find another confessor, but the protests of the friar forestalled her: "Stay here; there are very bad people in this place." He then began speaking the amorous words that eventually landed him before the Holy Office.[61]

Gregorio de Tapia's version of the story differed from Mariana's, but it suggests the same sense of liminality about the act of kneeling. When she approached him in the confessional, Gregorio asked if Mariana had come for a confession. If she had, then they would not be able to joke around—the sacrament of penance was serious business. Mariana responded that she had not, "and with that [he] began to joke around with her, speaking crass words [*palabras de chocarrerias*], and some of them were lewd." After he had flirted harmlessly for a bit, as Fray Gregorio saw it, Mariana got up and left "without confessing or speaking about confession then or ever after." The content of their discussion, he claimed, had nothing to do with the sacrament; it was all "joking, crass chitchat, and laughing together."[62] The Franciscan's explanation of what occurred, true or not, says a great deal about popular beliefs. One did not chat or flirt with a woman who had come to disclose her sins. However, despite being in a confessional setting and kneeling before a priest, Mariana had not sought absolution. As long as she had not initiated the confession by crossing herself and reciting the accompanying prayer, Gregorio considered himself innocent.

The particulars of the ritual used by different priests or in different geographical areas varied, but laypeople participated in the sacrament from an early age. They knew what to expect and developed a sense of proper decorum. Thus, just as the act of kneeling evoked a sense of moving into the sacred experience, the performance of the *santiguado* formally initiated the sacrament. Penitents made the sign of the cross from forehead to chest, left shoulder to right, and prayed in the vernacular: "By the sign of the cross, ✠ from our enemies, ✠ free us, Lord our God, ✠ in the name of the Father, ✠ and of the Son, and of the Holy Spirit. Amen."[63]

The *santiguado* gained its popular importance because, from early on, Spanish bishops repeatedly emphasized the need for priests to make sure laypeople knew it. Well before Trent, churchmen frequently encouraged lay Spaniards to internalize this minimal prerequisite for confession. Thus the bishopric of Badajoz mandated in 1501 that confessors should teach their penitents "the things that they must know and believe for their salvation," especially "how they must perform the *santiguado* and sign themselves with the cross." The priests should teach the people to carry out the ritual in the vernacular "so that they might better understand and receive it."[64] In 1521 the Synod of Córdoba published similar instructions and denied penitents absolution if they could not comply.[65]

After a penitent had performed the *santiguado,* the confessor asked her to demonstrate knowledge of a number of additional prayers, although these varied by region and date. In Toledo, the 1566 synod obliged confessants to recite the Pater Noster, the Ave Maria, the Apostles' Creed, and the Salve Regina.[66] In 1601 Archbishop Bernardo de Rojas y Sandoval (r. 1599–1618) likewise urged confessors to refuse communion to penitents who could not recite the four prayers, although he did not explicitly tell them to deny absolution in such cases.[67] The 1682 synod demanded considerably more. It ordered priests not only to withhold the Eucharist but to refuse confession to those unable to recite "the Creed, the Commandments of the Law of God, and of the Church, and that which they must understand and do in order fruitfully to receive these Sacraments [of penance and the altar], and also the Lord's Prayer, the General Confession, the Ave Maria, and the Salve Regina."[68] According to the letter of the law, therefore, failure to memorize these forms entailed failure to fulfill one's Easter duty.

In spite of these rising expectations, strong evidence exists that Old Christians in Castile, at least, kept pace. They not only knew how to perform the *santiguado* but also could recite the prayers of the church and the components of Christian doctrine required by synods. Yet, unsurprisingly, a learning curve existed, a point demonstrated by Inquisition cases for the lesser offenses of blasphemy and lewdness tried by the Tribunal of Toledo. In these cases, inquisitors asked defendants to recite the prayers of the church and perform the *santiguado* when they first appeared before the court. Of the more than five hundred sixteenth- and seventeenth-century *procesos,* the overwhelming majority of defendants performed the rites and prayers adequately.[69]

Early in the sixteenth century, inquisitors often did not ask defendants to perform these acts (or, if they did, it went unrecorded by scribes), but by the late 1540s the majority of people asked already knew how to make the sign of the cross and recite the accompanying prayer. Beginning around midcentury, when inquisitors started asking the questions more frequently, a rash of failures appear. Pedro Sánchez of Calzada de Calatrava (Ciudad Real) knew how to make the sign of the cross but erred significantly in reciting the creed, the Pater Noster, and the Ave Maria, and he did not know the Salve Regina at all.[70] Diego Granizo, a farmer living in Caravanchel near Madrid, erred in all of the prayers. Even in performing the *santiguado,* he failed to "say the words well."[71]

And in 1562, Catalina, a gypsy originally from Andalucía, could not sign herself or say any of the prayers except for a bit of the Ave Maria.[72] These, however, were anomalies. Most people knew what to say; individuals who had trouble doing so tended to belong to marginal, migratory, or poorly acculturated social groups: slaves, servants, foreigners, manual laborers, fruit pickers, beggars, shepherds, and gypsies.

At the same time, while most early modern Castilians knew how to perform the *santiguado* and say the appropriate prayers, some confessors continued to absolve penitents who could not do so well or at all. In 1588 Domingo López, a Gallegan living in Talavera de la Reina, made a successful Lenten confession to a friar in the monastery of San Gines, although he did not know how to perform the *santiguado* well. The following year, another priest refused him absolution, not because of his difficulties with the ritual but because Domingo denied that fornication was a sin.[73] Estevan Gomez did not know the *santiguado,* the Salve Regina, or the Ten Commandments, but he had confessed to one Fray Antonio in 1593 and communed at his parish church in Montalbán.[74] This clearly contravened episcopal orders.

## The Confession of Sins

During the confession proper, the main event of the experience, penitents revealed their sins to the divine representative. The church obliged them to disclose all mortal sins in type and number, along with the pertinent circumstances surrounding the offense. Priests attempted to elicit a "complete and fruitful" confession, and advice literature provided them with a wide array of strategies to achieve success. However, these strategies often made the situation in which local priests found themselves more complex, for advice varied from author to author, and at times these authors even contradicted one another. This in turn reinforced or undermined episcopal commands circulated via synodal constitutions. Confessors on the front lines found themselves having to navigate a cacophony of advice and decrees. The messy process of negotiation in which they engaged with confessants invariably influenced how they would approach the sacramental encounter as well. Eliciting good confessions from penitents was no simple matter, and the priest who lacked pastoral sensibilities or ran an assembly-line confessional found them hard to generate.

Yet few laypeople could be expected to get the most out of the sacrament without priestly direction, which made strategies to elicit complete and fruitful confessions all the more necessary. At the most basic level, this meant that priests needed to carry out their pastoral responsibilities by creating an environment where penitents felt encouraged to speak candidly about their sins. Many penitents found this type of pastoral care important. Ambiguous language could create tension and result in the loss of trust. When, for example, a confessor rated Catalina Flexas, a frequent confessant in the parish of Santa Cruz in Mallorca, the prettiest of all her sisters, she informed him that he "shouldn't care if penitents are beautiful or not, that he shouldn't care about those sorts of things but listen to their sins and nothing else."[75]

Advice literature encouraged priests to prohibit any discussion of other people's sins unless absolutely necessary, and above all to refrain from mentioning them himself. But some confessors found this difficult. In 1584 Ana Hernández of Moncejon (Toledo) confessed, for the last time, with her *cura,* Juan Fernández. He had already solicited her sexually two years earlier during a confession. This time, he told her about a man and a woman, both of whom he named, engaged in an illicit relationship. "Why are you telling me such things?" she wondered. Ana believed that the priest had spoken "with evil intentions," and his behavior scandalized her. This was the last straw: "She didn't confess with him ever again because he had a reputation for saying things in confession."[76]

Revealing illicit relationships proved to be a temptation for more than one priest. In 1625, while confessing Juliana Texera, Pedro Galindo of Honoraria (Cuenca) called a certain María Ventera a libertine who "lived badly." Juliana, who had always taken María to be an upstanding and devout virgin, covered over the awkward moment with a laugh. Pedro, perhaps encouraged by her good humor, expanded upon the subject: He knew that María could not be a virgin because she had had sex with a cleric, Martín de Albandea. Shocked, Juliana admonished Galindo: "Watch what you are saying!" The priest, however, pushed on, calling Juliana a ninny (*boba*) and explaining that he had confessed both Martín and María; they had separately acknowledged the liaison. Astonished, Juliana asked, "If this is a confessional matter, why are you talking about it?" Galindo's response did not calm her fears: "Yes, I know. I'm not telling anyone but you."[77] Behavior of this sort created uncertainty among the laity. Would confessing hidden sins damage their own reputations in the end?

Indeed, a priest's knowledge of carefully guarded secrets made him a potential threat to the public reputation of everyone in the community. A priest who spoke freely under the influence of too much *vino tinto,* lorded it over a penitent, or threatened to expose his penitents could wreak havoc. Few priests went to trial for having broken the seal, but laypeople often expressed fear that something might be let slip. Joan Reyner, a fifty-year-old Frenchman living in the Diocese of Barcelona at the end of the sixteenth century, speaks for this group: he just knew that priests shared confessional stories with one another and laughed among themselves at penitents.[78] Unsurprisingly, some priests who behaved badly during confession found themselves less busy than their colleagues.[79]

To combat this threat, advice literature stressed both clerical morality and the conspicuous public display of that morality. Priests needed equally to be good and to be *known* and *seen* as good in order to elicit complete and fruitful confessions. If a confessor avoided sexual encounters with penitents but the laypeople among whom he labored believed him guilty, the damage was done. In 1636 Diego Garoz, a priest in the parish of San Juan in Yébenes (Toledo), ruined his credibility as a confessor by mismanaging his relationship with several female confessants. There was no clear proof of illicit behavior, but several members of the community charged Garoz, in effect, with *mala fama*. The evidence? He had displayed excessive friendship toward certain women. He had visited their homes and they his. The result was a popular consensus that the priest had carried on sexual liaisons with them.[80] The scandal arose because his parishioners *believed* that Garoz had behaved inappropriately, an assumption that arose out of his excessive amiability and insufficient care for his reputation. While it hardly solved every problem, conspicuous clerical morality made it possible for penitents to trust their confessors.

In practice, creating an environment that encouraged confession often went beyond merely appropriate behavior. It became a matter of attending to the station and addressing the particular needs of diverse confessants. Indeed, episcopal examinations emphasized that priests needed to know the right questions to ask people of the various *estados*.[81] Manuals often included long lists of such questions. They encouraged confessors to distinguish between penitents and to lead each person through the sacrament in a fashion tailored to his or her own specific needs, for the temptations and sins of a merchant differed from those of a monk or a pubescent boy. The former needed to be challenged on the details of his financial transactions and whether or to what degree his pursuit of material wealth had led him to sin. Such complexities demanded a learned confessor whom the penitent could not overawe or confuse.[82] By contrast, a reluctant *muchacho* had to be coaxed into admitting that he disobeyed his parents, did "dishonest things" with other boys or girls, or withheld sins "out of shame." These encounters demanded not only different sets of questions but rather different approaches as well.[83]

Cataloguing the likely sins of very specific groups in this way stemmed from a number of concerns. Writers worried about teaching the innocent new ways to sin. Particularly when examining a penitent with regard to affairs of the flesh, one had to exercise caution. The historian Arturo Morgado García has also noted that these moral profiles reflect a particularly early modern obsession with the ordering of society.[84] But confessing penitents with specific reference to their likely sins probably also gave confessors an advantage in the confessional. Once they knew what sort of person had come to confess, priests could ask very pointed questions. When they did so wisely, they caused their penitents to consider the implications of their behavior in a more profound way and elicited a more complete confession. Records that would allow us to see these catalogues in use during confession do not exist, but episcopal examination and pastoral formation clearly sought to instill in confessors a deeper awareness of the group identity of their confessants and to use that knowledge to engage the individual sinner.

Confessors had other tricks up their sleeves. Here again one finds that hallmark flexibility of the penitential encounter. It could be adapted to suit the disposition of both confessor and confessant. Some priests structured the sacrament by working through the Ten Commandments or the seven deadly sins.[85] Others used the *estado* questions provided in manuals.[86] Sometimes confessants made a *confesión general* in which they sought forgiveness for all past sins and a new life of spiritual conversion.[87] Manuals encouraged confessors to have at the ready "certain places of the scriptures, and of the saints," with which to remind penitents of God's wrath toward Adam and Eve or the fallen angels, or of the great sufferings that Christ endured on their behalf.[88] Thus one confessor assured Domingo de la Peña, reluctant to make a complete confession, that he would go to hell if he died without owning up to all of his mortal sins.[89] Penitents who had an internal desire to repent but did not feel equal to the task might receive encouragement from their priest with reports of God's mercy and the power of Christ's "most holy blood to supply the defects" in their confessions.[90]

Confessants used this flexible modularity in confessional format by requesting the type of confession that would help them achieve their goals. Some penitents, for example, saw the general confession as a way to avoid revealing particular sins while still receiving absolution for them. José Gavarri warned confessors about allowing laypeople to dictate procedure. There were those who knelt and said, "My Father, I've come to make a general confession, so let's go through the Ten Commandments." But Gavarri suggested that the confessor should respond, "Gladly, my daughter, but first tell me the sins that you have kept quiet out of shame, and then we'll do a general confession. So tell me, what are they?"[91]

Juan Pan, a Frenchman living in Cerevera in Catalonia, provides a concrete example of this mindset. A neighbor admonished him for having sworn and talked a bit too openly about sins of the flesh. Encouraged to confess his offenses sacramentally, Juan responded that he had already made a general confession in which he had been absolved of all his sins. Witnesses to this exchange explained to him that he needed to "specify his sins and how many there were and their circumstances." Later, Juan described his position on the matter to the Inquisition. He had believed that by making a general confession with contrition, he had "already told all of his sins."[92] The Holy Office demurred and exiled the Frenchman for one year, ordering him to confess twice and to make a pilgrimage to the shrine of Our Lady of Montserrat.[93]

During the busy Lenten season, or whenever an indulgence had been granted, participating in the sacrament could become an assembly-line experience. In early August 1588, when Ana Rodríguez went to the Franciscan monastery of San Antón in Cadalso, she found more than thirty people waiting to confess for the Portiuncula and too few priests to manage the work.[94] Other confessors found themselves struggling to cope with their own success. In 1563 and 1564 the three confessors at the Jesuit college of San Gil in Avila had to schedule visits from penitents to manage the demand.[95] They claimed to have confessed 5,265 penitents in the first quarter of 1564. If all three confessors worked seven days a week, this would have amounted to nearly twenty confessions each day per priest.[96]

For the penitents who sought them, good spiritual directors were always at a premium, and the devotee who looked to establish an intense devotional regimen in the confessional could run into trouble when her chosen priest became popular. By the early 1570s, for example, María Bravo had confessed to Fray Alonso Sánchez of Almagro for fifteen years. Although she described Sánchez as a model confessor, called him an "angel," and claimed that he had treated her kindly over the years, María found another director, as Sánchez was "very busy with confessions."[97] Although elderly, the friar had recently begun confessing the female religious at a monastery in Calatrava. Another former confessant of Fray Alonso, Dr. Luis Sánchez, told a similar story: he had stopped confessing with the friar because he was "old and somewhat worn out."[98]

While some penitents found the phenomenon of the busy confessor dis-agreeable, others used the seasonal rushes, especially around Lent, to their advantage, since they meant that priests lacked the time to examine confes-sants as thoroughly as they might have done. As Juan Bernal Diaz cautioned, if *curas* allowed it, parishioners would all come to confess just before Easter. This, he warned, "cannot be done without great danger" to the consciences of both the penitents and the confessors. In quick confessions, "neither are [the penitents] able to say everything that is appropriate nor can the *cura* examine their consciences as he should."[99] Even Teresa of Avila admitted to having, early on, "always contrived to make a speedy confession," although in her case a fear of God supplied the motivation.[100]

While confessants might employ various penitential strategies to achieve easy, though valid, absolutions, priests had ways of asserting their authority. They could remind penitents that they confessed not simply to a man but to God's representative.[101] When a priest feared that his status as divine inter-mediary no longer carried the desired effect on his flock, he could draw on the authority of the saints themselves. Priests might display religious sym-bols to penitents to overawe and help them remember forgotten (or withheld) sins. In an Inquisition case from the New World, we learn that after hearing a Native American man confess a sexual indiscretion, the Franciscan Esteban Rodríguez produced "an image of our Lady" and asked whether the penitent had committed similar sins with other women. To this, the startled confessant replied that he had already declared all his sins and had "confessed himself completely and that he had no more to tell."[102]

On the other hand, some guidebooks admonished the confessor to bridge the gap between himself and his penitents by identifying with them. A priest could assuage his confessants' fears of offending or shocking a man of the cloth by admitting that he too was a sinner.[103] As Gavarri put it, a priest might tell his penitent, "It is better to confess [your sins] with me who am a sinner like you, than with the devil in hell; so tell them to me and with that you will be saved."[104] Martín de Azpilcueta advised priests not "to marvel at [serious or obscene sins], or give any sign of abomination or fright by spitting, making the sign of the cross, or becoming agitated," but rather "to pretend as if they heard nothing."[105]

On the surface, these strategies appear contradictory. Were priests supposed to threaten penitents with the fires of hell and the power of saints, or were they to cozy up to them and thus gain their confidence? In fact, the two approaches demonstrate again the flexible and dialogical nature of the confessional. Priests recognized that confessants needed to be treated differently in order to produce the desired results. As Alonso Fernández explained, "one single exhortation does not suit everyone because not everyone has the same habits. And many times what benefits some harms others, and often the feed that that fattens some animals kills others."[106]

This diversity demands serious consideration. One finds at nearly every turn a variety of opinions, even contradictory ones, telling confessors how they should conduct their business. In a climate where the influence of Probabilism held sway among moral theologians, a local confessor, unless he was extremely isolated, had no single authoritative voice that dictated procedure in the confessional. In this environment confessors could toss aside even the hard and fast rules of confessional wisdom, such as never questioning penitents too deeply about sexual offenses. Gavarri, for one, believed that most Spaniards had unconfessed sexual sins on their conscience; they feared to reveal them out of shame. He advised confessors to ask "one, two, even three times" if penitents had committed such sins. And he had a ready riposte for those who objected that this would teach the innocent, especially women, how to sin: "It was one thing to speak speculatively and another to speak practically." Gavarri claimed to have brought thousands of people to confess hidden sins through intense prodding and plying. His hard-won experience and wisdom trumped those who believed themselves to be authorities because they had read a *summa* or two.[107]

The variety of procedural advice requires that we reconsider assumptions about the usefulness of the sacrament as an instrument of social control or oppression. The use of confession to that end would have necessitated a particularly strong-willed priest and unexpectedly passive laypeople. At times, the variety of advice might have resulted in a sort of chaos where confessions were run according to the whim of the priest. But at other times the complexities of the situation worked to the confessants' advantage, as their obligation to adhere to the provisions of episcopally mandated confessional regimens became relaxed. Penitents found that, in allowing them to shop around for an obliging priest, learn the ins and outs of confessional practice, and rely upon loopholes, this chaotic situation provided room to maneuver.

After all the strategies had been employed, however, the confessor still had to determine whether a confession was complete, as the penitent claimed, or incomplete. Prescriptive literature enjoined clerics not simply to believe a confessant's claim, and with good reason. Many people made incomplete confessions in spite of their priests' best efforts. For instance, Diego de Torre of Roda, an *hidalgo*, or gentleman, apparently believed that one could "rise from the feet of the confessor without telling the truth and that [in doing so] you didn't sin."[108] Then there were the cases in which people claimed ignorance about the seriousness of their sins. Apparently, despite an intense inquisitorial assault in the late sixteenth century, a significant portion of the population maintained that fornication was a venial, not a mortal, sin and that it did not require sacramental confession. Thus, although Cristóbal González admitted in 1640 that he had had sexual relations with his betrothed, he "did not sin, nor did he view [his actions] as sinful, nor did he understand why he needed to confess them because they were venial and not mortal."[109]

Confessants sometimes used ignorance as a "weapon of the weak," in James Scott's terms. In the mid-sixteenth century, for example, a confessor asked Rodrigo Sanz if he had committed fornication. He responded that he had not, but Rodrigo's confessor knew that he had visited a local brothel. When pressed, rather than admit the lie, Rodrigo played the fool. He explained that when the confessor had asked whether Rodrigo had engaged in carnal relations with "some married or single woman," the layman had responded truthfully that he had not. The priest had never asked Rodrigo about prostitutes, whom he apparently considered a *tertium quid*.[110] And this was among Old Christians!

Authorities assumed that Spanish peasants (*rústicos*), African slaves (*negros*), and natives of Latin America were even more prone to make incomplete confessions.[111] In the case of the first two groups, "from whose capacity we cannot hope for any fruit," Benito Remigio Noydens advised confessors to expect inadequate confessions. Even if given two weeks to prepare, he warned, their confessions would still be perfunctory.[112] Remarkably, in view of these expectations, Noydens and others actually advised a relaxation rather than an intensification of confessional procedure. Thus, although *rústicos* and *negros* would invariably fail to prepare themselves adequately, priests should not refuse to confess them. Instead, the priest should simply proceed with the sacrament. Juan Machado de Chávez advised that if a confessor knew that a certain *rústico* was a teachable person of "good will" who promised to follow instructions, then he could be absolved in spite of his ignorance.[113] With regard to native Mexicans, the Franciscan Joan Baptista offered even more shocking advice.[114] Do they lie when asked if they have committed mortal sins? Then do not ask them. Do affianced couples tell different stories of their carnal relations? Rather than having one priest shrive both parties, let them be confessed by different priests, so that neither confessor catches the lie.[115]

These writers considered wooing marginal penitents more important than proper procedure. Here, authorities even moderated the basic requirement of completeness in confession. When Noydens addressed the problem of prostitutes and those who kept concubines (*amancebados*), he noted that learned opinion was divided. Some argued that absolution should be granted, even if the penitent could not recall every sinful act, while other authorities were more hard-nosed.[116] Noydens himself did not take a side, but in a theological culture that viewed such moral questions through the lens of Probabilism, he effectively validated the more lenient stance.

Noydens's approach, as well as the contradictory advice offered by the many manuals, again demonstrates that no strict formulaic application of a Tridentine norm regulated confessants' sacramental experiences. Rather, a much more complex set of variables determined procedure. These included the theological leanings, personality, and scrupulosity of both confessor and confessant; the amount of time available; their social, ethnic, and economic status; the confessant's gender; and even the preexisting relationship between priest and penitent. Given the sealed and private nature of the encounter, especially for sins that did not affect the public life of the community, significant latitude existed. While confession certainly could become a means by which priests could terrorize their penitents, confessors might equally be influenced by the needs and demands of the laity, making concessions and bending rules in order to avoid conflict, show favoritism, and secure mutually beneficial results.

Determining whether a confession was sufficiently complete could thus be a complicated process. This was true even of seemingly simple activities. Some guidebooks, for example, urged priests to pay close attention to the behavior and countenance of the penitent. Azpilcueta advised the priest—at the "beginning, middle, and end" of the encounter—to look at the penitent to see if he bore "the proper contrition."[117] Others, however, urged confessors not to look directly at their confessants, so as to avoid causing them shame or suggesting inappropriate intentions toward female penitents.

Surreptitious glances and the careful scrutiny of the confessant that accompanied them could hardly have been carried out formulaically. Women often wore veils over their faces, and in some churches grates and screens separated priest from penitent. In dimly lit churches, confessors must have found reading a penitent's countenance difficult. Even when they could see confessants, what exactly did proper contrition look like? Tears of repentance were the most obvious sign, but they eluded some and could be faked by others.[118] Joan Baptista found reading contrition among native Mexicans so difficult that he began his manual by assuaging scrupulous priests who hesitated to absolve native penitents when their visible contrition did not match expectations.[119] Baptista's argument centered on the notion that confessors needed to trust in the power of the sacrament, which was not communicated on the basis of merit or disposition but by a divine ordinance for the forgiveness of sins. While Baptista's emphasis on the efficacy of the sacrament was striking, many authorities advocated giving penitents a similar benefit of the doubt.

## Reserved Sins, Penance, and Absolution

With the confession proper at an end, another question loomed. Could absolution be granted? Even if both parties agreed that the confession had been "complete," absolution was not a foregone conclusion. Reserved sins stood outside the bailiwick of simple priests and required papal, episcopal, or inquisitorial absolution. The papal bull *In coena Domini,* first promulgated in 1363 and reissued annually thereafter into the eighteenth century, listed cases that could be resolved only by the pope or his representatives in the papal penitentiary. While the specific sins that demanded papal absolution varied into the seventeenth century, the bull generally focused on heretics, lay attempts to appropriate ecclesiastical privileges, and those who falsified papal documents or seals, usurped church goods, or molested or did violence to clerics.[120] Additionally, each diocese had its own list of episcopally reserved sins. Near the end of the sixteenth century, Toledo's list included twenty-seven offenses, including contracting clandestine marriages, not communing within fifteen days of Quasimodo Sunday, eating meat when forbidden, and public blasphemy.[121]

The Holy Office reserved to itself a number of offenses as well, such as the obstruction of its work, bigamy, heresy, and lewdness.[122] From 1561, it also reserved the absolution of penitents who had been sexually solicited during confession. In a process that must have been emotionally taxing and personally humiliating, the church required that the penitent present herself to the Inquisition before a confessor could pronounce her sacramentally absolved. Although the Holy Office did not regard the solicited individual as the offending party, the seriousness of the crime demanded this inconvenience.

In practice, however, matters proved less formulaic. The *bula de la cruzada,* taken by a large portion of the adult Spanish population, allowed its bearers to be absolved of all reserved sins except heresy. And in 1552 Pope Julius III granted Jesuits the authority to absolve even that grave offense.[123] Furthermore, some confessors took reserved sins less seriously than others. Juan García, a

Gallegan cobbler living in Madrid, was chatting with his co-workers on the subject of women. Having sex with a prostitute, Juan alleged, could not be a sin, since Spanish law allowed for brothels and the Crown taxed them. The other *zapateros* warned him that he was mistaken, but Juan disagreed. Later, however, when he reflected upon the discussion, he decided that perhaps he had erred. The next morning he made his way to the Jesuit *colegio* and confessed with one Father Clemente, who absolved him without a fuss. The Jesuit never mentioned that what Juan had said was a mortal sin, let alone a matter reserved to the Inquisition.[124]

Like so many other aspects of confession, determining what acts of satisfaction to impose upon the penitent was a delicate procedure. Generally, more serious sins demanded heavier penances, and sins that directly affected others required restitution. Francisco de Toledo suggested that penances should not be "arbitrary" but "contrary" to the sins committed: "If they are sins against chastity, the penance should be some fasts, disciplines, or a hair shirt. If perjuries or blasphemies, they should be penitential prayers, masses, and spiritual exercises." The confessor also needed to consider the "quality of the person." The poor should not be commanded to give alms, or servants to make pilgrimages.[125]

The performance of penance sometimes saw private confession enter the public realm. Neighbors, seeing a penitent completing his *opera satisfactionis,* might guess at what had been confessed, particularly if the punishment fit the crime. For this reason, Azpilcueta cautioned priests not to impose fasts or heavy penances lest, in so doing, they inadvertently break the confessional seal.[126] Better to impose penances that people could complete privately. Although confession continued to have public components for many decades, this approach from one of the most influential moral theologians of the age marks a break with the more community-focused penance of previous centuries and points in the direction of confession as individualistic, if not anonymous.[127]

Of course, in practice much depended upon one's confessor. Lazaro de Amaya of Madrid, for instance, committed the sin of public blasphemy, saying in the presence of two women that he renounced God. This was an episcopally reserved sin. However, when he confessed the matter at Nuestra Señora de Atocha, the friar absolved him and assigned a penance of just one Our Father and one Hail Mary.[128]

Penitents might not accept the penance assigned by their confessor, and authorities disagreed about whether they could do so licitly.[129] If the sentence seemed overly harsh, the penitent might request its moderation. If the priest refused, some authorities suggested that the confessant could ignore the penance and confess again with another priest. Even if penitents did accept their penance, some believed that they could commute it by taking indulgences or performing other pious works.[130]

Finally, at the end of the process, the priest spoke the words of absolution, the assurance that the offender's *culpa* had been forgiven by God and his church, even if acts of satisfaction (or, barring their completion, a stay in purgatory) might still be required before all necessary *poena* had been meted out. Some authorities suggested that the penitent should offer a prayer requesting forgiveness before receiving absolution.[131] The priest, however, performed the fundamental work by declaring the penitent's sins absolved in the name of God. While the church demanded that the minister at least speak the sacramental words *Te absolvo,* he might also use an extended version of the formula or the vernacular equivalent. The ritual thus completed, the penitent rose and left the confessional to perform his penance (or not), enjoy the freedom of having been forgiven his sins, worry about whether she had confessed everything, or forget about the experience entirely until the following Easter.

## Conclusions

Confessing clearly could be an elaborate process. Even the long exposition attempted here by no means accounts for the many variations or modular components that might find their way into the confessional. Nor could it possibly relate the diversity of opinions on every matter. Rather, by working through the main components of the penitential encounter, this chapter has emphasized three points. First, during the early modern period, the ecclesiastical hierarchy in Spain attempted to implement a strict prescriptive confessional regimen. It legislated rules about the location and space of confession and closely monitored priestly behavior. The goal of these dictates was the reformation of abuses in confessional practice. These measures, it was hoped, would free the sacrament to serve as a means of reforming the population.

Second, the wide variety of opinions offered by the regular authors of confessional guidebooks made putting this program into practice very difficult. These works sought to improve penitential practice through the formation of a pastorally minded clergy, but exactly what that meant depended upon one's theological leanings, personality, and experience. While manuals of confession went a long way toward creating a more able and canny pastorate, they also wore away at the clear guidelines propounded by bishops. This in turn gave rise to a greater diversity of practices than would otherwise have been the case. As a result, no single Tridentine voice dictated confessional procedure. Rather, one hears a cacophony of authorities, each contradicting or approving other authors, ameliorating rigid guidelines, and asserting proper practice.

Finally, while councils, popes, and bishops legislated procedure and guidebooks offered advice, the daily workings of confession came down to a tête-à-tête between two human beings. In that context, making or eliciting a good confession usually meant arriving at a mutually satisfying compromise rather than a simplistic imposition of clerical authority or submission of lay volition. Most people in Spain knew the sacrament well, and their wills did not cease to function when they entered the confessional. On the contrary, it seems that very often they proved to be just as canny as the priests who served them.

## REGULATING THE EASTER DUTY

Entre la mano y la boca
desaparece la sopa.
—SPANISH PROVERB

The fathers at Trent viewed confession as an integral part of reforming the church. They reinforced the significance of the sacrament in no uncertain terms, anathematizing those who denied the Lateran precept requiring that all Christians commune and confess annually. In 1561 Juan de Avila offered his thoughts on the matter in a *memorial* to the Council's third convocation: "It is well known from long and certain experience that there is no other remedy equal to the frequenting of these two sacraments [i.e., confession and the Eucharist] to pull a soul out of the mud, as the saying goes, and to set it going lightly in the clear and beautiful way of the Lord. And if the people could be made to frequent them, given a few reasonably good and learned confessors, it would be a simple and painless way of reforming the Christian people."[1] Despite this optimism, using the sacrament of penance to reform the people of Spain proved to be a less straightforward process than Juan de Avila had imagined.

Because confessors acted as representatives of God, the information exchanges that occurred in the confessional had about them a certain hierarchical quality. Penitents learned a worldview and reflected it back to priests by reciting Christian prayers and doctrine as well as by revealing their specific sins. They expressed their obedience to the ecclesiastical system through submissive postures and respectful behavior. In turn, the confessor—as judge, physician, and pastor—interpreted their confessions, instructed them in the faith, offered spiritual counsel, and granted absolution. Noting this hierarchical quality of the sacrament, historians have depicted confession as a fundamentally top-down institution foisted upon the people.

Yet confession was as much a bottom-up as a top-down experience, for laypeople made it their own. In this chapter we turn to the most highly bureaucratized and regulated episode of the penitential year in the largest and most prestigious ecclesiastical domain in Spain: the Lenten confession in the Archdiocese of Toledo. While the Roman church may have mandated annual use of the sacrament, it did not actually control confessional practice. Although the structure, space, and theology of the encounter empowered the clergy over the laity, the laity did not passively accept the implementation of clerical initiatives meant to regulate the sacrament. Laymen and women exercised real agency in confession; they had goals and the means of achieving them.

Most laypeople accepted the need to fulfill their Easter duty. To be sure, some shirked this obligation in shocking fashion. In Blanca, north of Murcia, for example, one cleric complained at the end of the sixteenth century that three-quarters of his mostly *morisco* flock failed to confess.[2] Most Spaniards, however, did more than merely comply. Despite highly bureaucratic legislation meant to regulate confessional practice, they demonstrated remarkable adaptability and flexibility as they found ways, within limits, to confess where and with whom they wanted while skirting the wrath of authorities.

The connection between bureaucracy and sacramental confession stretches back well beyond the early modern era. Few medieval people, save the very holy or the bizarre, sought to confess much more frequently than the once per year mandated by the Fourth Lateran Council in 1215.[3] The degree to which the remainder of the population attained even the minimal level of compliance remains difficult to piece together, but some evidence suggests that many failed to fulfill the Lateran precept.[4] In Spain, from at least the mid-thirteenth century, bishops attempted to record whether parishioners were confessing annually to their *proprio sacerdoti,* a phrase that most understood to refer to the parish priest or his lieutenant. As a consequence, local parishes became involved in regulating confession.

At the archiepiscopal level, Pedro de Albalat, archbishop of Tarragona (r. 1238–51), produced the *Summa septem sacramentorum,* which was included in the 1241 Synod of Barcelona. In order to establish parochial compliance with the Lateran mandate, Albalat ordered each parish to draw up a *memorial* that recorded the names of confessants.[5] Provincial councils held in Salamanca (1335) and Toledo (1339) obliged *curas* annually to compose lists of parishioners, indicating who had confessed and communed that Lent.[6] In 1345, noting the many failures in his diocese to adhere to the Lateran decree, Bishop Blas Fernández de Toledo (r. 1343–53) enacted a similar statute for the churches of

Palencia.[7] Four years later he obliged *curas* or their representatives to bring their lists to the annual synod.[8] Synodal statutes compiled in 1354 for the Archdiocese of Barcelona ordered similar lists to be made every year.[9]

At his 1498 synod, the primate of Spain, Francisco Jiménez de Cisneros (r. 1495–1517), invoked the *memorial* convention when he ordered the *curas* in the Archdiocese of Toledo to produce parish registers.[10] Other dioceses followed suit. By the middle of the sixteenth century the precept had become universal in the Kingdom of Castile and in the Crown of Aragon.[11] Nevertheless, few parishes appear to have actually produced these *libros de matrícula* or *padrones* for many decades.[12] Indeed, throughout Spain, the degree to which priests actually produced the episcopally mandated *matrículas* depended upon diocese, bishop, parish, *cura,* and *visitador.* In the Archdiocese of Tarragona, for example, they seem to have become important only in the second half of the eighteenth century, and in Pamplona not until the mid-nineteenth. But in Huesca examples exist from the late sixteenth century.[13] The parish of Saint Michael the Archangel in Escariche near Guadalajara had one as early as 1593, but the nearby church of San Miguel in Fuentelviejo still had no *libro de matrícula* a century later.[14] The failure of so many parishes to comply with episcopal attempts to regulate Lenten confessional practice raises questions about the relationship between the center and the periphery. In order to address these issues, we turn to a case study of Spain's wealthiest and most influential episcopal see.

## Confessional Legislation in the Archdiocese of Toledo

The Archdiocese of Toledo held pride of place and set the tone for the rest of Spain. During the sixteenth and seventeenth centuries, the archbishops of Toledo, who claimed the title primate of Spain, convened numerous synods and provincial councils. The published constitutions enacted during these convocations provided *curas* with a set of rules to implement in their parishes. By tracking this legislation for confession we can discern the strategies developed by the ecclesiastical hierarchy of Spain to regulate sacramental practice in the parishes.

In 1536 Archbishop Juan Pardo Talavera (r. 1534–45) followed the practice initiated for Toledo by Jiménez de Cisneros in obliging *curas* to produce parish registers and present them before the archbishop or his vicar-general by Pentecost or face a fine of two florins. The synod commanded all parishioners to confess between Palm Sunday and Quasimodo Sunday and required that priests admonish those who failed to do so. Those who remained unshriven two weeks after the deadline were to be excommunicated. The synod noted the "hardness" and "contumacy" of some who refused to comply, and tasked vicars-general with denouncing them as publicly excommunicate and proceeding against the obstinate with the full weight of the law in order to gain their submission. A placard was to be erected in every church listing the names of those who had been excommunicated, and, for the sake of the illiterate, the priest was to read the names aloud every Sunday and on compulsory feast days. Because of concerns about the disorderly performance of the sacrament by members of the regular orders, Archbishop Talavera forbade them to confess his sheep without episcopal approbation and license. Finally, he commanded *curas* to retain the services of extra confessors for their congregations during Lent and Holy Week.[15]

In 1566, while the famous Archbishop Bartolomé de Carranza (r. 1558–76) languished in the jails of the Holy Office under suspicion of heresy, Gómez Tello Girón, the diocesan administrator, convened the first post-Tridentine synod in Toledo. To speak generally, he implemented a more rigorous policy of confessional regulation than had Cisneros or Talavera. Tello sought to enforce ecclesiastical jurisdiction by doing away with vague parochial boundaries. Each household was assigned a parish church at which its members were to complete the Easter duty. The *cura* of one parish was to refuse to confess the parishioners of another. If a penitent received special privilege to confess to some other priest, he was required to present a *cédula* (confessional receipt) to his *cura* before communing. Failure to do so would result in the penitent's being punished as if he had failed to complete the Easter duty. And, for the first time, the synod formally denied confessants absolution if they could not recite the mandated prayers.[16]

In addition to posting and announcing from the pulpit the names of excommunicates, parish priests were ordered to share the information with other *curas* and the guardians of local monasteries so that the recalcitrant could not confess surreptitiously. The synod also stipulated a policy for dealing with those laypeople who had been excommunicated for more than a year or who had missed two Lenten confessions in sequence. The degree of punishment depended upon the amount of time they had been excommunicate and the degree of their pertinacity, but the priests were to deal with them as with those suspected of heresy.[17]

In 1582 and 1583 Archbishop Gaspar de Quiroga (r. 1577–94) convened first an episcopal synod and then a provincial council. The council said relatively little about regulating confession but reinforced the 1566 synod's plan for assigning households to particular parishes and enforcing parochial jurisdiction.[18] Intriguingly, Quiroga's episcopal synod did not reconfirm some of his predecessors' policies.[19] It made no mention, for example, of denying absolution to those unable to recite the prayers of the church or of treating those who had been excommunicate for more than one year as suspect of heresy.[20] On the other hand, a great deal of new legislation appeared under Quiroga. For the first time, in a synodal constitution at least, a monetary penalty of two *reales*—described as a "customary" fine—was imposed for failure to confess. Quiroga may not have explicitly required knowledge of Christian doctrine for absolution, but he did, for the first time, include in the synodal constitution copies of the prayers of the church, the articles of faith, the Ten Commandments, the commandments of the church, the *santiguado,* and a number of other common formulae such as the beatitudes and the deadly sins.[21]

Archbishop Bernardo Sandoval y Rojas convened the next Synod of Toledo in 1601. He reaffirmed many of the policies that had disappeared under Quiroga, but he also advanced new legislation. He increased the "customary" penalty of two *reales* for failing to comply with the Easter duty to four. The synod spelled out exactly what the *libros de matrícula* should look like and even provided a mock-up. Parish priests were ordered to remind their flocks every week, beginning the third Sunday before Lent, of their obligation to complete the Easter duty and to explain to parishioners what would happen if they failed to comply.[22] The pre-Quirogan policy of denying absolution and communion to confessants who failed to recite the four prayers was reinstated. The synod urged episcopal *visitadores* to inspect the parish's *libro de matrícula* and charged them with seeing that the sacrament of confession was properly administered.[23]

The 1622 synod met in Toledo under the authority of the *cardenal infante,* don Francisco de Austria (r. 1620–41), but since the archbishop never actually visited his archdiocese, it was presided over by Dr. Alvaro Villegas, don Francisco's co-administrator. Villegas strongly believed that confessions, especially Lenten ones, should be conducted by *curas* rather than regular priests.[24] No surprise, then, that he emphasized the crucial role of the parish priest and warned against allowing *clerigos* or *frailes estrangeros* to confess in parish churches, especially if they were not just unknown but actual foreigners. Villegas reminded his *curas* that they held the primary responsibility for administering the sacraments. Others could be brought in when the need arose, but "they [were] only there to help, not to excuse." Similarly, only for "very serious reasons" could *curas* grant licenses allowing parishioners to confess outside the parish during Lent.[25] The minimal doctrinal knowledge required of penitents was increased.

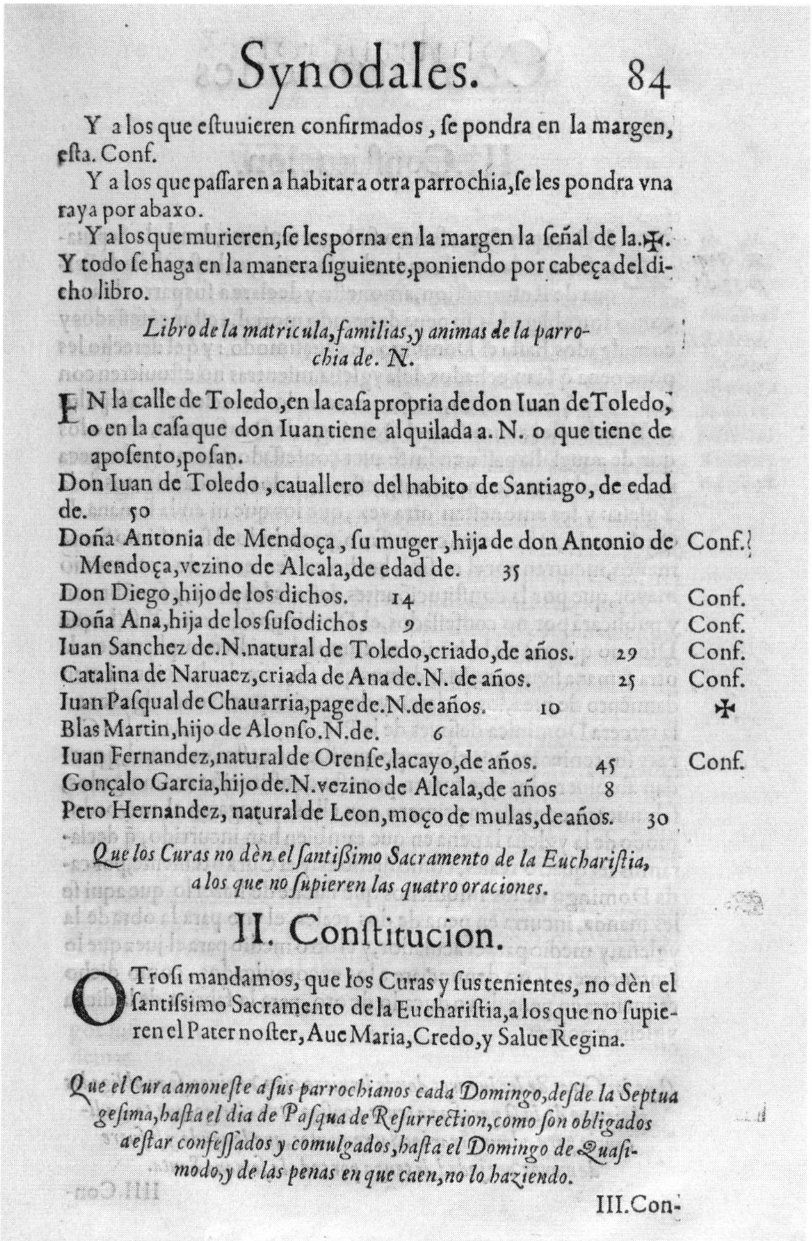

Y a los que eſtuuieren confirmados, ſe pondra en la margen,
eſta. Conf.

Y a los que paſſaren a habitar a otra parrochia,ſe les pondra vna
raya por abaxo.

Y a los que murieren,ſe les porna en la margen la ſeñal de la.✠.
Y todo ſe haga en la manera ſiguiente,poniendo por cabeça del dicho libro.

*Libro de la matricula, familias, y animas de la parro-*
*chia de.* N.

EN la calle de Toledo,en la caſa propria de don Iuan de Toledo,
o en la caſa que don Iuan tiene alquilada a. N. o que tiene de
apoſento,poſan.

Don Iuan de Toledo, cauallero del habito de Santiago, de edad
de. 50

Doña Antonia de Mendoça, ſu muger, hija de don Antonio de Conf.}
Mendoça,vezino de Alcala,de edad de. 35

Don Diego,hijo de los dichos. 14      Conf.

Doña Ana,hija de los ſuſodichos 9      Conf.

Iuan Sanchez de.N.natural de Toledo,criado,de años. 29   Conf.

Catalina de Naruaez,criada de Ana de.N. de años. 25   Conf.

Iuan Paſqual de Chauarria,page de.N.de años. 10      ✠

Blas Martin,hijo de Alonſo.N.de. 6

Iuan Fernandez,natural de Orenſe,lacayo,de años. 45   Conf.

Gonçalo Garcia,hijo de.N.vezino de Alcala,de años 8

Pero Hernandez, natural de Leon,moço de mulas,de años. 30

*Que los Curas no dèn el ſantiſſimo Sacramento de la Euchariſtia,*
*a los que no ſupieren las quatro oraciones.*

## II. Conſtitucion.

OTroſi mandamos, que los Curas y ſus tenientes, no dèn el
ſantiſsimo Sacramento de la Euchariſtia,a los que no ſupieren el Pater noſter,Aue Maria,Credo,y Salue Regina.

*Que el Cura amoneſte a ſus parrochianos cada Domingo,deſde la Septua*
*geſima,haſta el dia de Paſqua de Reſurrection,como ſon obligados*
*a eſtar confeſſados y comulgados,haſta el Domingo de Quaſi-*
*modo,y de las penas en que caen,no lo haziendo.*

III.Con-

Fig. 3   A model *libro de matricula*. From Don Bernardo de Rojas y Sandoval, *Constituciones*
*synodales del Arçobispado de Toledo* (Toledo: Pedro Rodriguez, 1601). Used by permission
of the Biblioteca Nacional de España, Madrid.

Instead of just reciting the four prayers, confessants also became responsible for the "commandments of the decalogue and of the church" and for knowing "what they should do to receive the sacraments fruitfully."[26] Instead of a two-week grace period following the Easter season, tardy penitents had only one week before excommunication. Finally, the synod ordered confessors to keep with them a list of papally reserved sins, lest they mistakenly absolve penitents out of ignorance.[27]

The final two synods of the seventeenth century, convened in 1658 by Baltasar de Moscoso y Sandoval (r. 1646–65) and in 1682 by Luis Manuel Fernández Portocarrero (r. 1677–1709), saw few developments, but neither did the old legislation disappear. Moscoso imposed a stiffer monetary penalty upon those who missed their Lenten confession. They now had to pay an additional two *reales* for every additional week that passed before they confessed.[28] The 1682 synod emphasized that only the archbishop himself or members of his council, and not his *visitadores* or *vicarios,* could license confessors, and ordered priests not to administer the sacrament on Good Friday. Finally, the synod offered a clarification, explaining that tardy penitents who failed to confess received excommunication *latae sententiae,* that is, automatically and regardless of whether a formal declaration had been pronounced.[29]

From an episcopal perspective, regulating confessional practice clearly entailed an elaborate bureaucratic structure, but the provincial and synodal constitutions of early modern Spain legislated very few *completely* new practices. Innovations such as erecting confessionals in parish churches and testing confessants' grasp of Christian doctrine had antecedents, but they tended to be occasional, unenforced, or characteristic of monastic life. More frequently, procedures that had long been on the books in some form—*libros de matrícula, cédulas,* episcopal licenses, and punishments for flouting the Easter duty—became more important and their use more clearly explained. The whole system developed into a complex information network of rules, certifications, and lists designed to provide bishops with regulatory oversight of all Lenten confessions in their dioceses. The presence of episcopal *visitadores,* the circulation of synodal constitutions and diocesan decrees, and mandatory attendance at synods helped remind parish clergy of their duty to implement and enforce legislation. And fines for noncompliance kept both priests and penitents on the righteous path. But how would laypeople respond to the decrees of a reforming episcopacy fortified by Trent as it attempted to implement new layers of confessional bureaucracy? And how would parish priests deal with their role as enforcers of those decrees?

## Confessing Outside the Parish Church

Opportunities to confess outside the parish and at times other than Lent set the stage for the responses of *curas* and laypeople to these developments, for as Spanish bishops began to ratchet up confessional bureaucracy, two other important developments had already begun to take root. The practice of confessing more frequently than once a year became typical, and members of the regular orders began flooding the market with vernacular guidebooks and devotional literature that addressed penitential practice.

The later Middle Ages had seen a remarkable increase in penitential activity across Europe, especially among the religious, members of tertiary orders, and lay holy folk. The late fourteenth-century Dominican nun Catherine of Siena (1347–1380) became a pioneering figure in popularizing frequent confession and the potential of the relationship between a spiritual director and directee.[30] And in the early fifteenth century, the influential Parisian theologian Jean Gerson had encouraged laypeople to go beyond merely making an annual rehearsal of their sins.[31] While Franciscans had long been known as preachers of penitential sermons and Lenten confessors, it was ultimately the Society of Jesus that brought the practice of frequent confession to the laity in the early modern period.[32] One Jesuit, for instance, reported the effects of the Society's ministry in Valladolid at the end of 1555, noting that the "accustomed exercise of hearing confessions increases day by day, as does the number of confessants, especially this Christmas season, so that I doubt if a larger number could be seen in Lent or Holy Week itself."[33]

In addition to those who confessed *ocho a ocho,* a growing number of Castilians began to shrive for jubilee indulgences and at feast days throughout the year, not just at Lent. Indulgences, which often required a confession before a devotee could enjoy their benefits, became increasingly available and popular. In small towns and rural areas, regular missionary preachers depicted their visits as extraordinary opportunities to obtain pardon from God, inviting auditors to begin their lives anew by making general confessions of their entire lives and participating in the sacrament more frequently.[34] Moreover, these same members of the regular orders, not their secular counterparts, produced the overwhelming bulk of published literature on confession.[35]

Confession also became a growing concern for the Holy Office. During its early years, the Inquisition focused on heresy cases: Judaizers, *moriscos, alumbrados,* and Protestants. For the hundred years or so beginning in the mid-sixteenth century, however, it turned to reforming Old Christians; nearly two-thirds of its defendants during that period claimed purity of blood.[36] And many of the sins that the Inquisition took responsibility for prosecuting had links to the sacrament of penance.[37] In 1561 sexual solicitation in the confessional came under inquisitorial jurisdiction. Likewise, tribunals began to try individuals for committing "minor heresies," which included statements against, scandalous words about, or the blaspheming of the sacrament.[38] In fact, cases of *proposiciones malsonantes* (ill-sounding statements) tried by the Tribunal of Toledo between 1575 and 1610 had to do with confession more often than with any other subject. Sacramental confession played a pivotal role in more than 10 percent of Toledo's entire caseload of 1,177 trials during that thirty-five-year period.[39] Between 1531 and 1560, 43 out of 814 cases (just over 5 percent) tried by Toledo involved statements against confession. Between 1561 and 1620, however, the figure rose to more than 9 percent (68 of 720) for uneducated defendants (artisans, farmers, and agricultural workers) and nearly 13 percent (86 of 667) for cases involving clerics and educated laypeople.[40] While these trends certainly indicate that the Inquisition became concerned about attacks against the sacrament during this period, they probably also indicate that Spaniards were discussing confession more frequently than they had previously.

At about the same time, inquisitorial trials began to demonstrate attentiveness to confessional behavior in another way. Beginning around 1550 and with increasing regularity and detail over time, defendants were asked about their confessional practice, particularly at Lent. These questions came during the portion of the trial known as the first audience (*primera audiencia*), when the accused supplied his name, lineage, occupation, and so forth; that is to say, this was part of the preliminary material gathered before the investigation of actual guilt. In 1561 the inquisitor-general Fernando de Valdes made these sacramental questions mandatory.[41] Initially, inquisitors merely asked whether defendants confessed and communed "when the Holy Mother Church" commanded it, and the defendant answered with a simple yes or no. Within a few decades, however, scribes added more details, eventually including where, when, and with whom defendants had last confessed and communed, and whether they had confessed that year outside Lent.

## Complying with the Church

The answers supplied by defendants accused of "minor heresies"—blasphemy, lewdness, and scandalous words—offer a useful way to study confessional behavior.[42] Although extra-Lenten use of the sacrament increased during the early modern period, the weeks around Easter remained the most significant penitential moment in the church calendar. The rigorous episcopal legislation for confession focused primarily upon the Easter duty, making it of particular interest. Fortunately, then, the answers provided by defendants allow us to chart the course of certain aspects of lay confessional practice in the Archdiocese of Toledo.

Before considering the data, however, a word of caution is necessary, since determining whether and how laypeople fulfilled their Easter duty is tricky. Given the spottiness with which *curas* created *libros de matrícula,* visualizing a complete picture is impossible. The benefit of using the questions asked by inquisitors to track confessional behavior is that they offer a large sample of information otherwise unavailable over a significant span of years. Yet those answers were given by people tried for religious misbehavior. This raises two questions. Can the answers be trusted? If so, since these respondents had been accused of religious misbehavior, did their answers reflect the larger society?

To the first question we can cautiously answer yes. In most cases the court could easily verify the information by gathering testimony about confessional practice from priests and other community members, checking the defendant's *cédula,* or consulting the parish's *libro de matrícula,* when it existed. The Inquisition rigorously pursued perjurers, which must have caused defendants to think twice before attempting to deceive the Holy Office. Furthermore, the specificity of the answers gives them the ring of truth. While defendants occasionally proved unable to identify their confessors to the Inquisition—"with an old Franciscan whose name he couldn't remember"—most could provide names or at least offices. While none of this proves that all the answers were true, it suggests that many of them were.

The second question—whether the individuals in the sample reflect the larger society—can also be answered affirmatively. Blasphemy, scandalous words, and lewdness were Old Christians crimes, since when a *judeoconverso, morisco,* or foreigner made similar missteps, they were viewed as indicative of more serious depravity. Inquisitors treated these lesser offenses as examples of crassness and ignorance or as irreverent exclamations. Certainly, we find no indication that the Holy Office pursued these defendants because of their confessional practice. Many of them exhibited altogether routine penitential compliance. Moreover, they typically viewed themselves as good Christians and frequently defended themselves, not by denying that they had made the offensive statements but by denying the moral implications imposed upon their words by inquisitors. Blasphemous, lewd, and scandalous words merely "slipped from the tongue," as one young man explained in 1582.[43] These defendants differed from most of their counterparts only in having been summoned before the Holy Office.

Hundreds of *procesos* dating from before 1700 remain from the Toledan Tribunal's campaign against minor heresies. Scribes recorded defendants' answers about their confessional observance in about five hundred of them. Most of these cases occurred after 1550, when it became typical for inquisitors to ask about confession. In only twenty-three cases did defendants admit to missing their Lenten confession during the trial year, and the later one proceeds, the fewer the failures: ten occurred before 1560, and only two after 1600. Eleven happened between 1560 and 1599, but that period accounts for the bulk (329) of the trials. This indicates that more than 96 percent of the sample fulfilled their Easter duty and that, in fact, the later sixteenth century saw a significant decline in failure to comply.

In general, those tried by the Inquisition for blasphemy or scandalous words came from humble backgrounds: agricultural laborers, foreigners, an old beggar, an escaped convict, and so forth. Less marginal members of society had a higher rate of compliance. Some who failed to confess could offer reasonable explanations. Frequently, for example, jailors denied access to the sacrament. For instance, Juan López de Cuerva of La Guardia, arrested in 1568 for lewdness, belonged to a confraternity whose members all confessed toward the end of Lent. Juan had been arrested during Lent but before his confraters had observed this tradition. He had been denied the opportunity to confess while in custody, leaving him unable to complete his Easter duty.[44]

Some individuals who had confessed the previous Lent were unable to cross themselves or recite the *santiguado* properly before the Inquisition. Since episcopal synods required that everyone perform these rituals before confessing, it follows that those who could not do so should have had difficulty finding a priest to absolve them, but apparently someone was willing to do the job. Chronologically, the same trends appear among these individuals as among those who did not complete their Easter duty. Of the thirty-nine failures, seventeen occurred before 1560, twenty-seven before 1580. Of the twenty-two defendants who could not sign themselves or recite the prayers after 1560, six were French, four Italian, and one German. One hailed from remote Galicia and another identified herself as a gypsy.[45] Members of stable communities rarely had problems, but itinerants and members of lower social groups (agricultural laborers, weavers, servants, slaves, muleteers, and so forth) failed more frequently. This may, however, merely indicate that inquisitors evaluated the performance of these individuals more severely than they did the less marginal elements of society.

In about two hundred *procesos,* the scribes recorded enough information for us to determine whether defendants had made their most recent Lenten confession to their *cura* (or his parochial representative) or to someone else. This information indicates whether the episcopal bureaucracy promulgated via synodal constitutions succeeded in compelling laypeople to fulfill their Easter duty *proprio sacerdoti.* Between 1540 and the end of the 1570s, more than half—roughly 60 percent—of defendants confessed and communed in their parishes at Lent. Failure to do so was often the consequence of legitimate impediments.[46] For example, one Frenchman who had lived in Toledo for many years explained that he had not confessed and communed at his parish, St. Thomas, in 1561 because the overworked *cura* had granted his parishioners license to fulfill their Easter duty elsewhere.[47] Francisco López, a knife maker, confessed to a Carmelite in 1570, but he had permission from his *cura,* who had included Francisco's name in the parish register.[48] This 60 percent level of compliance proved to be the high-water mark.

In the last decades of the sixteenth century, parish confessions declined significantly, to just less than half of the sampled individuals. In addition to this general trend, defendants more frequently failed to offer good reasons for not confessing at their parish church. They did not merely find themselves in situations where they could not make parish confessions; they actively began to pursue them. For example, in 1587 Alonso Chamorro publicly made a lewd statement but wanted to avoid inquisitorial entanglements. His parish priest knew about the sin, and Alonso knew that his *cura* knew. Hoping to beat the system, Alonso received absolution that Easter from a Franciscan; presumably he confessed the lewd statement, but we cannot know for certain. He had successfully made a Lenten confession and should have been permitted to commune. However, when he tried to do so at his parish to complete his Easter duty, the *cura* refused him.[49] While Alonso's gambit failed, many others had greater success.

By the end of the sixteenth century, and increasingly in the early years of the seventeenth century, laypeople began overwhelmingly to complete their Easter duty outside the parish.[50] The sample sizes for these years are small, but they remain highly suggestive. In the 1590s, ten out of twenty-five individuals confessed to their *curas;* in the first decade of the new century, two out of fifteen did so; and in the 1610s, only one confessant in ten. This suggests that the most dramatic moment of change in confessional practice corresponded strikingly with the onset of the new century. Yet this trend does not indicate that the parish system had broken down entirely. Rather, laypeople had made common the practice of confessing outside their parish church and then, like Alonso Chamorro, returning to their *cura* to take communion *para cumplir con la iglesia*, to comply with the church.

In about half of the cases from the late sixteenth and early seventeenth centuries, defendants explicitly described using this strategy. Sometimes they had obvious reasons for disobeying the synodal decree. Pedro Gutierrez from the Diocese of Burgos, for instance, confessed with a Carmelite friar in Alcalá de Henares in 1594 or 1595 because he was a student at the Complutensian University.[51] Others would have had a more difficult time explaining their actions. Luis Ramírez, a twenty-six-year-old Toledan tailor, confessed on Holy Thursday of 1608 with a Dominican in the monastery of San Pedro Mártir and then, on the very same day, took communion at his parish church, St. Mary Magdalene.[52] According to the 1601 Toledan synod, this should not have happened without some grave need. Nevertheless, Luis offered no explanation and neither his *cura* nor the inquisitor expressed concern.

For the remainder of the seventeenth century, tracking compliance becomes even more difficult, for two reasons. First, the Holy Office prosecuted fewer cases of minor heresy than in previous decades. Second, laypeople seem to have confessed more frequently than in previous decades. Thus their answers to the inquisitor's question "When and with whom did you last confess?" increasingly refer to confessions outside the Easter season. Only twenty-six *procesos* provide clues to Lenten confessional behavior between 1620 and 1699. But of those twenty-six, ten defendants confessed in their parishes, which may indicate that *curas* regained some of their lost market share. Even if this is true, the parishes still lagged far behind the levels of compliance they had commanded in the mid-sixteenth century.

## Explaining the Trends

These trends demand explanation, and a number of lines of possible inquiry exist. Gender, as it turns out, probably is not the key. Women were tried for minor heresies much less frequently than men, and even when they were tried, inquisitors typically recorded less useful information about their confessional behavior. Nevertheless, those women who appeared before the tribunal for

lesser offenses fulfilled their Easter duty just as creatively as the men did. Ana
Sánchez of Toledo, for example, attended Mass and heard sermons at two different churches: the hermitage of Nuestra Señora de la Estrella and the parish
of Santiago del Arrabal. Just so, when Lent came around she confessed at
la Estrella but communed at both churches.[53] Conversely, in 1572 Guitaria
López, a servant at the Convent of the Conception in Madrid, confessed and
communed twice: once with the *cura* of her parish and a second time at La
Concepción.[54] In 1574, 1578, 1583, 1591, and 1596 the *procesos* offer examples
of women who confessed at their parish churches during the Easter season.[55]
However, numerous counterexamples can be cited.[56] Conclusions based on
such a limited sample must be tentative, but it appears that the transition
toward confessing outside the parish occurred at around the same time for
both men and women.

Demography, by contrast, clearly did matter. As population rose during
the sixteenth century in New Castile, *curas* found it difficult to cope with massive flocks and often failed to regulate paschal compliance effectively, even
as bishops expected parishes to provide more careful oversight.[57] In 1587, for
example, owing to rising population and demographic shifts, the Archdiocese
of Toledo had 167,051 households and only 817 parishes, an average of more
than two hundred households per parish.[58] While the number of unordained
or merely tonsured secular clerics rose dramatically in the seventeenth century, their energy was directed toward satisfying the equally dramatic rise in
demand for masses for the dead, not confessing.[59] The members of regular
orders necessarily picked up the slack.

This situation helped to create a Castile in which, by the end of the century,
parish confessions during Lent were falling sharply. That laypeople continued
to act as conscientiously as they did suggests that many of them had internalized the obligation and saw the Easter duty as tied to the parish. Population
losses in the seventeenth century allowed priests to catch their breath, so to
speak, especially in a city like Toledo, which saw massive demographic decline.
After the sharp drop, however, many urban centers experienced slower population growth throughout the remainder of the seventeenth century and an
eventual return to sixteenth-century heights.

While the number of Castilian parishes remained relatively stable, the number of regular clergy surged. Between 1591 and 1623 the population of Franciscans more than doubled in Spain, from about sixty-seven hundred to fourteen
thousand. The numbers of Dominicans, Augustinians, Calced and Discalced
Carmelites, Trinitarians, Mercedarians, and Jesuits lagged behind the Friars

Minor, but each order experienced rapid expansion. In all, membership in the regular orders in Spain grew from about thirteen thousand in 1591 to almost three times that figure by 1623; their numbers continued to rise into the 1660s.[60]

Regular clerics often received better training for administering the sacrament of penance and were more enthusiastic about participating in it than their secular counterparts. Consequently, devout Spaniards frequently looked to regulars as spiritual directors. Even for the less devout, however, the religious orders could be useful. Those seeking easy absolution might consider visiting a regular priest a tempting alternative to their *cura*. If one's *cura* refused absolution, the matter could typically be resolved only through repentance or by remanding the confessant to a higher authority, which might prove complicated, undesirable, or both. If, on the other hand, a regular refused to absolve a penitent, in most cases she could simply go to another confessor, and then another, until she found a friar who would oblige her. The Salamancan Franciscan Felipe Diaz described the situation in these terms:

> You go to confess with one [priest] and he won't absolve you because he would really sin in doing so, since you are not in the right disposition to be absolved. So you go to another confessor and he absolves you, and thus casts you into perdition. You go to a learned consultant who tells you that you can't do something, that your business is illicit. So you seek out another and another until you find one that says, "Fine, you can do it," and you give that one more credit because his opinion conforms to your desire even though he is ignorant and doesn't know what he's talking about.[61]

Fray Felipe's comments also emphasize another matter that merits consideration. The picture of a penitent going from one confessor to the next assumes a very particular physical environment, one in which laypeople had access to multiple priests. Confessing in an urban as opposed to a semi-urban or rural setting was potentially a very different experience. Cities abounded not only with overfilled parish churches but also with monasteries, hospitals, oratories, and chapels. All of these provided alternative venues for confession. Influential ecclesiastical institutions controlled by regulars dotted the landscape of the great cities of Spain. San Juan de los Reyes in Toledo and, in Madrid, Nuestra Señora de Atocha and San Francisco el Grande frequently drew lay confessants.

Overpopulated urban parishes and an abundance of regular confessors made slipping through the administrative cracks easier, but the situation was different in small villages. Avoiding the watchful eyes of *curas* and neighbors was more difficult when everyone knew everyone else. Urban centers claimed the lion's share of religious institutions and individuals. In 1591 about 75 percent of the monasteries under the jurisdiction of Toledo's inquisitorial tribunal were located in cities. Just over 3 percent were located next to villages. Of the 3,837 regular priests, 67 percent lived in cities, with most of the remainder residing in towns. Similar figures hold for the population of secular priests. In 1591 there were 3,912 secular priests; more than half lived in cities, nearly 14 percent in towns, and about 32 percent in villages.[62] The comparison of these figures with the relative population densities (27 percent in cities, slightly more than 21 percent in towns, and about 51 percent in villages) indicates that at the end of the sixteenth century, clerical population (and hence the population of confessors) was thickest in the most heavily urban settings.[63]

The roughly two hundred inquisitorial trials for minor heresies that we have used to study Lenten confessional practice in the Archdiocese of Toledo also offer some useful data for analyzing the impact of demography. If the population represented by the sample data is divided into those people living in the largest cities (Toledo and Madrid) and everyone else, some real divergences appear.[64] The statistics demand caution since the individuals might have been away from their parishes during Easter, or their villages may have been located near large cities. Dividing the sample in this fashion also does not account very well for the differences between smaller cities, towns, and villages. Nevertheless, the trends are worth noting. The two large urban centers began with a very high rate of parochial compliance in the mid-sixteenth century—77 percent—but a continual decline in parochial confession occurred over the long term, especially after 1590. On the other hand, the remaining locales began with lower rates of compliance but saw an initial spike in parish confessions in the 1570s, before declining steadily through the early seventeenth century. After bottoming out at about a 26 percent rate of parish compliance, confessions to *curas* increased sharply throughout the remainder of the seventeenth century, eventually approaching pre-Tridentine levels.

Comparing the enforcement of confessional jurisdiction between the largest cities in New Castile and the remaining communities thus provides insight into parochial compliance, especially in the seventeenth century. The data suggest that the Spanish church succeeded in drawing people back to the parishes for their Lenten confessions, but only in smaller demographic centers. In Madrid and Toledo, episcopal attempts to restrict confession to parishes proved ineffective. Population loss during the seventeenth century may have helped urban

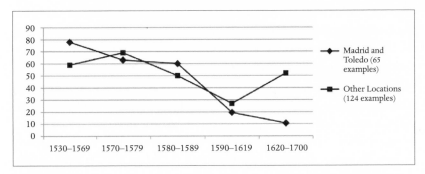

*Fig. 4*   Effects of city life on Lenten compliance (in percentage of confessions made to *curas*)

parishes slow the decline, but it did not stop it. The less rigorous bureaucratic policies of confessional regulation in the early and mid-sixteenth century under the synodal constitutions of Talvera (1536), Tello (1566), and Quiroga (1582) correspond with the highest level of parochial compliance. Yet the data also suggest that rates of Lenten compliance were not simply negative responses to episcopal attempts to enforce parish confessions through fines, threats, and rigid bureaucracy. If that were the case, we would expect to see parochial confessions increase after Quiroga's synod, which actually relaxed some of his predecessors' legislation. Instead, it is precisely at this point that one sees the beginning of decline in all groups.

It is tempting to view Quiroga's imposition of a monetary penalty of two *reales* for noncompliance as the straw that broke the camel's back, driving people away from confessing in the parishes.[65] But this is unlikely, as the monetary penalty was already "customary." And, in any case, the fine was applied only to those who missed their Lenten confession, which was never a very large number—less than 5 percent over the long term and declining over time. Nor did the movement away from parochial compliance occur simply because laypeople wanted to avoid having to recite Christian doctrine and prayers when confessing to their *curas*. Whether or not people wanted to memorize such things, they did so.[66] The small percentage who failed to confess or to learn their prayers does not account for the flood of laypeople who abandoned their parishes for regular confessors.

More likely, people feared the *potential* imposition of penalties and fines should they confess to their *curas*. This certainly proved to be one of the major advantages of going to a regular cleric and obtaining a *cédula* with which to certify paschal compliance. Not only did regulars often have better training as confessors than seculars; they also found it much more difficult, and often impossible, to impose upon their occasional confessants the sorts of penalties that episcopal legislation mandated. Regulars might refuse to absolve penitents if they came to the sacrament unprepared, unrepentant, or having committed a reserved sin. In the last case, they might even order the confessant to appear before the Holy Office or the bishop for absolution. Nevertheless, in large cities with many confessors and multiple venues for sacramental participation, some laypeople preferred to avoid those complexities. Instead, taking advantage of the opportunities afforded by the rise of Probabilism, they sought out a less scrupulous priest who *would* absolve them.

## Navigating the Bureaucracy of Confession

All of this leads to an important, if now obvious, conclusion: as post-Tridentine bishops imposed bureaucratic structures to regulate Lenten confessional behavior in the parishes, laypeople took their sins elsewhere. This conclusion carries with it two corollaries. First, Old Christians did not meet ecclesiastical attempts to regulate confession with widespread refusal to confess. Such refusal was fundamentally unusual religious behavior for most people.[67] Rather, confession formed a valuable, even fundamental, component of most Old Christians' religious lives. At the end of the seventeenth century, for example, Alonso Gómez saw confessional practice in Madrid as remarkable not in view of its defects, of which everyone was fully aware, but because *madrileños* kept coming in spite of them.[68] Early modern Spaniards believed in sin; they desired a remedy that would absolve them of guilt, keep them out of hell, and shorten their stay in purgatory. At the same time, they wanted some control over their religious lives in order to avoid public scandal and protect their honor. They accomplished both goals by learning to navigate the always complicated and often porous penitential system.

The second corollary is that the factors discussed above—demographic change, gender, social status, urbanity, the rising population of regular confessors, even episcopal bureaucracy—only created a situation in which laypeople *might potentially* have learned to navigate that system. None of these factors determined whether or how this might happen. Laypeople not only found ways to navigate the layers of prescriptive legislation that regulated confession; they also learned to employ strategies, both legitimate and potentially less legitimate, for overcoming or ameliorating those prescriptions. This fact highlights the remarkable intentionality that Spaniards exercised in their sacramental activities and the degree to which their behavior influenced the practice of confession.

Among the potentially less legitimate loopholes, from the church's perspective at least, were making incomplete confessions, refusing to confess during a single Lenten season or for a period of years, and producing counterfeit confessional receipts in order to commune. Even in Spain, some people, mostly foreigners or New Christians, eschewed sacramental confession to a priest in favor of direct confession to God. It is impossible to know how frequently confessants made use of these methods, although making incomplete confessions was anecdotally believed to be quite common, especially for *moriscos* and *judeoconversos*.

The more legitimate ways of navigating confessional waters are, if anything, more intriguing than the illegitimate. The early modern church in Spain produced a remarkable number of loopholes that worked at cross-purposes with the enforcement of parochial confessional regulation. Often, these loopholes evolved out of the jurisdictional tensions between regular and secular clergy. Some orders claimed the right to hear confessions and grant absolution without episcopal approbation. In spite of Tridentine support for episcopal authority, this debate raged for generations. Manuals of confession, invariably written by regular priests, frequently listed the many exceptions to the Lateran precept to confess *proprio sacerdoti*. Did one's priest solicit? Was he uneducated? Did he break the seal? Had one sinned against him or his family? Was life threatened or honor at stake? If so, according to some authority or other, confessing to an alternative priest, even without the *cura*'s permission, was permissible.[69]

If a layperson wanted to confess outside her parish at Lent and none of these exceptions pertained, she could follow a number of different paths that might provide satisfaction. If the penitent had the resources and inclination, she could request a dispensation from the pope or bishop. She could make a complete confession to a regular priest and then, when called to the parish to fulfill her Easter duty, legitimately make a perfunctory confession, since she could not be obliged to confess the same sins twice. Or she might simply ask her parish priest for a license to confess elsewhere. Synodal legislation indicates that granting such licenses was discouraged from the 1620s, but, as with so much else, the decision to grant them was made not at the diocesan but at the parochial level. If one were a student, traveler, or soldier, then extraparochial confessions automatically became licit, since distance made appearing at one's own church impractical.

Even within the parish itself, there was often a great deal of flexibility. Only those dwelling in the smallest, poorest, and most remote communities truly found themselves limited to a single priest. For instance, the remote Castilian town of Deza (Sigüenza), with about fifteen hundred inhabitants and no resident *cura*, still had at least eight different priests in and around town at the end of the sixteenth century, including a parish vicar, whom *morisco* confessants avoided because of his close ties to the Holy Office. Franciscans from the convent at Almazán also frequently ran missions and helped confess during high holy days.[70] If a trip to the nearest city was out of the question, laypeople might still find a monastery in relatively close proximity. In a pinch, one could always try the *cura* of a neighboring village. Some Dezanos, for instance, traveled seventy-five miles to confess with the obliging parish priest of Pozuel.[71] In the rural reaches of Galicia, some traveled thirty miles or more for a Jesuit confessor in the early 1560s.[72] Many parishes in Spain had multiple confessors, which enabled penitents to avoid a particular priest if they so desired.

Every sixteenth- and seventeenth-century Toledan synod obliged *curas* who tended churches of one hundred parishioners or more to provide extra confessors at plague times and during Lent.[73] From the mid-sixteenth century, synods stipulated that churches with more than one hundred people had to have a sufficient number of priests to allow church members to fulfill their sacramental duties in the time allotted. Smaller parishes were expected to provide an extra confessor to help administer the sacraments around Holy Week, when confessions and communions reached their peak. Synods even admonished *curas* to announce explicitly that parishioners were free to confess to these other priests if they desired.[74]

Finally, the indulgence known as the *bula de la cruzada* became perhaps the most popular loophole in the system of confessional regulation. Its development stemmed not from jurisdictional conflicts between regular and secular clergy but from the legacy of Iberian crusading and the exigencies of royal and papal finance. Among other benefits, the *cruzada* indulgence permitted the millions of Spaniards who took it to confess with any episcopally licensed confessor, even at Lent and regardless of episcopal decrees. To the degree that priests could and sought to implement synodal and conciliar precepts by regulating confession at the parochial level, it was to the *cruzada* that most people turned in order to facilitate their complex confessional behavior during the Easter season. Indeed, the *cruzada* ultimately made the enforcement of confessional jurisdiction a practical impossibility.

## Conclusions

Early modern Spaniards increasingly found ways to navigate and use the confessional system, with all of its loopholes, to their advantage. They cared about forgiveness because they believed in the reality of sin, and they expected to go to purgatory after their death.[75] They had internalized a strong, if sometimes skewed, sense of the difference between mortal and venial sins. They therefore saw confession as a necessity of life and afterlife. They might argue about what constituted a proper confession; they might seek out a more capable, agreeable, or lenient confessor than their parish priest. Very few of them, however, wanted to do away with the system entirely. Early modern Castilian laypeople were deliberate in choosing with whom they would confess. Those confessants, concerned about finding forgiveness but also about maintaining public honor, found ways to achieve both goals. They worked within the system established by the church, but they used that complicated, niche-filled, loophole-ridden system in surprisingly creative ways.

# CONFESSION ON CRUSADE

Tener bula para todo: To take the liberty of acting at pleasure, according to one's own fancy.

—NEUMAN AND BARETTI's *Dictionary of the Spanish and English Languages* (1851)

In 1585 Ysabel Martínez found herself in a predicament. Pedro de Ortega, her confessor, was making her feel uncomfortable. Rather than listen chastely to her sins, he made a habit of touching her face and speaking in an altogether inappropriate manner. Ysabel could have reported Ortega to the local representative of the Holy Office; technically, she should have, since sexual solicitation during confession fell under inquisitorial jurisdiction. But rather than take that drastic step, she initially sought to defuse the situation by turning to a popular indulgence for which she paid the modest sum of two *reales*. Unclear about the specifics, she consulted another cleric in the church, Juan de Belmonte, asking whether "by virtue of the *bula de la cruzada*" she could confess with someone other than Ortega. Belmonte assured her that she could choose any confessor, as long as he had an episcopal license.[1]

As we have seen, bishops and synods vigorously enacted programs to regulate confessional practice, while most Spaniards found ways to confess with whichever priest they wanted. The laity's failure to comply with episcopal legislation more often entailed the exploitation of loopholes in the bureaucracy of confessional regulation than a wholesale refusal to work within the system. Ysabel's indulgence, the *bula de la cruzada,* proved the most substantial of these loopholes. Its proliferation significantly undermined episcopal attempts to regulate the sacrament. While this situation greatly frustrated many bishops, it enhanced the flexibility of the confessional experience for many early modern Spaniards.

Most historians have largely ignored the impact of the bull of crusade on religious practice. Instead, emphasizing its importance to royal income during the early modern period, they have typically described it as a tax.[2] Others have viewed the *bula* as the dénouement of medieval crusading.[3] Henry Lea, who always described indulgences in the worst possible light, saw it as a tool for oppressing the masses and a means of instilling fear in the people under the guise of religious devotion.[4] Yet millions of *bulas de la cruzada* were taken every year. And the indulgence's vibrancy suggests that viewing it merely from an institutional perspective—whether secular or ecclesiastical—fails to capture its popular significance.

By the early sixteenth century, for most people, active crusading as an expression of piety had been replaced by contributing alms, which the Crown used to fund military campaigns against the enemies of the faith, who frequently happened to be Spain's enemies as well. However, the indulgence was not just a function of growing state power. Available to anyone living in the Spanish dominions who contributed alms, the *cruzada*'s popularity suggests that we also need to consider those who stood outside the echelons of power.[5] In fact, the indulgence became an integral part of life for most Spaniards, who, as the saying went, had their *bula para todo,* their *bula* for everything. This was particularly true when they went to confess.

The proliferation of the *bula de la cruzada* transformed confessional practice in early modern Spain because it allowed bearers to elect their own confessor. The demands of royal finances engendered a peninsula-wide campaign that promoted an affordable and papally sanctioned opportunity for confessants to avoid their parish priest. As a consequence of the *cruzada* indulgence, enforcing a strict policy of confessional jurisdiction became virtually impossible. Only in remote locations with no alternative to the local parish priest, or among the destitute unable to acquire the indulgence, could a *cura* claim a monopoly even over the Easter duty. Instead, those clerics who felt a special vocation to confession jockeyed for prominence, hoping to attract the most devout and influential penitents to their confessional. The *bula de la cruzada* made this possible.

## The Medieval Background of the *Cruzada* Indulgence

The *bula de la cruzada* flourished in the early modern period, but the indulgence's origins were rooted in Spain's crusading past. The sign of the cross toward which the *cruzada* gestured, explained Alfonso Pérez de Lara, author of the official manual on the subject, was a multivalent symbol. It pointed not only to the instrument of Christ's sacrifice but also to the military standard of Constantine, the crosses taken by the Holy Land crusaders, and the insignia of the Spanish military orders.[6] Like his medieval predecessors, Pérez saw all of these as compatible.[7]

Crusading, of course, had a long pedigree in Spain. In the early eighth century, Islamic armies had overrun all but the northern extremes of Iberia. In subsequent centuries, the remnants of Christian kingdoms struggled, in fits and starts, against the Muslim conquerors. At times, these conflicts took on an overtly religious character. After the success of the First Crusade (1095–99), Iberian monarchs, prelates, and nobles adopted a robust crusading ideology, and the first quarter of the twelfth century saw crusade indulgences arrive in Iberia.[8] While the Latin kingdoms in the Levant rose and fell, Iberia became the most successful medieval crusading theater. Popes granted legates and participants received indulgences, engaged in cross-taking ceremonies, and used crusading imagery.

By the 1480s most of Iberia had been restored to Christian governance. The Catholic Monarchs sought to complete this process by overthrowing the last remnant of Islamic rule, the Kingdom of Granada. The papal indulgences granted for this crusading endeavor proved to be the immediate context out of which the early modern Spanish *bula de la cruzada* developed.[9] It differed from its medieval antecedents in that preachers distributed thousands (and in later years millions) of vernacular broadside summaries of the indulgence, known as *buletas*. Almsgivers walked away with the printed documents and often saved them for years after they had expired. Some hung them on the walls of their homes; others were buried with their copy.[10] The distribution of *buletas* demonstrates the impact of the print revolution on the preaching of crusading indulgences as well as a dramatic shift in popular participation in the crusade. In previous centuries, crusading enthusiasm had tended to be active, dangerous, and largely limited to elite members of society and their entourages, but by the early modern period, Spaniards of all types participated in the endeavor in a relatively cheap, safe, and uncomplicated fashion.

During the summer of 1482, the representatives of the Catholic Monarchs negotiated with Pope Sixtus IV (r. 1471–84), seeking financial support for their Granadan crusade. In early June of that year, the parties signed the Accord of Córdoba, which granted Ferdinand and Isabella a tenth of all ecclesiastical incomes in Castile, Aragon, and Sicily and promised a new crusading indulgence.

In August the pope made good by promulgating the bull *Orthodoxae fidei,* which arrived in Castile in March of the following year. The Dominican monastery of San Pedro Martír quickly printed the *buletas* for this first mass-produced bull of crusade.[11] The effort proved a resounding success. The Florentine ambassador Francesco Guicciardini recalled that in 1487 alone, Spaniards had contributed some eight hundred thousand ducats.[12]

*Orthodoxae fidei,* which became a model for subsequent bulls of crusade, offered substantial privileges, to say the least. The pope bestowed a plenary indulgence upon all who personally fought in the campaign or sent another to fight in their place. He extended the same indulgence to members of religious communities who jointly supported combatants financially. The pope also granted a similar privilege to the poor who wanted to contribute but could neither campaign themselves nor support a replacement. Those with useful skills, such as doctors, cobblers, carpenters, blacksmiths, nurses, preachers, and even manual laborers, could receive the indulgence if they devoted their talents to the campaign for at least three months.[13]

Yet these provisions hardly exhausted the bull's treasures. If individuals could not participate directly, the pope still permitted them to demonstrate their support by contributing alms to the cause. *Orthodoxae fidei* established a sliding scale for contributors based upon socioeconomic status. The king and queen could take the indulgence for one hundred gold florins; high ecclesiastical officeholders, the wealthy, and social elites could have it for ten. Those worth less than three hundred ducats paid one gold florin or four silver *reales*. For *pauperes* worth less than sixty ducats, the sum of two silver *reales* sufficed.

In addition to the indulgence, those who took the *cruzada* received a number of privileges that had their origins in the harsh reality of the crusade campaign.[14] They could hear Mass and obtain Christian burial in a land under interdict and ignore otherwise mandatory dietary restrictions during periods of fasting; they were even allowed to consume dairy products (and meat in certain cases) during Lent.[15] They could marry in the third and fourth degree of consanguinity and establish private oratories. Absentee ministers could receive income from benefices, and clerics were released from following the canonical hours.

The bull also granted bearers special opportunities to take advantage of the sacrament of penance. Rather than confess at Lent to their parish priest, they could choose another "appropriate" (*idoneum*) confessor. Instead of undergoing their *cura*'s annual scrutiny, crusaders, and by extension *cruzada* bearers, could confess with any licensed confessor, whether secular or regular. Furthermore, under normal circumstances, reserved sins demanded the attention of the Holy Office, the bishop, or the pope. But, with only a few exceptions, such as heresy or conspiracy against the pontiff, any priest could absolve *cruzada* bearers of any reserved sins. Finally, in the event that one died suddenly without having confessed, the indulgence granted forgiveness for sins committed since the bearer's last confession, as long as the decedent showed some evidence of contrition. These privileges, which continued to be a defining aspect of early modern *bulas de la cruzada,* significantly affected confessional practice and the enforcement of ecclesiastical jurisdiction in Spain. During the early modern period, very few people actually went on crusade, but many acquired a *buleta* and the freedoms it provided.

Although Granada surrendered to Christian forces in 1492, Pope Alexander VI (r. 1492–1503) granted yet another bull of crusade to the Catholic Monarchs in 1494. He hoped that they would take the fight into North Africa and restore the church there.[16] But despite the papal blessing, Ferdinand and Isabella failed to mobilize a successful crusade. The Duke of Medina-Sidonia captured Melilla in 1497, but Spanish troops had their hands full in Italy, and the idea of a large-scale African campaign seems never to have captured Ferdinand's attention.

At home, a major *morisco* uprising, the first of two revolts of the Alpujarras, was crushed at the beginning of the sixteenth century, but it awakened Castilians to the Muslim threat on their southern border and led some to call for a new crusade. The queen and her confessor, Cardinal Francisco Jiménez de Cisneros, were particularly enchanted by the idea.[17] Even on her deathbed in 1504, Isabella urged King Ferdinand to devote himself "unremittingly to the conquest of Africa and the war for the Faith against the Moors."[18] Cisneros fought on and urged the king to do likewise. In the autumn of 1505 an expedition from Malaga captured Mers-el-Kebir, and Spanish troops seized Oran in 1509. Although Cisneros sought to capitalize on these military successes, Ferdinand contented himself with the creation of a buffer against Muslim encroachment. Their conflicting agendas contributed to a parting of ways. In the end, the Spanish merely captured and garrisoned a few key ports, leaving the rest to the Moors.

Other enemies of the faith also came into view—Protestants, Native Americans, and a waxing Ottoman Empire. Given the rich traditions of crusading Spain, it is no surprise that papal crusading indulgences continued to be offered in the early modern period. Yet medieval bulls of crusade had been extraordinary opportunities granted for and limited to participation in particular campaigns. From the mid-sixteenth century, by contrast, they were preached annually, almost without fail, to support the Spanish monarch in his defense of the church generally, rather than for any specific martial enterprise.

While the great era of crusading as an expression of popular religious devotion had passed, early modern states eagerly appropriated crusading ideology.[19] Monarchs often found it difficult to distinguish their own best interests from God's will. As Philip II commented to one of his ministers, "I hope in God . . . that he will give you good health and long life, since you are employed in his service and in mine, which is the same thing."[20] By the seventeenth century, the Crown could rely on papal willingness to grant the *cruzada* and the right to spend the income more or less as it saw fit. From 1601, Clement VIII allowed King Philip III to employ *cruzada* finances in crusading activity against any enemy of the faith and in the defense of his realms rather than merely in Mediterranean conflicts.[21] However, this transformation of the *cruzada* into a nearly inviolable tool of the Spanish state was a long process that began in the late fifteenth century and took decades to run its course.

## The Cruzada as a Tool of the State

Medieval crusade indulgences had enticed arms bearers to take the cross and fight in the defense of the faith; even in the late fifteenth and early sixteenth centuries Spanish *bulas de la cruzada* evidenced a strong connection to the martial ethos of the pious knight.[22] Later in the sixteenth century, they lent support to Spain's Mediterranean conflicts against the Islamic Ottoman Empire and Barbary corsairs. Spanish monarchs adeptly leveraged their role as defenders of the faith to gain these papal boons, and they enjoyed the stable and long-lasting revenue streams produced by the *cruzada* indulgence.[23] Yet this same institution undermined episcopal control of confessional practice, and consequently placed the Crown's own domestic agenda of religious reform in danger.

The administrative developments that made the bull of crusade a tool in the royal arsenal coincided with the growing power of the monarchy over the Spanish church. From the late fifteenth through the mid-sixteenth century, popes granted Iberian monarchs a wide variety of privileges, such as the income of vacant sees, the lands and revenues of Spanish military orders, and authority to appoint high ecclesiastical officeholders, first in the New World and then in Spain, a privilege known as the *patronato*.[24] The Crown also claimed oversight in the publication of papal bulls in Spain and appeals to the Holy See.[25] Additionally, it gained various extraordinary ecclesiastical incomes. These included, from 1494, two-ninths of the tithes paid to the Castilian church as well as a tax on clerical rents and incomes known as the *subsidio*.[26] In 1567 the *excusado*, which consisted of the entire tithe of the most valuable piece of property in every parish, was added to subsidize the war in Flanders.[27] And, of course, there was the most lucrative of the Crown's ecclesiastical incomes: the *cruzada*.

During the reign of Emperor Charles V, who ruled the Spanish dominions as King Charles I from 1516 to 1556, the *cruzada* verged on becoming a regular source of royal revenue. The Crown spent considerable time and energy convincing popes that the indulgence could not be done without if Spain was to continue as champion of the Catholic faith. Not every pope, however, was equally inclined to accept these arguments, not least of all because massive systemic abuses accompanied *cruzada* preaching. Some who took the indulgence on credit found their goods confiscated when they could not pay their debt. Some preachers exaggerated the benefits of the *cruzada;* others palmed fraudulent *buletas* off on unsuspecting and illiterate laypeople.[28] Spaniards also complained about the frequency of sermons. Every time the pope granted a new bull, he suspended the previous one and its privileges. From the Crown's perspective, these "suspensions" were absolutely necessary, since if the old bull "be not suspended there would be few to take the new one." In fact, one commentator estimated, the preaching campaign would cost more to mount than would be raised.[29]

Most frequently criticized, however, were the pressure tactics that *cruzada* preachers (nicknamed *echacuervos*, "crow-throwers") used to persuade their audiences to take *buletas*. As early as 1480 the Catholic Monarchs decreed that no one should be forced to give alms for an indulgence, yet complaints of such practices continued to appear. In 1512 and 1520 the Cortes of Catalonia lodged protests against *echacuervos* who forced people to attend sermons and extorted alms.[30] The Cortes requested that authority over *cruzada* preaching pass from the hands of a commissioner-general, who was jointly appointed by the pope and king, into those of local bishops. As matters stood, *cruzada* preachers operated outside episcopal jurisdiction.[31] The royal position, however, allowed for no flexibility on this point.[32] The commissioner-general appointed *cruzada* preachers, and it was his duty to examine their learning, life, and habits.[33] Commissioners, however, appear not to have taken that task too seriously, since their success depended upon strong sales. An *echacuervo* who knew how to bend the rules a bit could prove lucrative.

The Cortes of Valladolid and Toledo complained of abuses in 1523 and 1525.[34] A group of Augustinian and Dominican monks from Salamanca protested that the multitude of bulls and the tactics of *echacuervos* demonstrated a "contempt for the blood of Christ." They claimed that the people of the *pueblos* were kept from working their fields until they paid two *reales* for the indulgence.[35] *Cruzada* preachers received commissions for selling bulls, which encouraged them to pressure their audiences to take the indulgence.[36] The Florentine ambassador Guicciardini suggested that by 1513 few city dwellers were taking the indulgence. Rather, *rústicos* contributed most of the alms, and they only did so "out of fear, being nearly forced."[37]

Monarchs made unenthusiastic reform efforts during the first half of the sixteenth century, but to little effect. In 1524 Charles V formally forbade a number of abuses, among them punishing people for not attending sermons, unnecessarily keeping peasants from their labors, compelling them to purchase *buletas* against their will, and causing people "any vexation."[38] If the decree had an effect at its initial promulgation, the multiple petitions against abuses submitted to the king in 1548 suggest that it did not provide a long-term solution.[39]

Near the end of his reign, in 1554, Charles attempted a more substantive reform.[40] However, in that same year the anonymous author of the early picaresque novel *Lazarillo de Tormes* enshrined the caricature of the corrupt *echacuervo* in Spanish literature. The eponymous character, a Sevillano youth, roamed aimlessly, serving a series of masters. Among them was a *cruzada* preacher whom Lazarillo described as "the most adept and shameless and also a better hawker of [bulls] than I ever saw or hope to see or than I think anyone has ever seen, for he had and sought out ways and means and very clever tricks." The preacher used a remarkable series of deceptions to bilk the gullible out of their money and persuade them to take the indulgence. This led Lazarillo to wonder how many other *echacuervos* were, like his master, swindlers of the innocent.[41]

Such misuse of power led some Spaniards to question the validity of the bulls. The Holy Office, for example, tried Gabriel de Carvajal, the *cura* of Lilla on the Valencian coast, as a Lutheran sympathizer for doubting the indulgence's efficacy.[42] In 1579 or 1580 Cathalina de Quebo, a lay holy woman (*beata*) from Baeza (Jaén) explained that she never took the indulgence because, for the same price, she could get more forgiveness (*perdones*) by endowing four masses for the dead. The king, she lamented, used bulls of crusade to take away all the money.[43] In 1589, while preaching the *cruzada*, a *cura* in the Diocese of Lugo rounded on one of his congregants, Pedro Fernández Ligero. Since Pedro had not confessed in four or five years, the priest urged him to take the *bula* so that his sins could be absolved. The layman responded by intoning a popular refrain: he claimed that *bulas* were farces (*que no eran bulas sino burlas*). He considered the *cruzada* no more than a royally imposed sin tax.[44]

Abuses sparked even more disturbing questions about the power of the pope and his authority to grant indulgences. In 1583, for example, the Holy Office summoned Juan de Osguevillas, an elderly man from Sigüenza, who had wondered, "How can it be that a man on earth is able to pardon sins?"[45] Francisco García had expressed similar uncertainty two decades earlier in Rodilana, south of Valladolid. He and his neighbor, Marcos de Bonilla, attended a *cruzada* sermon together, after which Marcos decided to take the indulgence. But Francisco responded, "Why would you want to spend two *reales*? What's the benefit?" Marcos explained that whatever the pope bound on earth, God would bind in heaven, but Francisco had his doubts. Maybe Saint Peter could bind and loose, but could all popes? Certainly, Peter or Gregory the Great could grant indulgences; they were saints. Maybe the current pope could, too . . . if he was a saint as well. Whence, the inquisitors later asked Francisco, did these doubts arise? He responded that, in the past, when popes granted pardons and indulgences, it was like a miracle. But now, "So many come, and for that reason I doubt them. . . . Every day [the preachers] hawk their pardons."[46]

Twice during the second half of the sixteenth century, popes suspended the *bula de la cruzada*, at least in part to stem abuses. However, the suspensions also reflect the papacy's desire to assert its authority and limit the power of the Spanish monarch in religious affairs.[47] In May 1555 the newly elected Paul IV (r. 1555–59) had confirmed the indulgence, but growing animosity with Spain led him to rescind both the *cruzada* and the *subsidio* six months later. In spite of reservations, Pius IV (r. 1559–65) renewed the *cruzada* soon after his election, but on the condition that the Spanish Crown return a portion of the revenues, the *fábrica*, to support the rebuilding of St. Peter's Basilica in Rome.[48] The *cruzada* was consequently preached for the triennial of 1561–63 as well as in 1564 and 1565. In December 1565, however, as Philip labored to secure the indulgence for the subsequent triennial, Pius IV died.[49] Philip needed the new pope, Pius V (r. 1566–72), to reconfirm the indulgences granted by his predecessor. Negotiations proceeded slowly, however. The king tasked his ambassador at Rome, Juan de Zúñiga, with guarding the "substantial" and "principal" parts of the *cruzada*: the ability to elect confessors, the absolution of reserved sins, the commutation of vows, "and other things of this sort."[50]

In January 1569 Pius V finally indicated his willingness to grant a new crusade indulgence. Philip was concerned that the pope would use this opportunity to

diminish the *cruzada*'s substantial privileges, but the king feared worse repercussions if he refused outright. He encouraged Zúñiga simply to accept
changes made by the pope, noting that it would be "easier to make up what
is missing and increase [the privileges] afterward" than to win everything at
once.[51] For his part, Zúñiga assured Philip that as long as the *cruzada* still
allowed people to eat eggs and drink milk on holy days, Spaniards would continue to take it.[52] Pius's new bull, however, proved even more limited than
Philip had expected, for its main focus was to encourage individuals to take
up their crosses, bear arms, and actively defend the faith rather than to donate
alms to fund the king's professional army.[53] While Philip fumed, his bishops
responded by granting their own indulgences, even an episcopal version of the
*cruzada*. But Pius ordered them to desist, and, in any case, returns were never
as grand as they had been for the papal bull of crusade.[54]

Sincere concerns about abuses seem to have motivated the pope. Nevertheless, with Ottoman naval forces massing in the early 1570s, Pius needed Philip's
Spain to join the League of Venice and protect Christendom. The Ottoman
threat represented so grave a danger that the pope eventually granted concessions he had otherwise refused to make. On 21 May 1571, having secured
Spanish support for the League, he granted the *cruzada* for two years, and the
following day extended it for four more.[55] Whatever doubts Pius had harbored,
saving Christendom from the Turkish threat outweighed them. From 1571
until the indulgence's final dissolution in the mid-twentieth century, popes
would deprive Spanish monarchs and their subjects of the *cruzada* rarely and
only for brief periods.[56]

Philip had his bull, but Pius V imposed some reforms upon the *cruzada*. It
was no coincidence that the pope had suspended the indulgence in the wake of
the Council of Trent.[57] Although the first two sessions had discussed the abuses
and possible reformation of the Spanish bull of crusade, the Council did no
more than condemn those who sold indulgences on commission.[58] Only on the
very last day did the fathers approve a decree on indulgences. Yet even here,
the official canons and decrees made only oblique reference to the *cruzada* and
never mentioned it by name.[59] Thus, although abuse of indulgences in Spain
had been a major subject of scrutiny and debate among the delegates, Trent
offered only a weak condemnation.[60] The Council had expressed fear that if
indulgences could be acquired with "excessive facility," ecclesiastical discipline
would be debilitated, but because so many different abuses existed, the decree
did not offer specific condemnations or order detailed reforms. Instead, it urged
bishops "diligently to correct, each in his own church, all abuses of this nature,

and to report them in the first provincial Synod," that they might be made known to the pope.[61]

Pius leveraged Tridentine condemnations of these abuses into a more practical program when he granted the new bull of crusade in 1571. Most significantly, he forbade the paying of *echacuervos* on commission in hopes of eliminating the pressure tactics for which they had become notorious.[62] Priests and religious were forbidden to eat dairy products during fast days, since they were to set an example for laypeople, and the bull could no longer be used to absolve usury, simony, the gaining of goods by illicit means, and similar offenses.[63]

Pius's successors, especially his immediate successor, Gregory XIII (r. 1572–85), proved more pliable and less scrupulous by relaxing some of the harshest restrictions.[64] The degree to which Pius's brief reforming program may have helped alter the corrupt atmosphere that lingered around the *cruzada* remains an open question. To judge from inquisitorial trials, however, complaints declined in the late sixteenth century. Some continued to express theological doubts about the power of the pope, concerns about the impoverishment of the peasantry, or questions about how *cruzada* funds were administered and collected. Yet few mocked the bull or complained of rampant abuse at the local level. Perhaps more significantly, while the *cruzada* may not exactly have become a benevolent institution in early modern Spain, many Spaniards came to consider the indulgence worth the two *reales* they paid for it.

## The Popularity of the *Cruzada*

Throughout much of the sixteenth and seventeenth centuries, the *cruzada* brought millions of *reales* into the king's coffers every year, which indicates that a vast number of people contributed alms on a regular basis. But how many *buletas* were taken, and by whom? These are difficult questions to answer with precision. Although *echacuervos* were supposed to preach the indulgence in all population centers, "no matter how small," they seem to have bypassed some remote villages.[65] Demographic historians have just begun to work out how many people purchased bulls of crusade, at what price, and in which regions.[66] Moreover, counterfeiting appears at times to have plagued the distribution of the bull. Some preachers made more money by pocketing income from false bulls than from selling real ones![67]

The situation is further complicated by the fact that various forms of the early modern *cruzada* existed. The *bula de difuntos* sped loved ones' transition from purgatory to heaven; the *bula de lacticiones* allowed priests to consume dairy products during Lent; and the *bula de composición* legitimized ill-gotten gains. But the most popular version of the *cruzada* by far was the bull for the living (*bula de vivos*), which came in two versions. For the vast majority of people, the *bula común* sufficed, but elites (*ilustres*) had their own, which offered the same benefits at quadruple the cost. Members of the ecclesiastical hierarchy, inquisitors, members of the nobility, high government and military officials, royal secretaries (and their wives), and representatives at the provincial and city level took this more expensive version. The *bula común*, affordable for all but the poorest, could be had for just two silver *reales;* the *bula de ilustres* cost eight.[68] In the year 1592 the press at San Pedro Mártir in Toledo, which printed half of the *cruzada* indulgences, produced 2,472,330 *buletas*.[69] The *bula de vivos* accounted for 2,232,400 of these. At the end of the year's preaching campaign, only 8,050 *buletas* went unclaimed.[70]

The current state of research rarely allows us to know with certainty the exact number of bulls sold in any given year, or the identity of almsgivers. However, since the *cruzada* made up a portion of Crown income, the amount of money it brought into the royal coffers often can be determined. This provides a rough sense of the *cruzada*'s popularity from the mid-sixteenth to the mid-seventeenth century. Excluding Spanish holdings outside the Iberian Peninsula, the income for the triennial 1552–54 amounted to 672,668 ducats.[71] Between 1561 and 1563 the *cruzada* brought in 916,840 ducats. Constantino Gentil of Genoa acted as treasurer-general of the *cruzada* during the triennial beginning in 1563 and estimated an income of 1,376,133 ducats, but the election of Pius V in early 1566 put the future of the *cruzada* in doubt, as he effectively suspended the indulgence for the remainder of the decade.[72]

When Pius renewed the bull of crusade, financiers anticipated a drop in sales. In October 1571 Juan Fernández de Espinosa considered 684,000 ducats a good estimate for two years of *cruzada* income.[73] In 1573 Leonardo Donato reckoned that the annual income would be about 350,000 ducats, still substantially less than what Gentil had bid a decade earlier.[74] This decline probably reflects the uncertainty that surrounded the *cruzada*'s future and the impact of Pius V's reforms on income.

As it turned out, *cruzada* income climbed dramatically in the final decades of the sixteenth century. In 1584 the Venetian ambassador Vincenzo Gradenigo estimated that *cruzada* sales for mainland Spain alone accounted for 600,000 ducats of royal revenue, which corresponds roughly with official records.[75] For the years 1578 to 1589, the historian Modesto Ulloa has assessed the sums gathered annually as well as the number and varieties of bulls purchased.[76] During that decade the *cruzada* garnered between 613,832 and 784,988 ducats per year. Occasional spikes skew the data, but the *cruzada* indulgence experienced healthy growth near the end of the century.

We also know something about the quantities and varieties of bulls that Spaniards took during those years. The *bula común de vivos* accounted for between roughly 80 and 90 percent of the total number of bulls taken. Variations depended largely upon whether preachers offered the *bula de composición* in a particular year. In *composición* years, the percentage of *bulas de vivos* declined, but actual sales held steady.[77] The *bula común de vivos* remained the biggest moneymaker.

*Cruzada* proceeds between 1589 and 1598 contributed an average income of 732,535 ducats to the annual royal income of about six million ducats.[78] Clearly, no long-term crisis of confidence in the *cruzada* occurred—quite the contrary. The reform of abuses and the generous privileges stimulated public interest in the indulgence. Some may have taken more than one *bula de vivos* per campaign, but no one was permitted to take more than two. By the end of the sixteenth century, most adult Spaniards contributed two *reales* each year. Taking a *buleta* had become part of life.

From the perspective of governmental administration, the seventeenth century saw an ongoing bureaucratization of the *cruzada*. It became a more stable form of Crown income. The pope now granted the indulgence in sexennials but suspended the bull each year to allow for annual preaching campaigns. The Spanish Crown borrowed heavily against the revenue and pledged the *cruzada* income to creditors years in advance. By 1665 income from the Castilian *cruzada* was pledged through 1679.[79] The financiers who oversaw the complicated program now received a standard annual estimate from the Crown that they had to match either through *buleta* sales or out of their own pockets.[80]

*Table 1*   *Cruzada* income, 1578–1589

| Year | Ducats | Year | Ducats |
| --- | --- | --- | --- |
| 1578 | 731,169 | 1584 | 653,272 |
| 1579 | 613,832 | 1585 | 662,633 |
| 1580 | 643,973 | 1586 | 666,560 |
| 1581 | 632,036 | 1587 | 784,988 |
| 1582 | 690,151 | 1588 | 713,208 |
| 1583 | 628,141 | 1589 | 690,905 |

*Table 2*    Number of *bulas* taken, 1578–1589

| Variety of *bulas* | 1578 | 1579 | 1580 | 1581 |
|---|---|---|---|---|
| Vivos *(común)* | 3,711,000 | 3,539,000 | 3,750,000 | 3,660,000 |
| Vivos *(ilustres)* | 12,548 | 13,600 | 14,000 | 14,000 |
| Difuntos | 346,962 | 355,500 | 336,000 | 350,000 |
| Composición | 591,004 | | | |
| común as % of total | 79.6 | 90.5 | 91.4 | 91 |
| **Variety of *bulas*** | **1582** | **1583** | **1584** | **1585** |
| Vivos *(común)* | 3,660,000 | 3,600,000 | 3,760,000 | 3,768,000 |
| Vivos *(ilustres)* | 14,000 | 14,200 | 14,200 | 15,800 |
| Difuntos | 371,000 | 385,000 | 385,000 | 385,000 |
| Composición | 349,000 | | | 50,000 |
| común as % of total | 83.3 | 90 | 90.4 | 89.3 |
| **Variety of *bulas*** | **1586** | **1587** | **1588** | **1589** |
| Vivos *(común)* | 3,792,000 | 4,099,000 | 4,137,420 | 4,000,000 |
| Vivos *(ilustres)* | 13,800 | 13,800 | 13,800 | 13,800 |
| Difuntos | 385,000 | 385,000 | 389,500 | 385,000 |
| Composición | 53,000 | 500,000 | | |
| común as % of total | 89.4 | 82 | 91.1 | 90.9 |

*Table 3*    *Cruzada* income, 1589–1598

| Years | 1589 to 1590 | 1590 to 1591 | 1591 to 1592 |
|---|---|---|---|
| *Cruzada* income (in ducats) | 725,600 | 720,344 | 707,601 |
| **Years** | **1592 to 1593** | **1593 to 1594** | **1594 to 1595** |
| *Cruzada* income (in ducats) | 739,785 | 714,815 | 732,645 |
| **Years** | **1595 to 1596** | **1596 to 1597** | **1597 to 1598** |
| *Cruzada* income (in ducats) | 759,930 | 748,365 | 743,730 |

Between 1619 and 1643 the government expected the *cruzada* to contribute 779,733 ducats toward annual royal income (or, at least, royal debt), a figure based on the sale of some 4,300,000 *buletas*. In 1643 the anticipated income was lowered to 698,133 ducats, the equivalent of 3,850,000 *buletas,* to account for population decline. Yet these figures remain strikingly higher than in the years before the 1570s. Presumably, financiers did not continue to bid for the opportunity to oversee an unprofitable initiative. Rather, it seems, Spaniards consumed the *cruzada* indulgence with gusto.

## The *Cruzada* and Confession

Abuses must surely have continued, and, no doubt, preachers, neighbors, relatives, and local busybodies pressured some people to take the indulgence. The very poor, who could not immediately afford two *reales,* sometimes accepted charity, but the practice of purchasing on credit was more typical in times of dearth. The pope allowed the practice "in order that all might be able to enjoy the graces and powers" of the *bula,* even if they lacked the necessary funds at present. Yet this practice placed some debtors in serious financial straits, resulting in the seizure and sale of goods and property.[81]

In spite of these problems, the *cruzada* remained popular. But what attracted millions of people to take it every year? Somewhat surprisingly, contributing to the fight against enemies of the faith seems rarely to have motivated lay-people.[82] And while community pressure or heavy-handed *echacuervos* may have contributed to the success of preaching campaigns, many people were also drawn to the indulgence because of the truly significant benefits that it offered. Having a *bula,* for instance, could be important for establishing one's bona fides as a good Christian. In Catalonia in 1623, Joan Baptista demonstrated that his community "held and reputed [him] to be a good Catholic Christian," offering as proof that he "heard mass, gave alms, and took the bull of crusade."[83] Others were drawn to the luxury of eating eggs and drinking milk during Lent. Upper-class and even middling households used their *buletas* to establish oratories in their homes. And many Spaniards, like Ysabel Martínez, whom we met at the outset of this chapter, spent their two hard-earned *reales* on the indulgence because it afforded them a greater degree of freedom when they participated in confession.

Indeed, the *cruzada*'s popularity had much to do with how it affected confessional practice. This is seen clearly in the *advertimientos* (advice or warnings) prepared during the Crown's complicated negotiations with the papacy in the late 1560s. The recipient was probably King Philip's ambassador, Juan de Zúñiga, whom the document would have helped to engage in delicate negotiations at Rome. It spoke authoritatively on what, from the Spanish perspective, had to be won and what could be conceded, at least for the moment.

The *advertimientos* argued that the *bula*'s penitential graces—the privilege of electing a confessor, the power to grant absolution, the ability to commute vows, and so forth—attracted the largest number and widest variety of people. Should the pope do away with these, he would diminish the "substance and principal part of the *cruzada*." The *advertimientos* described the penitential graces as fundamental because, according to "many learned and pious men," being obliged to confess with one's parish priest during Lent or having to appear before his superior to receive absolution for reserved sins "has been the occasion for many people to abandon confession." Even worse, some who found themselves in that situation made "false and incomplete confessions." The result: "great inconveniences and scruples of conscience." Such "obstacles and impediments" had to be removed, especially "in these times."[84]

That the removal of such obstacles and impediments dramatically hindered episcopal programs, which championed a rigorous mode of confessional jurisdiction, seems not to have entered the author's mind. Decades later, Antonio Escobar y Mendoza, an eminent Jesuit Probabilist, quipped with reference to the indulgence's proliferation that the only laypeople in Christ's church allowed to choose their own confessors were "kings, princes, and, *per Bullam Cruciatae,* the peoples of Spain and Sicily."[85] No coincidence, then, that manuals of confession often included long sections that addressed the indulgence, and tortuous discussions of its impact on penitential practice.[86]

How did the bull of crusade shape the confessional encounter? We rarely catch glimpses of penitents showing confessors their *buletas* when they came to confess. Perhaps they had become so much a part of the warp and woof of the sacramental experience that there was no need to mention them. At least occasionally, however, confessors did request the document. In 1561, for example, Francisco García of Rodilana (Valladolid) wanted to make his Easter confession at San Juan de los Reyes in Toledo, but "because he did not have a bull by which to elect a confessor," he had to confess a second time in his parish.[87] In November 1614, when Beatriz de Espinosa of Madrid confessed to Fray Felipe de Laiz, he told her that "he could not absolve her until he saw her *bula de la cruzada,*" which she apparently had left at home.[88] The scarcity of such examples suggests that regular confessors may not have taken the enforcement of confessional jurisdiction too seriously, especially since so many Spaniards possessed *buletas* that allowed them to confess to almost any priest.

Yet being allowed to confess to *almost any* priest did not mean that *cruzada* bearers could confess to *every* priest. Theologians and churchmen often disagreed about which clerics could legitimately be chosen as confessors, and local priests and laypeople drew their own conclusions. Let us return to the case of Ysabel Martínez. She found herself saddled with a confessor, the sacristan Pedro de Ortega, who sexually harassed her. Rather than go to the Inquisition—a drastic but viable option—she asserted the privileges of her *buleta.* At one point in the drama, in fact, Ysabel raised the possibility with Padre Ortega of using the indulgence to switch confessors. He responded, either out of woeful ignorance or, more probably, out of fear that she would expose him to another confessor, that "the bull wasn't any good for that sort of thing without the license of the *cura*."[89] But Ysabel knew better; she took her *buleta* and went elsewhere. She never confessed to Ortega again.[90]

Among those with more level heads and better theological sense than Ortega, a range of relatively legitimate opinions developed. The more cautious approach, advocated by manual authors such as the Franciscans Francisco de Alcozer and Enrique de Villalobos and the Jesuit Antonio Fernández de Córdoba, argued that priests needed to receive approbation from the bishop in whose diocese they intended to administer the sacrament. Once that approbation had been granted, however, the cleric became a viable and "appropriate" confessor for any *cruzada* bearer in the diocese.[91]

Even within this position, a range of different views developed. Gaspar de Villaroel recalled having addressed this issue with a young but exemplary priest, Luis de Lagos, while living in Madrid in the 1630s. Several *beatas* sought Lagos as their spiritual director, but despite having passed the licensing exam and receiving episcopal approbation to confess in the archdiocese, he could not accommodate them; he was still too young to confess women. Villaroel interceded on behalf of his friend with the ordinary, asking him to make an exception, but the "holy and scrupulous bishop" courteously refused.

The *beatas* continued to court the young priest. "Considering the problem," Villaroel remembered, "I advised [Lagos] that he might confess them if they were to choose him according to the bull. . . . In spite of the limitation of age, he was an approved confessor, and the bull requires no more than that the chosen confessor be approved by the ordinary."[92] Luis de Lagos remained uncertain and worried that Villaroel might merely have relaxed his theology to accommodate a friend. Eventually, they forwarded the query to the faculty of theology at the University of Salamanca. In 1625 the Congregation of the Council replied negatively to the same question, but in 1634 Villaroel received favorable replies from two eminent Salamancan theologians.[93]

In contrast to stricter positions on the indulgence, a more flexible approach concluded that although a confessor needed the approbation of the ordinary to be considered "appropriate," the bull did not stipulate from *which* ordinary that approbation had to come. Thus a minister in good standing, who had received episcopal approbation anywhere in Christendom, could hear the confession of any penitent who had taken the *cruzada*.[94] Juan Machado de Chávez admitted that some "grave authors" disagreed with this position but claimed that "many more numerous and most grave Doctors" took a more favorable approach. The *bula,* he explained, "asks no more prerequisite than that the Priest whom the penitent wants to choose as a confessor by virtue of [the *cruzada*] be approved."[95]

Other works, like Pérez de Lara's official handbook for the *bula de la cruzada,* wisely did not even attempt to resolve the issue. It noted only that the indulgence required that the chosen confessor had received "the approbation of the bishop."[96]

All of these positions, even the most cautious ones, evidence the broad range of confessing opportunities available to most Spaniards. As the influence of Probabilism grew, this flexibility became even more apparent. The regular clerics who wrote the confessional manuals and *cruzada* handbooks formulated arguments that strengthened their position vis-à-vis the authority of the secular clergy and the bishops. Ultimately, their approach to confessional jurisdiction and their interpretations of the *cruzada*'s benefits carried the day.

During the papal negotiations of the late 1560s, the Crown asked Archbishop Pedro Guerrero of Granada to comment on the problems and controversies surrounding the *cruzada* indulgence. He offered a thoughtful and at times daring response. If things did not change, he warned, there would be consequences. Extraordinary grace had become commonplace; even the pope could not keep track of all the indulgences and dispensations. Someday, Spain would reap the whirlwind, for Guerrero believed that the long-term consequences of "so many easy and frequent confessions" would be a decline of "reverence and devotion in the souls of the faithful."[97] Perhaps he was not far off, for the phrase *tener bula para todo*—to have a *bula* for everything—became slang for being free to do whatever one wanted.

## Conclusions

During the early modern period, the blurring of jurisdictional boundaries that resulted from the proliferation of the *cruzada* made attempts to enforce confessional jurisdiction a nightmare. The ease and regularity with which most Spaniards could legitimately steer clear of a confessor whom they found offensive, overly harsh, or ineffective belie expectations. If wicked priests wanted to use confession as a tool of oppression, or if ecclesiastical and secular authorities saw it as a vehicle for social control, it proved to be a remarkably unwieldy instrument to those ends.

Like the jurisdictional conflicts between regular and secular clerics, the exigencies of royal finance wore away at episcopal attempts to implement a clear and rigid program of penitential practice for lay Spaniards. Members of the religious orders, particularly the writers of confessional manuals, co-opted the Crown's prerogative to have the crusade indulgence preached in its domains. They pushed the limits of the *bula*'s provisions in their favor in order to wrest control of confession from the parish. In so doing, they undercut the church's ability to use parochial Lenten confession as a disciplinary tool to reform the laity.

Yet the Crown and the regular orders were not the only ones responsible for this turn of events. The men and women of early modern Spain took the indulgences and used them to legitimize their confessional behavior. Institutions like the bull of crusade created an environment in which the practice of sacramental confession could remain flexible. Because the *cruzada* loosened episcopal restrictions, the laity rarely found themselves trapped in intractably poor relationships with confessors. They could usually find a way out. Nor did many people find that the intricate confessional bureaucracies devised by bishops weighed upon them too heavily. Such programs should have rigidly controlled how, when, and with whom the people confessed, but in practice they had a great deal more bark than bite. But if confessional practice at the local level was not chiefly a top-down institution foisted upon the masses by those in power, we must consider other conditions—class, gender, and race—if we are to understand how people experienced the sacrament.

# CONFESSION AT THE INTERSECTIONS OF SOCIETY

¿Diga, picaro, es mi confessor, o mi galan?
—DOÑA ANGELA DE BORJA to her confessor

Theologically, the sacrament of penance divided society into two groups: representatives of God and everybody else. All penitents took an equally subservient position before their confessor. While prescriptive literature enjoined priests to pay close attention to their confessants' position in society in order to effect the best confession possible, extraconfessional social status ought not to have affected the laxity or rigor with which the confessor carried out his duty. Earthly wealth and power had no bearing before the divine judgment seat; God could not be bribed, cajoled, deceived, or cowed. Confessors, however, sometimes could be.

Social status affected confessional experience, but not always in the most straightforward or obvious of ways. Constructing confession as a series of crude power relations might lead us to expect that those with worldly authority always received preferment and imposed their wills upon their confessors, and that those confessors in turn held sway over their poor, marginal, and female penitents. Such two-dimensional characters rarely exist in reality. While priests sometimes treated the wealthy better than the poor, some confessors demanded submission from powerful confessants. Sometimes priests exploited the weak and marginalized in confession. Sexual solicitation in the confessional, for instance, was a crime usually committed against those with limited means of retaliation. But people from every social group exercised power, criticized bad priests, demanded redress of grievances, and exerted influence on the confessional experience. The obverse is also true: some confessors treated even their humblest penitents with deep respect.

This diversity was hardly random, but explaining it demands a nuanced description of the social fabric within which confessional activities unfolded in order to isolate the factors that deeply influenced—even if they did not necessarily determine—confessional practice. The professed religious had different experiences from laypeople. Nuns had a different experience from other women. Belonging to a particular parish or lay confraternity mattered. Possessing worldly power, as in the case of members of the royal family, nobles, or local elites, and the webs of patronage that such power entailed, could transform the sacrament. Being poor, uneducated, or a *rústico* rather than wealthy, educated, or an urbanite carried its own set of limitations and opportunities. The devout confessant could find the confessional a very different place from those who participated only as part of an annual obligation. And, dramatically, the way women participated in and experienced the sacrament often differed from the experience of men.

## Social Status

The top of the social pyramid provides a useful point of departure for considering the impact of status on the sacramental experience, for the confessional lives of kings and queens *were* different from those of most laypeople. By and large, they had a great deal of freedom to choose their own confessors. They could also demand the attention of spiritual directors in ways that would have been presumptuous for most people. On his deathbed, for instance, Philip II *ordered* Diego de Yepes to conduct a "rigorous examination" of his conscience. The Jeronomite assented and spent three days shriving the dying monarch.[1] Even this attentiveness did not exhaust the penitential largesse available to royal persons, for Philip had also received a plenary pardon for his sins directly from Pope Clement VIII just a few weeks earlier.[2] At this level of society the encounter often played out differently than it did for most people. For example, in a display of mutual reverence and submission, both priest and royal penitent typically knelt during confession. The exception proves the rule; in the late fifteenth century one of the signal proofs of Queen Isabella's extreme humility was her willingness to kneel before her confessor, Fray Hernando de Talavera. At their first meeting, Isabella, noting that the Jeronomite had sat down, commented, "We ought both to be kneeling." The confessor, however, contradicted her: "No, *señora,* rather I should be seated and your Highness should kneel for this is the tribunal of God and I am his minister here." Rather than assert her royal prerogative, the queen submitted, "like a saint," and later commented, "This is the confessor for whom I was looking."[3] Talavera, subsequently named the first archbishop of Granada (r. 1493–1507), thus received approbation from the godly queen for taking his status as a representative of the divine judge seriously.

While other social elites never experienced the freedom or influence commanded by the royal family, they secured what privileges they could. Thus, especially in the seventeenth and eighteenth centuries, wealthy ladies often established private chapels, or oratories, in their homes, where they heard Mass, confessed, and communed.[4] Many commentators questioned the propriety of this trend and the degree to which it sprang from true devotion. The learned *madrileño* Dominican Bernabé Gallego de Vera complained in 1651 "that laxity and excess of luxury and ease have made saying Mass at a late hour in private houses so prevalent that it seems as if the churches were intended only for ordinary people." Even those of more middling status imitated the practice and, when they lacked a devoted space, converted dressing rooms, bedrooms, and pantries into temporary chapels. This led Fray Bernabé to comment, "In Madrid and other large cities, there is hardly a house of middling quality that does not have such an oratory." Consequently, such people never "entered a church to hear Mass or the word of God."[5]

The church made some attempt to restrict this behavior. In 1625 the inquisitor-general, Juan Sánchez de Avila, complained, "During the past several years the abuse has been introduced of administering the sacraments of confession and communion in private houses not only to the ladies of the establishments but to their servants as well." The ladies themselves, however, would not bear the brunt of Sánchez's reform. Rather, he forbade secular and regular priests to "administer the sacrament of penitence and the Eucharist in private dwellings . . . except to the ladies of such dwellings . . . and that all other persons shall have recourse to the churches."[6] Subsequently, the Spanish church and state attempted to curtail private oratories even further, restricting their use to the nobility. In 1640 the Royal Council secured a reformation of abuses from the papal nuncio, which declared that licenses for oratories should be granted only to royal councilors, people of recognized title, or in cases of necessity. Nevertheless, into the eighteenth century, people of more modest status successfully obtained the privilege.[7]

Yet social elites did not always enjoy easy confessions and absolutions. A strong confessor could demand humility and submission even from the powerful. The biography of the Jesuit Baltasar Álvarez (1533–1580) reported that his many aristocratic confessants "recognized in him a superiority of spirit so great that he outclassed their own grandeur." Confessants did not dare speak about worldly matters in his presence but, out of respect, let him choose the topic of conversation.[8] A rather different expression of confessors influencing powerful confessants surfaces in the 1570s in Murcia, where confessors interrogated members of the city council about the level of taxation.[9]

Nevertheless, as the reformation of private oratories suggests, the lower one descended the social ladder, the more often were attempts made to regulate confessional practice. In 1641, for example, the poor of Granada had their Lenten confessions scripted in a distinctive manner. A local knightly confraternity organized a banquet to allay the effects of high bread prices and fed five hundred people. In addition to providing food, the confraters saw to it that the *pauperes* confessed and communed before leading them in procession through the town.[10]

Indeed, some elements in society found their confessional activities receiving particularly close scrutiny. In an effort to restrict charitable giving to the deserving poor, the 1576 Synod of Santiago de Compostela deemed begging without having fulfilled the Easter duty illicit and ordered the city's priests to warn parishioners not to give alms to the unconfessed.[11] Episcopal synods frequently encouraged doctors to admonish their patients to confess and, in some dioceses, forbade treating those who could not produce a confessional receipt.[12] At least occasionally, such refusals seem to have occurred.[13] Seventy-year-old Monserrat Gitte, a beggar, admitted that she would rather confess to a stick than a priest, but she needed a *cédula* to get into the hospitals.[14]

Poverty could also affect one's relationship to the parish community and confessional practice. In 1608, for example, Barcelona's inquisitorial tribunal received statements from two priests denouncing forty-six-year-old Pedro Marco of Reus. Pedro, the witnesses explained, had refused for three years to pay a very small debt, which led to his public denunciation and excommunication. Consequently, he had failed to complete his Easter duty, thereby becoming a heretic. We do not know how Pedro incurred the debt, to whom he owed it, or the amount in question. But when the Holy Office called him to account for his behavior, Pedro explained that "he felt himself to be a sinner" for not confessing, yet he could find no solution to the problem: "He was very poor" and could not pay what he owed.[15] This explanation seems to have satisfied the inquisitor, for he did not pursue the matter. While the Holy Office reprimanded Pedro and advised him to pay the debt as soon as possible, it suspended the case and absolved him, the best outcome for which Pedro could reasonably have dared hope.

Both Spanish authorities and confessors found dealing with prostitutes a particularly difficult challenge. The syphilis epidemic of the 1550s pressed the Crown and local municipalities to regulate the trade, above all by secluding it in licensed brothels. This tacit acceptance of prostitution in Roman Catholic Spain caused some confusion for other Spaniards. Many individuals brought before the Holy Office on charges of lewdness claimed that sex with a prostitute could not be more than a venial offense, since brothels were regulated and taxed by the Crown! The women must have found the situation even more difficult to navigate. Although they lived in a state of publicly unrepentant sin, they were baptized Christians and therefore subject to the demands of the church.

The 1583 Synod of Toledo attempted to resolve the confusion by suggesting that "women who live and dwell in public houses should attend mass on Sundays and on required feast days, and confess every year as they are obliged to do, and show their *cédula* when the holy mother church demands."[16] However, this decree failed to clarify whether prostitutes could receive absolution. By 1660 a Toledan synod had concluded that priests should weigh the matter carefully and scrutinize the state of the *mujer ramera* before absolving her.[17]

The case of twenty-four-year-old Beatriz de Mansilla, originally from Consuegra but in 1583 a prostitute at a *casa pública* in Madrid, suggests some of the complexities involved in such matters. Beatriz had been catechized and could sign herself and recite the *santiguado*. She knew the Lord's Prayer, Ave Maria, Apostles' Creed, and Salve Regina "well" and by heart in both Latin and Castilian. The previous Lent she had dutifully confessed at the parish church of San Gínes. We do not know if she received absolution in this instance, but, as Beatriz explained, since she lived "in a public house where men came in to pick up on her," the *cura* refused her communion.[18]

Convicts and outlaws found their confessional lives restricted as well. Until the end of the sixteenth century, the Holy Office refused its prisoners the consolation of the sacraments in the hope that this would lead them to repent, but in later years Jesuits began to take an interest in confessing inmates. Francisco de Prada, for example, who had been held since Palm Sunday, confessed while in jail in Toledo on Holy Thursday of 1668 with a Jesuit who then gave him the Eucharist as well.[19] Mary Elizabeth Perry has argued that confessing prisoners served a dual role in Seville. The incarcerated believed that if they demonstrated sufficient contrition when they confessed to the prison chaplain, he might intervene on their behalf. By contrast, secular authorities encouraged priests to influence prisoners to confess their crimes sacramentally "so that they could use their confessions against them."[20] This strategy, however, would have been a patent violation of the confessional seal, and it is unclear when or how it could have been put into practice.

Yet Perry correctly draws our attention to the connection between spiritual and temporal authorities. Those living outside the secular or ecclesiastical law had to watch their step, for troubles with one arm could easily lead to entanglements with the other. In 1628, for example, the Holy Office arrested Antonio Suárez on charges of blasphemy. This was hardly his first misstep with the law; Antonio had formerly been incarcerated for assault and murder but had escaped. He subsequently spent two years on the lam, during which time he failed to fulfill his Easter duty.[21]

The confessional activities of itinerants were less stable and usually less rigorously regulated than those of the sedentary. Peddlers, muleteers, shepherds, and migrant laborers traveled for work; other picaresque wanderers went wherever fortune took them. The gypsies of Spain made every effort to live outside the regulatory structures of church and society. A nomadic lifestyle generally precluded the formation of a long-term relationship with a spiritual director. Even completing the Easter duty in one's home parish became problematic. Francisco Rivera, who sold linen, identified himself as a resident of Almagro, but in 1659 he made his Lenten confession in Zalamea de la Serena, 140 miles to the west, "because that was where he happened to be at the time since he [didn't] have any fixed residence but travel[ed] around selling from place to place."[22]

The church recognized itinerancy as problematic and tried to regulate it. Synods forbade *curas* to confess laypeople other than their own parishioners unless they could show a *cédula* from their own parish priest or a bull of crusade.[23] Of course, given the prevalence of the latter, few penitents would have felt the full weight of such restrictions. And, in any event, this rule pertained only to parish priests shriving for the Easter duty. It had no bearing on confessions to regular priests or outside Lent.

Some individuals, however, found any attempt to rein in their free-spirited roaming onerous. In a rare inquisitorial case for failure to observe the precepts of the church, just such a *picaro* appears on stage. In 1558, at the age of seventy, Juan Sánchez of Escalonilla (west of Toledo) had spent much of his life wandering as an itinerant laborer. He returned to his hometown occasionally, but he never stayed long. We know little of his youth, but it may have been a difficult one; he could not identify his grandparents and had never met his father, whom Juan understood to have been named Bartolomé. His mother, María Gonçales, seems to have raised him on her own.

Sánchez's trial occurred before the 1566 Synod of Toledo required confessants to memorize the prayers of the church. Nevertheless, Juan did not know how to sign himself or recite the *santiguado*. Of the four prayers, he claimed to know only the Ave Maria, but when asked to recite it, the defendant had to admit his ignorance of that one, too. The heart of the trouble, however, was a different matter. "Asked if he has confessed this current year, [Juan] said that he had not." And then, "Asked how long it had been since he confessed, he said 'twenty-six years.'" Juan assured the inquisitor that he had heard Mass during that span, but when "asked why he had not confessed in such a long time, he said '*por flojedad y bellaquería.*'"[24] Out of laziness and trickery.

The inquisitor leveled a barrage of questions at the accused. What trickery? Who told you to do this? Who were you with during those twenty-six years? Did you know that you were obliged to confess and commune annually? To the last of these, Juan replied that he had known of his obligation when he was young. Did the defendant not understand that if he failed to confess annually he became excommunicate? Juan claimed ignorance. The inquisitor asked, "Since this witness knew [Christians] were obliged to confess every year, why had he failed to do it for so many years?" The defendant replied ambiguously: *por perdido.* Because he had been lost. "Who caused you to be lost in not confessing?" The answer: *la ventura.* Fortune. "But didn't anybody ask you why you weren't confessing?" No one had, Juan claimed.[25]

The trial record is incomplete and disappointingly lacks a resolution. It is, moreover, extremely difficult to know how to read the case. Was Sánchez really that ill-informed? Was he playing the ignorant *rústico* in the hope of securing leniency? Was he an obstinate old man nearing the end of his life who just didn't give a damn? Whatever his motivations, Juan was precisely the sort of individual that the early modern synodal legislation of confessional practice hoped to reach. Yet, in spite of it all, itinerant living could keep individuals below the radar and provide a degree of freedom for those who chose not to confess, whether because of laziness, the winds of fortune, or disregard for the demands of the church.

## Confession and the Devout

While social status went a long way toward determining one's penitential experience, other factors mattered as well. Sometimes personal devotion toward the sacrament proved equally important. Many saw a deep commitment to confessional piety as risky; it could provoke gossip about false sanctity or sexual misconduct, the breakdown of family bonds, and even inquisitorial entanglements. Yet for some it remained attractive. The very devout could overcome the limitations of gender, low social status, even a problematic pedigree.[26] Ultimately, this allowed some unexpected confessants to command the sort of respect typically granted only to those with great worldly power.

Teresa of Avila offers the most famous example. Her family was devout and wealthy but bore the stigma of *converso* ancestry. Her paternal grandfather, Juan Sánchez de Toledo, converted to Christianity, but the Inquisition later condemned him as a relapsed heretic. Teresa's difficulties over the years with confessors have become almost legendary, for she frequently lamented them.[27] While some of her confessors, such as Francisco Borgia and Jerónimo Gracián, provided much-needed support and encouragement, she found others insufficiently learned, unable to live up to the moral standards outlined in prescriptive literature, and incapable of comprehending her visionary experiences or method of prayer. And, of course, Teresa also suffered the typical ignominy visited upon Spanish saints during the era: the scrutiny of the Holy Office.

Yet, as a confessant, she ultimately overcame the limitations of both lineage and gender. She not only found good confessors for herself but, temporarily, as it turned out, secured for the abbesses in her order the privilege of choosing confessors for their nuns without the approval of male superiors.[28] At times she even successfully subverted the structure of the sacrament and exercised remarkable authority over her own spiritual directors.[29] "What do you think of Teresa of Jesus?" asked one of her confessors to another. "Oh," replied the second, "you fooled me by telling me that she was a woman; by faith she isn't, but rather a masculine man."[30] In at least one instance, she even heard the confession of her own confessor.[31] As Teófilo Ruiz remarks, Teresa "was only one of many *Converso* descendants who made a mark in Spanish society and who, because of their intellect, unusual spiritual gifts and good fortune, were able to transcend the confines of their social order, gender, or the limitations of ancestral filiation."[32]

It was not only great mystic saints who overcame such hurdles and by virtue of their spiritual charisma commanded monarchlike respect in confession. The nearly illiterate *beata* Francisca López (1570–1650) of Alcoy (Valencia), born of "honest" but poor parents, commanded such authority that when she told her Jesuit confessor about God's favors toward her, he knelt with her in the confessional. It seemed to him that "the Holy Spirit was speaking through the mouth of that virgin."[33] Here was a striking inversion of the action taken by Hernando de Talavera, who sat while confessing the Catholic queen! Philip II could demand the undivided attention of a confessor for three days at his deathbed. However, for a period of perhaps three years, the doorkeeper at the convent Francisca frequented had explicit instructions from her spiritual director to notify him whenever the *beata* came to confess, even if he were sick in bed.[34] Whether out of jealousy or genuine concern, some tried to separate Francisca from her confessor, whispering that their relationship would surely attract inquisitors.

This phenomenon—the inversion of social status in the confessional—was as much the result of a confessor's devotion as the confessant's.[35] Every pauper or *converso* devoted to the sacrament needed a confessor who saw such individuals as worthy of attention. The secular clergy associated with the sacerdotal school of Avila, for example, labored to draw the poor into the confessional. They gave them alms, "consoled them, made their beds, swept their rooms, cleaned their drinking cups with great devotion and humility, and persuaded them to confess and purify their consciences in order to receive the Most Holy Sacrament with purity."[36] Charity afforded their spiritual advice gravity among the poor that it would otherwise have lacked.

The Ignatian emphasis on "divesting oneself of disordered love of relatives" played a role in the Society of Jesus's willingness to look beyond the background of its members and many of its spiritual directees.[37] Thus the Jesuit Luis de la Puente described his godly colleague Baltasar Álvarez as refusing alms from penitents and offering them his attention regardless of their status. "He accommodated himself to those with whom he dealt," wrote de la Puente, "of whatever sort they were, great or small, without disdaining the small or allowing his heart to gravitate toward the great." He despised confessors who worked only "with *gente honrada* and no one else."[38]

Yet Álvarez was not completely disinterested; he did not give all confessants equal attention. Rather, while he paid scant attention to social status, devotion itself became determinative when he chose whom he would direct spiritually. Thus he refused to take on more penitents than he could prudently manage, receiving the diligent rather than the great. Álvarez demanded a great deal from his confessants, and those who felt they could not live up to his standards "fled from him," which suited the Jesuit, since it gave him more time to focus on those "who truly sought the highest levels of perfection."[39] There may be a degree of hagiographical exaggeration at play here, but, as with Teresa of Avila and Francisca López, the ideal occasionally approached reality.

## Confessional Patronage

A sort of confessional patronage could also affect the experience of confession, and, despite episcopal legislation, the custom of paying confessors or giving them gifts remained common. Monarchs, for example, lavished upon their spiritual directors favors out of the reach of other penitents. Most royal confessors received at least one bishopric, and they frequently played an important role at court, influencing political decisions as royal counselors.[40] Famously, Queen Isabella nominated her confessor, Francisco Jiménes de Cisneros, to serve as regent of Castile upon her death. Even when a royal confessor rejected such gifts—for example, when Fray Juan Hurtado refused Charles V's offer of the archbishopric of Toledo—the monarch might find less obvious ways to extend patronage and favor by funding religious houses or pious works dear to the priest's heart.[41]

The wealthy imitated this practice by granting confessors grand favors. When, for instance, Simón de Rojas, an influential spiritual director, took over the impoverished Trinitarian house in Ciudad Rodrigo, he turned it into a center of confessional activity and drew in "a solid clientele of penitents from among the wealthiest citizens of the town," who responded by making donations to the establishment.[42] Early in the sixteenth century, the twice-widowed doña María Davila provided in her will for the foundation of a convent of Poor Clares outside Avila. She appointed as chaplain Alvaro de Castro, a relative and her personal confessor.[43]

For confessants with disposable income, like doña María, such patronage could continue even after death. Parishes in Granada frequently received sums ranging from a single *maravedí* to two *reales* from testators, "in honor and reverence of sacraments received."[44] This postmortem patronage becomes all the more evident in the remarkable proliferation of masses for the dead in early modern Spain. The average number of masses requested in the wills of *madrileños* grew from ninety in the 1520s, to two hundred in the 1550s, to nearly five hundred in the 1570s. By the 1590s it approached eight hundred, despite the rising cost of masses during the same period.[45] Similar evidence exists for Toledo, Cuenca, and Granada.[46] The desire to die well and assure oneself of a short stay in purgatory maintained an army of early modern Spanish priests, who did little more than recite anniversary masses for the deceased.[47]

In addition to requesting prayers for their souls, merchants frequently endowed pious institutions such as hospitals, convents, churches, and chapels in their wills in an effort to expiate their sins.[48] Testators could determine how these funds would be directed, and religious institutions relied upon the bequests. For many institutions, attracting and maintaining the good will of wealthy individuals became an important component in the calculus of confessional negotiations.

While granting ecclesiastical offices or endowing religious houses for one's confessor may have been limited to the extraordinarily wealthy and powerful, confessants of more modest means also gave gifts. Such transactions sometimes had a mercantile character. In the early 1580s, for instance, Lucía Hernandez of Piedra Buena (Toledo) confessed with don Gabriel de Osca, the curate of her parish, and as she knelt before him, she gave him some alms "in order to begin to confess."[49]

Determining the purpose of such exchanges is difficult. Across Spain, early modern diocesan synods legislated against the practice, either because they saw it as an attempt to purchase absolution or because they deemed it illicit for priests to demand money for performing their curatorial duty.[50] The 1583 Toledan synod explained that, because it desired "absolute purity and cleanness" in the administration of the sacraments, confessors should receive only what was officially due to them, even if a gift was offered "spontaneously."[51] Similarly, diocesan authorities prohibited priests from imposing penances that would directly benefit them, such as ordering confessants to pay for masses to be said by their confessor.[52] In 1594 the Franciscans enacted similar legislation.[53]

These prohibitions did not meet with complete success, since some priests continued to request donations and penitents continued to offer them. According to Fray Juan Campana's testimony before the Holy Office in 1594, the Theatines in Madrid had established a sliding scale ranging from fifteen *reales* to three ducats for their weekly penitents, which would surely have put their services out of the reach of most *madrileños*. And, apparently, if a penitent missed his confession, a cleric "would go to his home and denounce him right in front of his family for having gravely offended God."[54]

When Alonso de Higuera from Estemera confessed for Lent in 1585 to Fray Juan de Santiago, the Trinitarian asked for the more modest sum of two *reales* and promised to say a pair of masses for Alonso in exchange. The layman paid, but unfortunately the inquisitorial documents do not record what he thought about the request. As it turned out, Santiago had not actually been ordained to confess. When the Holy Office deposed him for *intruso en confesión*, the inquisitors asked whether he had received alms when performing confessions. Fray Juan admitted that some people had given him food and others had given money.[55]

One wonders exactly what people thought their donations would achieve. Did they give alms as an expression of charity for their confessor's own maintenance or with the intention of seeing it dispersed among the poor? Did laypeople view their offering as the just price for services rendered or as a token of appreciation for the priest's hard work? Some probably hoped that they would sway the impartiality of the one who sat in judgment. Others, perhaps, feared the repercussions—in onerous acts of satisfaction or refusals of absolution—should they fail to make a donation. Were these commoners really so different from kings and queens who made bequests to spiritual directors? Even monarchs and royal confessors recognized confessional gift giving as morally problematic. As in the case of Fray Juan Hurtado's refusal of the archbishopric of Toledo, it seems that a priest who accepted a donation from his penitent opened himself up, at least potentially, to charges of impropriety.

Nevertheless, individuals reacted very differently to priests who accepted or solicited alms. The Inquisition of Córdoba, for example, tried Hernan Sánchez in 1624 for pretending to be a confessor, but testimonies on his character and how he procured donations varied dramatically. Don Francisco de Villaepando, a lawyer of the royal appellate court in Granada, cast Sánchez and his confreres as "sensual and depraved people, [who] feigned virtue for many years in this region, that by doing so they might gain the trust of contemplative [*recogida*] and virtuous people, and once they had it, make money and commit sins." Even worse, "They seem[ed] to do this by means of confessions." Indeed, Sánchez traversed the diocese with an alms box that he used to "gather up lots of money, poultry, barley, and other things that he requested." Seemingly, he did so "in order to distribute them to the honorable poor," but in fact he kept the alms for himself. The widow doña Ynes de Molina, however, provided a rather different assessment. "It is true," she admitted, "that while she was confessing with . . . Sánchez, she dearly loved him and gave him gifts," but that did not mean she had been deceived or extorted. Indeed, doña Ynes believed that giving gifts to confessors was not only acceptable but appropriate, as long as it was done "without excess and always in a very wholesome way and with good intensions and without there being any offense in it."[56]

In Tarancón in La Mancha, a group of mendicants from nearby Huete came regularly to preach and confess in the region. In recompense for "such a useful and necessary thing," the friars customarily received food and alms. The bill for their maintenance was then passed on to the city council. In 1579 the town's mayor appealed to the *administrador perpetuo* of the Order of Santiago for a ruling on the appropriateness of the practice. He judged the situation "good" and ordered the council to pay up to ten thousand *maravedíes,* so long as receipts showed how the funds had been spent.[57] The issue here seems to have been less the appropriateness of receiving such alms than who would foot the bill. Yet this sort of maintenance fee was surely the norm for many priests who lacked other sources of support and poor parish clergy who relied upon donations to augment meager incomes.

Many laypeople, however, recognized a priest's refusal to receive gifts as a sign of godliness. María Bravo of Almagro, for example, described a former confessor, Fray Alonso Sánchez, in terms of highest praise, noting that he "refused to accept the alms that she wanted to give him out of gratitude for his hard work."[58] María found other ways to express her thanks and extend her own humble form of patronage. Since she had nothing else to offer, she gave Sánchez some strips of cloth for his nieces. Certainly, we must be aware of the possibility that priests extorted their penitents, but we see here as well a more subtle system at play. If priests earned a bit extra on the side, laypeople rarely complained too loudly. The giving of gifts helped construct mutually dependent relationships and greased the wheels of confessional justice.

## Confessional Networks

Like gifts and status, social networks also played a significant role in the sacramental experience. Usually, such networks supported confessional practice, reminding individuals of penitential obligations and often encouraging people to exceed them. While only two individuals interacted in confession, this fact belies the complexities engendered by kinship bonds and other, more artificial social relationships. Confessors were to prohibit penitents from discussing others in the confessional unless absolutely necessary, but the obligations and advantages engendered by community bonds and blood ties often affected confessional behavior. The sacrament continued to evidence a strong communitarian, rather than simply an individualistic, character throughout the early modern period, which could make the confessional feel rather crowded.

Family connections, for instance, often determined where and with whom one confessed. This was the case most obviously as a result of the parish structure and in the fulfillment of the Easter duty. For instance, Juan Bernal Díaz de Luco, concerned about the fact that many parishioners waited until the end of Lent to confess, offered the oft-repeated advice that *curas* should call their flock to confess by households in the weeks leading up to Easter Sunday.[59]

*Matriculas de confesión* recorded confessants by family, "designating them by their names and ages, more or less, and declaring specifically the heads of the household, husband and wife, children, maids and servants, and the people in their houses."[60]

Even outside Lent, family loyalty could pressure laypeople to frequent a specific priest. In Almagro, María Bravo's entire household confessed with Fray Alonso Sánchez in the monastery of the Comendadoras de Caltrava. In 1575 María found herself the object of Fray Alonso's unwanted sexual advances, and she seems quietly to have switched confessors, offering as an excuse that he was too busy confessing the nuns at the monastery. Nevertheless, when she fell ill, her family called Sánchez to her sickbed. Another resident of Almagro, the widow doña Ana de Torres, believed the friar to be a "good Christian and religious and of good habits and reputation," and ordered her daughters not to confess with anyone else because "he was very honest and religious and . . . he administered the sacrament of penance with great veneration and reverence."[61]

The head of household often set the tone for a family by directing relatives toward more or less frequent use of the sacraments. For instance, the Sevillano businessman Juan Antonio had long been accustomed to confessing and communing with Jesuits, and while visiting Madrid in 1617 he met with a father of the Society who persuaded him to confess daily. Having adopted the practice, he wrote to his wife in Seville urging her to do the same. Although willing to follow his lead, she "encountered great resistance from her confessor" when she broached the subject.[62]

Such influence could extend beyond the immediate family. Wealthy and elite households included servants, slaves, and retainers, and the attitudes of masters and mistresses established the pattern of practice for all. Juan García Álvarez de Toledo (d. 1619), Count of Oropesa, and his wife supported a group of *beatas* in their home who practiced frequent communion. Although they hoped for more, the *beatas* received permission to commune two or three times a week, and "no woman in the house received it less frequently than once a week, even the African slaves. Many of the male servants observed the same frequency, and anyone who failed to commune at least once a month was criticized by all as an impious person who did not behave like the rest."[63]

Confessants sometimes left their *cédulas* in the possession of relatives or landlords for safekeeping. The German Nicholas Buckholz, accused of having denied the necessity of priestly intercession in confession, left his *cédulas* with his landlady, Beatriz Marina of Madrid. Subsequent testimony proved that Nicholas was a rather frequent confessant, but had he been less pious, Beatriz would have known. When called to testify, she did her best to offer the sort of support that a family might normally have provided. She explained that she frequently saw Nicholas praying and going to Mass, both on feast days and during the week. He often read devotional books at night, and when he sat down to eat he thanked God, blessed the table, and did the same when they cleared the food away. She admitted that she had never actually seen him confess or commune, but every year during Holy Week he gave her a *cédula* proving that he had completed his Easter duty. As the landlady (*como dueña*), she passed these on to the parish *cura*.[64] Big cities meant constantly shifting populations, large parishes, a degree of anonymity, and, for many, the absence of family structure. In this context, regulating confessional behavior proved exceedingly difficult. Nevertheless, artificial kinship ties like this one, with Beatriz taking on some of the duties of a head of household, helped check the flouting of penitential obligations.

Yet the networks that usually endorsed and encouraged good confessional practice could break down, sometimes with disastrous results. Teresa of Avila's father, for example, refused to call a confessor when she grew ill. A "devastating regime of daily purges" had destroyed her already precarious health in the 1530s, but don Alonso Sánchez de Cepeda did not consider the matter serious and thought his daughter overly scrupulous.[65] The danger, however, proved real, and Teresa fell into a coma for four days. The saint later indicated that if she had died, her salvation would have been in peril.[66] For Teresa, who felt deeply the need for freedom to confess whenever and with whomever she wanted, this incident demonstrated how human, even familial, relationships could distract from and impede one's friendship with God.[67] "O all-too-fleshly love," she lamented, "although [don Alonso] was such a catholic and prudent father (which he truly was; this was not the effects of ignorance) he could cause me such grave harm!"[68]

## Opportunities and Limitations for Female Confessants

In the 1580s the Inquisition charged Father Pedro Chamorro of Trujeque with a number of crimes. Among them, he had made a young servant his mistress and lived with her in sin for some years. Falling ill, she asked Chamorro to send for a confessor, but first the priest persuaded her "two or three times" that "she shouldn't tell the truth or confess the sins that she had committed in having had carnal relations with him the whole time that she lived in his house." To his entreaties the servant replied, "Well, since I am [so ill], don't I have to confess the truth?" Chamorro responded, "Come on, there's nothing in that [*Anda, que no va nada en ello*]." He convinced her that a complete confession was unnecessary when one was in extremis; she did not need to reveal the affair. The confessor arrived and the servant followed her master's advice. Her soul burdened by mortal sins, she died without making a complete confession.[69]

Chamorro's rough treatment of his serving girl suggests not just the breakdown of the proper function of social networks but also the complexities that could arise from the highly gendered nature of early modern Spanish society. Merry Wiesner has commented pointedly concerning early modern women and religion: "At the heart of the issue was the control of female sexuality and maintenance of a moral order in which women were subservient."[70] This concern about control and moral maintenance was present in the penitential milieu, but it is also important to highlight some of the ways in which women asserted control over their confessional lives. This in turn helps explain why and how the sacrament became a popular aspect of early modern women's devotion.

People expressed conflicting sentiments about the complex relationships women formed with their male confessors. On the one hand, they saw confessional piety as absolutely licit. The church heartily approved of it as a devotional expression that stood in stark opposition to the theological platform of Protestantism. On the other hand, many viewed those relationships as problematic and sexually charged because of the dangers that theological reflection connected to the female body.[71] As the late medieval moral theologian Jean Gerson warned, "for even the most deeply religious men, no matter how great their sanctity, a common life and familiarity with women are not safe."[72] Indeed, the intimacy shared by confessors and their confessional daughters sometimes boiled over into sexual dalliance. Even when it did not, female confessants more frequently than men became the objects of overtly offensive priestly behavior and found their significance as religious people undermined. This contentious situation sometimes led to trouble, for both the devout female confessant and her spiritual director.

Misuse of the sacrament—whether real or imagined—continued to be a concern throughout the period. Nevertheless, confession remained popular at least in part because a variety of institutional and social forces corrected, albeit imperfectly, for the vulnerability of women. The social networks that female penitents formed with other women, the support of families and sympathetic clergy, and the reforming concerns of the church forestalled or redressed some abuse.

Confession also achieved new heights of popularity among early modern women because they had fewer acceptable alternatives for expressing their religiosity than in previous generations.[73] Direct communication with God, an important late medieval form of female religiosity, became much more contentious territory in the early modern period.[74] Determining whether women feigned sanctity, visions, ecstatic experiences, xenoglossia, or revelations became a pressing concern as Golden Age Spain was vigorously confronted by the Inquisition.[75] The rise of penitential devotion, which gained popularity in the later Middle Ages and soon became a fundamental expression of feminine piety, offered an important new outlet.[76] Pious laywomen, the professed female religious, *beatas,* and tertiary members of religious orders in Spain embraced the sacrament of penance. Yet confession formed only one part of a vast penitential society.[77] As Wiesner comments, "Women and men went on pilgrimages, bought and viewed relics, paid for memorial masses or special prayers, lit candles, founded lay confraternities dedicated to certain saints or devotional practices such as the rosary, and carried out a variety of other acts for religious reasons."[78]

Given the rise of penitential, especially confessional, piety among women, it is important to note that except in extraordinary circumstances generally deemed unacceptable by the church, women confessed to ordained male members of the priesthood. This gendered situation did not necessarily undermine the effectiveness of confession as a spiritual exercise. As Patricia Ranft cautions, "We must remember that the confessor–spiritual director relationship was first and foremost a spiritual relationship, and women and men of the Counter Reformation period considered it as such."[79] Yet gender did matter in confession.

Stephen Haliczer has argued that the rising prominence of confession among women collided with the agenda of the church hierarchy to reform the sexual conduct of the clergy.[80] Trent, for example, condemned concubinage and encouraged bishops to purge the practice among the clergy. Reforming bishops held synods, levied fines, and carried out visitations in their dioceses. The vow of celibacy, which had often gone unenforced in the previous era, became a reality for many priests. Controversially, Haliczer concludes that the combination of increasing frequent confession by women and the elimination of concubinage sexualized the confessional experience in a new way. It produced an increase in confessional solicitation, which the Spanish church attempted to combat by requiring the use of confessionals and bringing the crime into the bailiwick of the Inquisition.

Whether or not we accept Haliczer's thesis, historians have noted the eroti-cized overtones of relationships between certain confessors and their *hijas de confesión,* even when no sexual congress occurred. Some *beatas* and religious women experienced visions loaded with marital imagery when they bonded with a spiritual director.[81] Teresa of Avila had such a vision when she resolved to give her obedience to Jerónimo Gracián, her confessor. "It seemed to me," she wrote, "that our Lord Jesus Christ was next to me in the form that he usually appears, at His right side stood [Gracián] himself, and I at His left. The Lord took our right hands and joined them and told me he desired that I take this master to represent Him as long as I live, and that we both agree in everything because it was thus fitting."[82] Even when such marital visions were absent, the bond between a confessant and her confessor frequently became significant. It often lasted for many years and became one of the very few meaningful relationships that a woman could form with a man outside her family. And for many women who sought a relational context within which to express their piety, especially the professed religious and *beatas,* the "insti-tutional stamp of approval" a male director conferred could be of singular importance.[83] This proved to be the case even for someone like Saint Teresa, who "developed the gift," as one commentator put it, "of making men give her the orders she wanted to obey."[84]

Even women who did not aspire to heroic levels of sanctity saw confes-sion as a break from the confines of daily life. As Elizabeth Lehfeldt notes, "the lives of women—especially religious women—increasingly pivoted on the dis-tinction between a life of circumspect seclusion and the temptations of what lay beyond the doorway to the home or cloister."[85] Advice literature urged parents to keep daughters at home in order to protect their virtue. In a chapter titled "On the Solitude of the Virgin," the Spanish humanist Juan Luis Vives wrote, "An unmarried young woman should rarely appear in public, since she has no business there and her most precious possession, chastity, is placed in jeopardy."[86]

For at least some women, marriage offered little more freedom. Clerics and moralists depicted wedlock as a means of enforcing social stability through the institution of domestic enclosure.[87] Like Vives, Luis de León described the world as fraught with dangers and temptations to which women were espe-cially prone. Drawing on Plutarch, he suggested, "Women, following [the example of a tortoise, which has no voice], must remain at home and practice silence."[88] This "poetics of containment" became intimately connected with issues of honor and purity in Spanish society.[89] Such rhetoric has led Emilie Bergmann to argue that Spaniards defined feminine chastity in terms of "the almost complete absence of autonomous activity. The virtuous woman should be almost invisible, appearing on the street as seldom as possible."[90]

In practice, however, the behavior of Spaniards looks a bit different, for the confinement of women—nuns in the cloister, prostitutes in brothels, and laywomen in their homes—was never absolutely enforced or enforceable. A "permeable" sort of seclusion confronted early modern Spanish women.[91] The female peasants of remote Galicia, for example, commanded remarkable social, sexual, and economic freedom.[92] Likewise, women in Granada enjoyed an unexpected degree of uxorial independence, as they visited one another's homes and exchanged gifts. In the seventeenth century husbands increasingly provided their wives with pin money, which the women spent as they saw fit. The lay moralist (and, one hastens to add, bachelor) Francisco Manuel de Mello (1608–1666), whose *Carta de guia de casados* went through eighteen editions, worried about these trends. He feared that giving women control over their own rooms within the home and their own expenditures outside it would ultimately undermine the family.[93]

Like pin money and private rooms, participation in penitential activities could become a source of feminine freedom. It provided women with an opportunity to leave the house and engage their community. While this does not necessarily mean that devotion functioned as a façade for a desire to be sociable, it does suggest that a significant outlet for sociability coincided with attending sermons and participating in penitential confraternities, rosary masses, pilgrimages, and confession itself.

Yet even some of these areas saw restrictions imposed on female participation. Take, for example, Spanish confraternities, which uniquely in Europe often opened their doors to female members. Gender segregation in confraternities, at least in Castile, was as likely to be initiated by women as by men. Female participation in specifically penitential confraternities, which began to flourish in Spain in the sixteenth century, appears always to have been somewhat limited. Women were forbidden to flagellate themselves but permitted to participate as *cofrades de luz,* bearing torches in processions. Some imitated Veronica by wiping the blood and sweat from the bodies of male penitents. From the late sixteenth century, however, both church and state began restricting female involvement. By the seventeenth century, only men processed.[94] Confession, by contrast, remained accessible to women.

## Contradictions in Gender and Confession

In fact, one of the most significant aspects of confessional practice and its impact on religious life in the early modern Roman Catholic world is that women participated in the sacrament much more frequently than men. Like the rise in the frequency of confession generally, this gender divide is difficult to demonstrate quantitatively, but anecdotal evidence is abundant. In 1557, for example, the missionary Jesuits in Burgos described a situation typical of this feminization of confession:

> The fathers here are so intent upon the salvation of their fellow men that, as the saying is, they hardly have time to scratch their ears; the number seeking the holy sacraments is so great that there is hardly a day when we cease hearing confessions and giving communion, especially Sundays and holy days, when a great multitude of women burning with divine love fills our chapel. Men, however, are not at all well disposed toward us, with a few exceptions, and these, since space is limited, go to other churches lest they be intermixed with the ladies.[95]

Around 1590 an anonymous theologian, commenting on the controversial practices of frequent communion and long conversations in the confessional, noted that these were "very ordinary in women and very rare in men."[96] Luis de Granada thought it a "plague" that women had "made off" with frequent communion, which necessarily entailed frequent confession. "So it seems," he wrote, "that women need the bit and men need the spur, and I can think of none sharper than to tell [the men] that this omission and negligence of theirs is equivalent to the worst sins which have been committed in this world."[97]

For some critics, however, the problem went beyond the issue of frequency. They worried not simply that women participated in the sacraments more often than men but that frequent confession could actually be emasculating. In 1554 the Jesuit Peter Domenech wrote to Ignatius Loyola from Valladolid, explaining, "the fruit that had been expected from frequenting of the sacraments is now manifest to everyone. Some, and not just a few (although I do not have the number), made general confessions, rendering an accurate account of their whole life, such that those whom one previously feared as ferocious lions, now can be handled like tame lambs."[98] But others took a more negative view of the phenomenon. In 1557 the Dominican Melchior Cano (1509?–1560), who saw frequent use of the sacraments as a sure sign of the Antichrist's imminent arrival, wrote to Charles V's confessor criticizing the Jesuits for taming their male confessants. "One of the reasons," wrote Cano, "that I am dissatisfied with these Theatine fathers [i.e., Jesuits] is that the gentlemen whom they take in hand, instead of making them into lions, they turn them into chickens."[99]

We occasionally encounter men committed to confession with the same intensity as the most devout women, but examples are rare. The emperor Charles was commended for his religious zeal because he confessed four times a year toward the end of his life in monastic seclusion.[100] Under Jesuit influence, the Sevillano merchant Juan Antonio embraced daily confession, as we have seen. Yet far more laywomen than men made the sacrament a central part of their devotional lives, at least in part because the church endorsed far fewer outlets through which they could enact their religiosity. In the context of those limitations, and in spite of the risks associated with the relationships between women and their spiritual directors, confession became a mainstay of feminine piety.

It is, however, quite significant that the prescriptive literature of the age rarely reflected this fact. This paradox comes close to the heart of historiographical debates about what some scholars regard as the misogynistic spirit of early modern Christianity. By all accounts, priests confessed women more often than they did men. Yet one finds precious little advice in manuals of confession to help guide female penitents or their confessors in the making of good confessions. Manual authors devoted considerable time and energy to discussing the sins to which the different *estados* were prone. But they generally described those *estados* in terms of social position or occupation: nobles, doctors, tailors, students, laborers, priests, and so forth. Their ordering of society rarely allowed for discussions of the *estado feminil*. The uniqueness of girls, wives, virgins, mothers, and widows went unaddressed. Female servants, landladies, and even women of quality seemingly did not exist as discrete groups.

When manuals of confession addressed women directly, they accorded them only a secondary significance and rarely a distinct identity. Francisco de Alcozer, for instance, addressed the sins of "tailors, cobblers, leatherworkers, washer women, and seamstresses." He explained the various ways in which the first three groups might sin. This included a variety of work-related shenanigans such as stealing silk, damaging goods, passing poorer materials off as costlier ones, or attempting to pay less or demand more than the just price for their work. Fray Francisco dealt with the women after the men in a single sentence: "Washerwomen and seamstresses can commit these same mortal sins."[101]

Counterexamples to this trend do exist. In his *Noticias singularissimas* for confessors, José Gavarri, who so often challenged received wisdom in penitential practice, included a long section on women who wore low-cut or revealing clothing. But even Gavarri failed to offer real-life examples of confessing women who had sinned in this fashion, or to provide specific suggestions for dealing with the issue in the confessional, as he frequently did for other matters. Instead, he approached it as an abstract theological question: "whether women who nowadays go about in low-cut gowns sin mortally."[102]

The tendency for manual authors to focus on confessing men rather than women is surprising, since many confessors spent more of their time confessing women than men. While manuals persistently ordered priests to avoid illicit relationships with female penitents, whether during confession or outside it, the same works repeatedly dismissed or devalued women themselves as confessants. Azpilcueta offered no specific advice whatsoever for confessing women. Antonio Fernández de Córdoba penned nearly three hundred pages of specific questions, divided according to *estados,* for the use of confessors. He so thoroughly nuanced his categories that he addressed carpenters and weavers of damask and taffeta. Nevertheless, he referred to women on only three brief occasions, mentioning nuns, midwives, and reformed prostitutes.[103]

This dearth may indicate that authors regarded the confessions of women as simple, not requiring serious consideration. Some may have concluded that, being less exposed to the world, women had fewer sins to confess, but this seems unlikely given contemporary attitudes about feminine proclivities toward sin. Some believed that women's spiritual growth would have less impact than men's and therefore focused their energy on the latter. Another possibility, difficult to prove but attractive, is that clerical writers felt a need to express, even in print, a lack of interest in women in order to depict themselves as good shepherds above reproach. The advice given to the Jesuit Baltasar Álvarez, who became Teresa of Avila's spiritual director, ties together a number of these concerns. He was warned against spending "time with women, especially Carmelite nuns, in person or by letter," and encouraged to apply himself "to dealing with men wherein there is less danger and more and longer-lasting fruit."[104] Moreover, since confession in early modern Spain developed a reputation as a feminine and feminizing activity, authors may have wanted to disassociate the sacrament from its popularity among women in order to mitigate that concern.

Oddly, the silence of manual writers is out of step with other moral literature from the same era.[105] Juan Luis Vives's *De institutione feminae christianae* and Luis de León's *La perfecta casada,* merely the most distinguished examples of advice literature for women and family life, have already been mentioned. In fact, in León's work some see a heightened valuation of wifely duties, for León argued that wives pleased God not by behaving like nuns but by managing their homes well. In Spain as in other areas of Europe, according to James Casey, "the family was assuming increasingly the role of moral foundation of the godly community."[106] These works dovetail with the likes of Francis de Sales's *Introduction to the Devout Life,* a best-seller in Spain from its first printing there in the 1610s, which similarly placed morality "within the grasp of all, the married man as much as the celibate priest."[107]

Contemporary treatises that aimed at an educated clerical audience also attempted to come to terms with the issues of domestic life. The most popular of these, *De sancto matrimonii sacramento disputationum* (first published in Genoa in 1592 and then in three volumes in Madrid between 1602 and 1605), written by Tomás Sánchez (1550–1610), has been described as a "benchmark for confessors when judging the sinfulness or otherwise of specific actions."[108] The Cordoban casuist Sánchez, whose cleverness later made him a target in Blaise Pascal's *Provincial Letters,* pushed the boundaries of discussions on marriage and made the family an important topic of conversation in literature and preaching.[109]

Of greater popular importance than *De sancto matrimonii,* stories of saints' lives were disseminated widely among Roman Catholic women, providing readers with models for both holy living and good confessions. And while the stories of male exemplars proved popular, early modern women preferred saints of their own sex.[110] Between 1500 and 1700, Spanish printers produced approximately two hundred spiritual lives of women, and some went through numerous editions.[111] Women read them on their own and to one another, and confessors read to their illiterate penitents.[112]

This suggests an interesting conclusion about the formation of female penitents. While men could find themselves in manuals, *vitae* offered the clearest depictions of women participating in the sacrament. Thus the Jesuit Bernardino de Villegas's *Esposa de Christo instruida* offered advice to female penitents but did so as part of his *vita* for the Bernardine nun Saint Lutgarda. Such a divergence meant that devout women who relied upon spiritual biographies and autobiographies as the paradigm for the confessional experience would have had a different set of expectations from male confessants who drew upon confessional manuals. Most notably, the holy women of *vitae* were just that, holy women. Even those who did not participate formally in the religious life behaved like nuns as often as not. They tended to depict their good confessors primarily as spiritual directors with whom they shared not just their sins but also the experience of spiritual life and growth toward holiness. Busy parish priests who lacked a strong vocation for spiritual direction must have been a tremendous disappointment to such women. No wonder so many of them turned to confessors in the religious orders, who could provide the sort of confessional experience that women had learned to expect.

## Solicitation in the Confessional

Yet, as Teresa of Avila's often tumultuous confessional relationships suggest, those who desired spiritual direction only sometimes found kindred souls. This becomes particularly apparent with incidents of sexual solicitation in the confessional. To be certain, the Roman church saw such behavior as reprehensible and a heretical abuse of the sacrament. The ecclesiastical hierarchy understood that, in addition to its overt sinfulness, this offense undermined reforming work, which relied heavily upon confession, for it caused others to look with disdain upon the sacrament, seeing it profaned by the church's own ministers.[113] While some may have looked the other way or sought to protect offending priests, many in the church demonstrated outrage at what had become an all too common practice.

Sexual solicitation by priests of their penitents, especially female penitents, occurred with more frequency than can easily be explained away. And, of course, the records that remain represent only cases in which the victim (or some other witness) exposed the deed to the Holy Office.[114] We do not know what percentage of the total these records represent. Some women waited decades before coming forward; others must never have done so.

What is clear is that women reacted in different ways to the sexual advances of their confessors. Their reactions demonstrate the fluctuating dynamics of negotiated power in the confessional and influence our understanding of gender's role in the administration of the sacrament. Early modern moral treatises prepare us to expect women to have responded in a more or less passive and compliant manner, for their authors encouraged women to submit to male authority figures, whether fathers, husbands, or priests. Moreover, the penitential space underscored ecclesiastical authority by placing the seated priest, as divine representative, in a position of authority over his kneeling penitent. Nevertheless, laywomen did not necessarily confuse submission to God with submission to an individual priest.

Although it was not a uniform reaction, many solicited women disrupted their confession to scold a priest or simply stood up and walked away without receiving absolution or being granted leave. For example, Augustín de Cervera, a Carmelite, confessed an anonymous young woman in the town of Mora in 1578. When he reached out a hand to touch her breast, his confessant pulled back, indicating that "she did not want him to touch any part of her." The embarrassed priest "let her be and continued with the confession in a clean manner, carrying out his office as he was obliged."[115] In the 1570s, when Gabriel de Osca solicited one Francisca in Velasco, she responded by standing up, telling him off, exiting the church, and finding another confessor.[116]

Another of Osca's victims, Lucia Hernández, responded to his advances by rising to her feet and demanding to know "what he saw in [her] that he would do that." "Come, come, *señora*," the priest demurred, "confess [your sins]; I don't mean anything bad by it [*no lo hago por mal*]." Lucia stalked off into the nave of the church with the priest following in her wake. "For the love of God," he pleaded, "don't make such a scandal of confessing. Anyone who saw you sit down and then get up so quickly will talk about it." Lucia remained resolute and vowed never to confess with Osca again. Because her town, Piedra Buena, did not have many other confessors, this meant that she was unable to participate in the sacrament as often as she wanted.[117]

Doña Angela de Borja, a professed nun in a convent outside Valencia, knew how to set boundaries in her obedience to a spiritual director. In the early 1640s she began to confess and commune on a daily basis, but the misconduct of her confessor, Antonio Marigo, brought that practice to an end. Instead, the nun confessed only when prevailed upon by her sisters in the convent. During one encounter, six or seven years after the drama had begun, Fray Marigo told doña Angela that he would give her a mortification to perform and that whatever he commanded, she should obey. With that, the Mercedarian told her to lift her skirts and show him her "private parts." She replied that he was "a bold rascal" (*un picaro atrevido*). "Is this any way to obey?" asked Marigo. The nun responded that she knew the limits of obedience owed to a confessor; his request exceeded them.[118] The submissive physical posture that penitents adopted before representatives of the divine judge did not necessarily mean that they would put up with roguish behavior.

Confessants frequently shared their experiences of bad confessors with friends, family members, and neighbors. Female penitents often turned to other women, seeking support and offering warnings about confessors whom they should avoid. Ana Martín of Mocejón came home in tears after an encounter with her *cura*. Ana's mother asked what had happened and listened to her story. Her mother then informed Ana's father-in-law, who accompanied the young woman to the Holy Office. After being solicited by Juan Ribas in Barcelona, Mariana Boquina immediately told "other women, her friends," what had happened. They could sympathize since the same thing had happened to them. In 1593 a group of *madrileñas* appeared en masse before an inquisitor to lodge a complaint against a Bernardine monk who had solicited each of them individually.[119] The mutual support and encouragement that these examples suggest occurred over and over again in cases of women who came forward.

Indeed, when women joined forces they could become rather fearsome. The Franciscan Juan de Olomedo, who served as confessor to the nuns at the Monastery of the Immaculate Conception in Oropesa, found himself accused of sexual solicitation by many of his confessants. In his defense, the seventy-year-old priest offered context for the accusations. A dispute between himself and the abbess had turned the nuns against him and led them to accuse him falsely of solicitation. Fray Juan implored the inquisitor to look upon his testimony "with the eyes of a father, because I am alone, and [the women] are powerful."[120] The leniency shown him by the Holy Office—it merely restricted the friar from confessing women—suggests that, rightly or wrongly, his judges felt the weight of that concern.

Attempts to marshal support, however, sometimes backfired, as in the case of Juana López of Almagro, another of Alonso Sánchez's victims. After Fray Alonso kissed her during a confession, Juana stopped going to him. Instead, she turned to a local Dominican, Juan de Molina. She told Molina what had happened, but rather than champion her cause or take her to the Holy Office, he admonished her: "Shut up, daughter. Don't say that or let it come out of your mouth. Don't tell it to anyone." Later, Juana told the inquisitor, she allowed herself to forget the matter—perhaps the term repression is appropriate here—for a period of six years. When neighbors asked why she had stopped confessing with Fray Alonso, she simply responded, "He was old and didn't understand things well."[121]

Certainly, not all solicited women responded with self-confident outrage or indignation. Even the story of Lucia Hernández, whom we saw rebuff Gabriel de Osca's solicitation in 1579 or 1580, is complicated by a long period of silent submission. The first incident of solicitation actually occurred years earlier, when Lucia's family summoned don Gabriel to hear her confession as she suffered from a grave pain in her side. He sat at her bedside while someone (*alguna persona*) shut the door, leaving Lucia alone with the priest. During the confession—she could not remember exactly when—he "placed his hand on [her] breast." After recovering from her illness, Lucia continued to confess to the priest for four years, although "nothing ugly happened" until the solicitation of 1579 or 1580.[122]

Others exhibited even more willingness to overlook the behavior of soliciting confessors. At the end of the seventeenth century in the Canary Islands, Francisca de Santa Ana reported that more than a year earlier Francisco del Rosario, a Dominican, had told her to take off her cloak and had tried to embrace her inappropriately when she confessed with him. Yet six or seven months later she confessed with him again. When asked by the inquisitor to explain this behavior, Francisca claimed that she had acted out of convenience: "There were a lot of people confessing with the other confessors and she found [Francisco del Rosario] less busy and also because it didn't seem like he remembered her."[123]

Likewise, Agapita Donday from Valencia, whom the Mercedarian Estevan Verde solicited outside the confessional, continued to confess to him after the incident.[124] When pressed to account for her willingness to do so, Agapita explained that before the incident she had confessed more freely (con mas libertad) with Verde, but afterward she did so "with more caution," and very rarely. She only went to him "in those times when her regular confessor . . . could not confess her because of the press [concurso] of penitents" and especially when she saw that Verde was not busy.[125]

The purpose of inquisitorial trials was to expose and root out heresy, not to explore witnesses' feelings. Yet one longs to make sense of these events and the willingness of women to return to soliciting confessors. Modern psychological assessments of women who return to abusive men suggest that such relationships tend to exhibit significant imbalances of power and often alternate between cycles of punishment and indulgence.[126] This may help us to account for some situations in which solicited penitents remained attached to abusive priests, but we must be very cautious about importing contemporary North American psychological theory to the rather different social, cultural, and material context of early modern Spain.

The seemingly cavalier attitude of Francisca and Agapita toward the offenses perpetrated against them remains disconcerting. Perhaps, in their cases, inquisitorial scribes failed to convey outrage or shame as clearly as in Lucia Hernández's trial. Perhaps women simply considered the occasional solicitation to be a disagreeable but not unanticipated part of the confessional experience. Francisca and Agapita had other confessors to whom they could turn, but both women occasionally chose to visit a soliciting priest *merely out of convenience*. They did not exhibit great fear or anxiety toward the confessors, and the victims do not appear to have developed a strong attachment to the men who sexualized the encounter. Nevertheless, it is hard to believe that their attitude toward sexual abuse could have been so blasé. Would, as Agapita suggested, a healthy dose of caution really forestall recidivism?

## Honor, Familial Support, and Their Limits

Concerns about honor help resolve this incongruity, at least in part. Social scientists have often used honor as a central concept in describing Mediterranean society.[127] Drawing upon this theme, Teófilo Ruiz comments, "The honourable life was a goal to which most Spaniards aspired. The absence of honour, or the breach of honour, implied shame; in early modern Europe and in Spain in particular, there was nothing more shameful than sexual dishonour."[128] That dishonor fell not just upon an individual woman but also upon her family and entire community. Whether the offense was voluntary or involuntary was of secondary importance in this calculus.

Other scholars have questioned the rigid application of honor as an interpretive concept in early modern Spain, demonstrating that while honor mattered, it could be deployed in remarkably elastic ways. Ann Twinam, for example, describes how colonial elites in South America located honor "in the public sphere, where an individual's reputation was malleable and ultimately defined by other peers."[129] Similarly, Allyson Poska has argued that even among peasants, "a person's honour was constituted not by broad social norms, but by a combination of one's own articulation of one's behaviour and one's interaction with the community."[130]

In cases of sexual solicitation, women deployed the concept of honor in a variety of ways. Certainly, some women maintained their honor by refusing to be molested, upbraiding offending confessors, and telling their friends, family members, other priests, and even inquisitors about the offense. Cathalina Flexas of Mallorca, for instance, rebuffed Gabriel Canaves's advances on the basis that she was a *mujer honrada* and "greatly esteemed her honor," even when the priest insisted that the liaison would be kept "very secret."[131] For others, however, being *honrada* meant keeping their mouths shut. Spanish society emphasized avoiding scandal and maintaining the "good fellowship" necessary for a community to live in peace.[132] This motivated some women who experienced solicitation in the confessional to remain silent.

The story of thirty-year-old María Bravo, to whose interactions with Fray Alonso Sánchez we have returned a number of times, illustrates this point. The Inquisition first summoned María on 12 April 1575. In that interview she described her relationship with Sánchez in idealized tones. She called him an "angel" and claimed that she never experienced "any lewd behavior from him." He even refused the money that she tried to give him for "his hard work." After confessing with him for fifteen years, María had switched confessors, but only because he had a hard time managing all the confessants who sought his counsel.[133]

The next day, however, María changed her story. Her anxiety over admitting Fray Alonso's solicitation leaps off the page. She repeatedly referred to herself as an honorable woman; she only wanted to tell the truth. The first transgression, she explained, occurred when the friar kissed her during a confession. Angered and dismayed, she made Sánchez promise not to do it again, because she had taken a vow of chastity and did not want to break it. Alonso promised and, confident that he would keep his word, María returned. But the same thing happened three more times, including once when her family summoned the friar to confess María on her sickbed, "because in her house they didn't suspect anything bad." This time, having confessed and absolved her, Sánchez kissed the *beata*. Overcome with emotion and knowing that the parish priest was waiting to bring her the Eucharist, the exhausted woman began to cry. So did Fray Alonso. He told María that she needed to confess again to deal with the new infraction. She did so and again he absolved her.[134]

The priest's tears do not appear to have been an expression of true repentance. He asked María to continue confessing with him, whether to facilitate further sexual encounters or because he feared her revealing all to another priest. But María could not continue: "For the honor of both of [us]," she and Alonso could not continue to talk so often in the church lest "they" suspect the pair of improprieties. If Sánchez needed to talk to her, he could come to her home.[135] María explained that she then stopped shriving to Fray Alonso, some four years before her testimony. Concerns about public opinion and tarnished honor had pushed her to hide her shame from her family and to lie to the Holy Office, casting her violator as an ideal Counter-Reformation confessor. It may even have driven her to allow the friar access to her person in the less public confines of her own home.

Honor was malleable and socially constructed in early modern Spain, but that malleability had its limits. María found herself navigating them. She maintained that she was *honrada* but feared that the Inquisition, her community, and even her own family might dispute the claim. María's concerns do not speak for all of the women who quietly endured soliciting confessors, but her story provides a reasonable account for those who sought to avoid scandal and maintain their honor in the face of public scrutiny.

This approach also helps account for the rarity of honor killings in the wake of sexual solicitation. Male kin hoping to recover family honor attacked soliciting priests with remarkable infrequency. In 1623 the Galician Francisco de Quiroga y Taboada shot and killed both his visibly pregnant daughter and the priest with whom she was carrying on an affair "for the honour and good of his house."[136] Even this rare case does not pertain to confessional solicitation. Yet we intuitively view solicitation as more dishonoring than consensual concubinage with a cleric, which could sometimes be viewed as honorable.[137] Some families and communities must have looked to the Inquisition to restore tarnished honor. Certainly, ecclesiastical prohibitions against harming clerics helped restrain vengeance, as did the idea that priests were sacrosanct. However, the heat of righteous indignation might well have crowded out concerns about subsequent punishment, and laypeople frequently distinguished between honoring the priestly office and submitting to a bad priest. The lack of bloody vendettas against soliciting confessors continues to perplex, but the need to maintain community cohesion—to secure "good fellowship" at all costs—surely forms an important part of the answer.

The failure of early modern Spaniards to address tarnished honor by attacking soliciting priests suggests some of the limits of family support for female relatives. Confessional activities could also lead family networks to break down in other ways. In solicitation cases, family members sometimes valued "good fellowship" over honor or the protection of women's virtue. At other times, an opposite tendency surfaces: heterodox confessional behavior could prompt families to spurn relatives or provoke denunciations.

The case of the French tailor Guillermo Bononel expresses this dynamic. Guillermo, who lived in Madrid in 1630, had married Ana Ortíz about eight years earlier. Some considered him a bad husband. Ana's sister, María, said that Guillermo treated his wife poorly and "did not give her what was necessary." He laughed at her if she went to Mass in the middle of the week or if she confessed often.[138] Ana, María, and María's husband, Vicente Ramon, found Guillermo's religious behavior altogether suspect. This family network of witnesses accused the Frenchman of various infractions. They claimed he had desecrated a crucifix and that, instead of taking bulls of crusade, he mocked them. Most of the charges levied against him, however, pertained directly to his confessional behavior.

Vicente, for example, offered hearsay evidence that his brother-in-law never completed his penances. He claimed that Guillermo thought that the priest should do the penance instead, since he had imposed it. Ana testified that Guillermo refused to confess for indulgences because he "didn't want to do it, saying that he didn't have to confess more than once a year." In fact, one Lent, Guillermo had refused to confess at all. He ordered his wife to lie to the *cura* and tell him that Guillermo had already fulfilled his Easter duty. María's testimony provided additional details on this last point. Her husband had told her to say that he had moved away so the parish priest would not know Guillermo had failed to confess.[139]

Other neighbors portrayed the accused in a better light. Miguel Martín, also French, took his countryman for a "good Christian" who worked hard for his wife and children. Bartolomé de Cuellar believed that Guillermo had completed all of his religious obligations. Bartolomé Gonçalez, a familiar of the Holy Office, testified that Guillermo was a conscientious man who feared God. The tailor went to Mass when he was obliged to and on many feast days. Gonçalez had seen him praying and knew nothing that would suggest that the Frenchman was anything but a faithful Christian. In general, his neighbors viewed Guillermo as a bit rough around the edges but, all things considered, a good Christian and family man.[140]

Perhaps his wife and in-laws had seen through the façade in a way that his neighbors had not. Perhaps María sought to free herself from a man whom she despised. Indeed, her husband may well have been physically abusive, for he admitted to having broken the aforementioned crucifix when, in the midst of a row, he threw the closest thing to hand at his wife.[141] Whether or not the charges brought against him were true, they were the sort of charges that María and her supporters believed serious enough to demand the dissolution of the obligations entailed by familial bonds of support. Guillermo was no *madrileño* but a *lombardo frances,* from the "land of the heretics," as Vicente informed the inquisitors.[142] He engaged in sacrilegious behavior by mocking and attacking the trappings of Spanish religiosity. And emphatically, at every turn, he demonstrated that he was an outsider by flouting his penitential obligations. Under these pressures, family networks could and did break down, leaving individuals to face trial and tribulation alone.

# Conclusions

Early modern Spain was a hierarchical society in the confessional as in other areas of life, and one's *estado* affected penitential practice in striking ways. However, status and gender did not always prove determinative. The devout confessant, even the devout female confessant of problematic lineage, could transcend the limitations imposed by church, state, and society in such a way as to command remarkable respect. Confessors could demand submission from powerful penitents and show reverence toward the poor and illiterate. In spite of this important nuance in the relationship between the status quo and its subversion—there is no escaping it—the rich and powerful often received preferment, while the lower social orders found their confessional lives more firmly delimited and regulated.

Extraconfessional relationships could alter the experience dramatically. Gift giving became an important way to build a mutually dependent rapport with a confessor. Kinship bonds and even artificial social relationships—between a landlady and her tenant or between groups of women—helped to determine how, when, and with whom one confessed. When the penitential encounter went wrong, these bonds formed an important line of defense for the redress of grievances. When such networks broke down, the results could be disastrous.

Prescriptive literature often downplayed the significance of female confessants, and some people found the sacrament destructive or confining. Nevertheless, many people took ownership of their sacramental lives, demanding that confessors behave appropriately. Most early modern Spaniards refused simply to submit to the will of a clerical class imbued with the spirit of a baroque Counter-Reformation Roman Catholicism. "In theory," notes Jodi Bilinkoff, "the spiritual director, male, formally educated, imbued with the power of his office, guided the penitent, male or female, who then blindly obeyed his dictates."[143] But only in theory. In reality, penitential relationships exhibited remarkable variety. Most Spaniards learned to enter into that reality and made confession a part of their religious lives. Others, however, found tradition, familial identity, and ethnicity insuperable roadblocks to negotiating the sacrament successfully. We turn now to these individuals.

 **6**

## CONFESSION AND THE NEWLY CONVERTED

It is very strange that it should be Spain, which straddles sea and land, and which goes to the ends of the earth, east and west, to Chile, China, and Japan, to convert the infidel . . . that does not care for and fails to ensure the conversion or confirmation in the faith of these people it has within its own home.

—PEDRO DE VALENCIA

Most early modern Spaniards found themselves able to navigate confession with relative ease and experienced a remarkable degree of flexibility in fulfilling even their Lenten obligation. Yet Spanish society proved to be deeply concerned about purity of blood, and those who belonged to highly marginalized groups of dubious ethnic or religious pedigree often had a rather different experience. Perceived as dangerous and potentially heretical elements living within a Roman Catholic society, gypsies, *judeoconversos,* and *moriscos* became special targets for reforming bishops, missionaries, and inquisitors.

The sacrament of penance played an important role in the lives of these people. The ecclesiastical hierarchy viewed confession as essential to Christianization. Priests deployed the sacrament in order to reform and regulate behavior at the local level. If the parish and the Easter duty proved ineffective, regular priests and inquisitors might be called upon to engage New Christians who resisted conversion. Yet members of marginalized groups recognized the potential risks inherent in confession, and no matter how well they adapted to Christian practice, those who could not or did not desire to free themselves completely from their past found that they would never be entirely accepted. For most of them, there was no effective process of reintegration into Christian society once the authorities or their own community identified them as suspect. Even those determined to give up their old ways in favor of the new

The epigraph to this chapter comes from Valencia's *Tratado acerca de los moriscos de España* (1606), in *Obras completas,* 4:115.

found that the stigma of their past and the suspicion of their neighbors could result in accusations of heresy on flimsy evidence.

Some individuals and families, especially among the *judeoconverso* population, succeeded in passing into the larger Christian community and appropriating penitential piety, making it a part of their own lives. By contrast, gypsies responded to the implementation of religious reform at the parish level by withdrawing from society and retreating into their own highly mobile and separate communities, which often successfully evaded episcopal and inquisitorial scrutiny. These strategies did not work for everyone. Secular and ecclesiastical authorities ultimately concluded that their program of Christianization had failed for the *moriscos*. Even the ministrations of the Holy Office could not turn these false Christians into genuine ones and sometimes served only to reinforce their obstinacy. Because political authorities considered them a military threat, the Spanish Crown expelled some three hundred thousand *moriscos,* nearly the entire population, in the early seventeenth century. The failure of the sacrament to effect change in this situation highlights the fragility of confession as an instrument of transformation.

## The Conversion of the *Nuevos Conversos*

By the end of the fifteenth century, both Muslims and Jews had long shared in Iberia's history. Jews had lived in the peninsula and practiced their religion there from at least the second century BCE. Muslims had entered Visigoth Spain in force in 711, conquering all but the mountainous north in a matter of decades. After more than seven centuries of Muslim political presence, in 1492 the Catholic Monarchs negotiated the surrender of the last holdout of the Islamic era, the Kingdom of Granada. As Christian rule extended southward over the centuries, however, it did not coalesce into a single united kingdom. Rather, the peninsula fragmented into a variety of political entities, each with its own traditions and customs.

Many areas developed a rough sort of coexistence (*convivencia*) in which Muslims and Jews continued to practice their own religions under Christian dominion.[1] The largest populations of practicing Muslims (*mudéjares*) were located in the regions around Granada and in Aragon and Valencia. In the cities, many worked in artisanal trades and as gardeners or, as in the case of Granada, in construction and the production of silk textiles.[2] More rural *mudéjares,* especially along the east coast and in the north, tended to work as servile farmers on the lands of nobles or as muleteers. Jews achieved a greater geographical diversity, constituted an urban minority, and engaged chiefly in commercial, professional, scholarly, and artisanal occupations.[3] In cities, both groups tended to reside in ethnic quarters: *morerías* and *juderías*.

In the later Middle Ages, occasional anti-Jewish pogroms—most notably those of 1320–21 and 1391—resulted in forced conversions to Christianity. However, the most significant moment of transition came in the wake of Granada's fall, when the Catholic Monarchs expelled all Jewish inhabitants who refused to convert.[4] As for *mudéjares,* the royal plan after 1492 appears initially to have been to allow them to practice their religion quietly under Christian rule. Archbishop Talavera of Granada implemented a slow, gradual program of evangelization and assimilation that earned him the good will of the Andalusian Muslim community.[5] That program, however, was soon replaced by a more hard-line approach overseen by Cardinal Cisneros.

Beginning in 1499, Cisneros advocated burning Islamic books, converting mosques to churches, arresting Christians who converted to Islam, and forcing conversions. The combined effect of these initiatives incited a Muslim revolt in 1500. Once the Crown had crushed the uprising, it forbade the practice of Islamic religion, and, like the Jews, the Muslims of southern Spain had either to convert or to depart. In the early 1520s the popular Christian uprising known as the Germanías Revolt precipitated similar developments in the Kingdom of Valencia, leading to the forced conversion of *mudéjares* there. The irregularity of the situation sparked an inquisitorial commission in 1524, which pronounced the conversions valid because they were only conditionally, not absolutely, forced—the Muslims *could* have refused baptism, even if doing so had cost them their lives or livelihoods. In 1525 Charles V made the policy official and universal: conversion or expulsion for all *mudéjares.*[6] While some communities resisted, the Crown brought them into line. Thereafter, anyone who practiced Islam in the peninsula did so in secret or suffered the consequences.[7]

## The Jewish Problem

After its establishment in 1478, the Holy Office focused most of its attention on newly baptized Jews because inquisitors tended to doubt the sincerity of Jewish conversions.[8] *Judeoconversos'* confessional behavior was sometimes used to test their sincerity. In 1492, for example, the Tribunal of Cuenca tried Pedro Bernal for Judaizing. His neighbors were asked if Bernal "confessed and communed at least once a year at Lent, as a catholic and good Christian should, with his *cura* or, having his *cura*'s license, with other clerics and friars."[9] The confessional activities of New Christians interested inquisitors because the sacrament necessarily intruded and interrogated. Crypto-Jews (*marranos*), by contrast, sought privacy and solitude when confessing their sins.[10] Hence, echoing the practice of many Judaizers, Marina Fernández told the Toledo Tribunal that she preferred "to make a hole in the ground and say her sins there" rather than reveal them to any "earthly man."[11] Blasco Rodrígues, a sincere convert, described the difference between his current and former coreligionists in 1491 by saying, "we [Christians] confess to a man and they [confess] to a wall."[12] Old Christians who had become habituated to the practice found confession a thorny issue; it was even more so for those who had only recently been initiated into the mysteries of the faith.

Some *marranos* continued to practice Jewish rites in later decades. In 1572 the *judeoconversa* Elvira de San Juan suggested that "confession should be made to God alone." Elvira's sister explained that their mother "had told her she shouldn't confess, even if the confessors asked her to."[13] Into the seventeenth century inquisitors turned up *conversos,* especially Portuguese immigrants, who told similar stories. Beatriz Enriquez, for example, believed that the law of Moses "was good for saving her soul" but had not mentioned this to her confessors "because she knew they would not absolve her." Although she had confessed and communed, she did so only out of obligation. To her, it was a "joke," for "priests could not pardon sins."[14]

This sort of behavior may even have begun to spread outside *converso* communities. In 1594, for example, the Tribunal of Córdoba tried María Jiménez of Lucena, a thirty-six-year-old widow. María was not identified as a New Christian, yet she had said that if a confessor refused to absolve her of a certain sin, she could make a hole in the earth or lean over the edge of a well and confess it there.[15] In her defense, María claimed to have learned the practice from her husband before he died.

Most *conversos* who remained in Spain after 1492 eventually embraced Christianity, or if they did not, then their descendants in the second and third generations did. They often became religiously indistinguishable from their neighbors. However, some problematic elements remained, such as the *alumbrados,* members of an eclectic religious movement that emphasized internal spirituality.[16] Most of the *alumbrados'* early leaders—Isabel de la Cruz, Pedro Ruiz de Alcaraz, María de Cazalla, and Gaspar de Bedoya in early sixteenth-century Toledo—were of *converso* stock.

A devaluation of Roman Catholic formalism and ritualism constituted one of the movement's more coherent themes. Alonso Manrique, archbishop of Seville and inquisitor-general, offered forty-eight propositions against *alumbrado* beliefs in a 1525 edict of faith. He opposed their notion that prayer must be mental and not vocal, their belief that perfectibility was attainable on earth, and their "contempt for the cult of the saints, the worship of images, bulls, indulgences, fasting, abstinence and the commandments of the church."[17] Manrique also accused *alumbrados* of denying that the sacrament of penance was divinely ordained.[18] Pedro Ruiz de Alcaraz, for example, encouraged the household of the Marquis of Villena to forsake fasting, pious works, confession, and vocal prayer. All that was necessary for salvation was a state of abandonment (*dejamiento*) in which one's will was given over to God.[19]

While inquisitors believed that this last claim drew upon Lutheran ideas, it also resonated with more indigenous expressions of late medieval Spanish theology. In 1478 Pedro de Osma, professor of theology at the peninsula's premier institution, the University of Salamanca, denied in his *De confesione* that confession was divinely instituted. He asserted that contrition alone sufficed for the forgiveness of sins, which obviated the need for clerical absolution.[20] Evidence from his inquisitorial trial indicated that some readers had stopped confessing sacramentally as a result.[21] Some of the early *alumbrados*—among them Rodrigo de Bivar, Juan de Vergara, and Bernardo de Tovar—were believed to have adopted Osma's view.[22] But Bivar claimed to have heard the message preached in Alcalá de Henares by Pedro de Lerma (1461–1541), the Erasmian chancellor of the Complutensian University.[23] Although later *alumbrados* tended to tread more warily, their critics continued to charge them with heterodox views on confession.

In the first half of the sixteenth century, *judeoconversos* often found themselves pegged as adherents of the movement. Trials against *alumbradismo* stood between two great waves of inquisitorial attention, the early trials against Judaizing and the later ones (from the 1550s) against Protestantism. *Conversos* became the bridge upon which that transition was built, for *alumbradismo*, with its disregard for the institutional trappings of the church, proved attractive to Jewish converts.[24] Later in the sixteenth century, some New Christians helped circulate Lutheran literature. Of course, not all *judeoconversos* were *luteranos*, *alumbrados*, or *marranos*. Nor were all *luteranos* or *alumbrados* of Jewish descent. Nevertheless, presumed Jewish disdain for the sacraments bound all of these heresies together in the minds of many inquisitors. But why were they so worried about the confessional lives of *nuevos conversos*?

The concerns stemmed from a sense that multiple heretical groups had begun a demonically coordinated attack on the sacrament of penance. From the church's perspective, confession deserved respect from those who partook of it, even those who had been compelled to do so. Ecclesiastical leaders believed that *judeoconversos* (and other marginal groups) mocked the sacrament by withholding their sins. And when these false Christians did confess sins, it was only to stay out of trouble, not for the good of their souls.[25] While some authorities permitted incomplete confessions in certain situations, allowing Judaizing *conversos* to do so was unthinkable.

Roman Catholic assumptions about the sacramentally transformative nature of confession itself further heightened the tension for religious authorities. As a sacrament, penance worked grace in the hearts of those who received it.[26] It helped form those who participated into better Christians. However, *conversos* seemed to be misusing the sacrament by making invalid confessions. Like Beatriz Enriquez, mentioned above, they saw the ritual as a joke and doubted its efficacy. Their irreverent behavior toward confession mirrored the stories of Jews who desecrated the body of Christ by stealing communion wafers. In keeping with long-held assumptions about the devious nature of Jews, inquisitors molded anecdotal evidence elicited from defendants into a profile that presumed the infidelity of *judeoconversos* as a group. They withheld mortal sins, resting instead upon the law of Moses as the better way to salvation. According to church authorities, such sacrilegious confessions destroyed rather than built up grace, thereby subverting the sacrament's transformative effect.

Moreover, ecclesiastical reformers expected the confessional experience to provide an opportunity for instruction and correction. It was supposed to allow priests to assess the lives of laypeople in an annual face-to-face meeting. But this could be effective only if participants actually revered the sacrament, faithfully confessed their sins, and humbly received correction. Failure to do so stripped confession of its corrective power. Doubting that priests could pardon their sins, *marranos* deceived their confessors and refused to be molded by the sacrament except in the most formal of ways. They might comply with the church's demands externally, but internally they maintained their own traditions and beliefs. While some Old Christians undoubtedly approached confession in a similar fashion, the Holy Office singled them out much less frequently.

Finally, while crypto-Jews came under inquisitorial scrutiny first, they were not the only ones who questioned the validity of confession. Rather, they represented one column of what ecclesiastical authorities saw as an all-out assault on the sacrament of penance. Jews, Muslims, gypsies, Protestants of every stripe,

Erasmians, and *alumbrados* all challenged Roman Catholicism's penitential system. They thereby showed themselves to be diabolically led heretics.[27] This context made discovering the confessional behavior of marginalized groups living in the midst of God's people a matter of particular concern for the Holy Office.

Once discovered by the Inquisition, the stain of impurity (both theological and hereditary) lingered for generations. Even after reconciled heretics completed their allotted period of public penance, the sackcloth garb (*sanbenitos*) worn by the *penitenciados* was hung in parish churches in perpetuity, a reminder for the convicted, their descendants, and the larger community of previous bad faith—the children would pay for the sins of their fathers.[28] Some wealthy families and devout individuals rose above the stain after a few generations, but many *conversos,* even when otherwise indistinguishable from their Old Christian neighbors, found their pasts difficult to bury.

## *Judeoconversos* and Confessional Success

Although many Spaniards continued to view Jewish *conversos* as categorically different, the Spanish church had remarkable long-term success in drawing them and their descendants into the faith. Like Teresa of Avila, whose grandfather was a first-generation *converso* condemned as a relapsed heretic, many *conversos* adopted Christianity enthusiastically as the only religion they had ever known. They abandoned Judaism and became saints, bishops and archbishops, religious of all stripes, and high government officials. That people suspected and denounced Jews had as much to do with their perceived success in times of economic downturn as with actual heterodoxy. In moments of crisis, they became easy scapegoats. Moreover, cases of crypto-Judaism uncovered by the Inquisition led to others' being found guilty by association. While forced conversions, by their very nature, inevitably led to both actual deception and expectations of it, the persecution of *judeoconversos* reflects specific assumptions about Jews' deceptive nature. Thus, for many observers, the hollowness of their original false conversions extended in later years to confessional dissimulation.

As all of this suggests, the vexed question of why Jews converted has long been the subject of historiographical debate. Suffice it to say that three general approaches exist. The first proposes that most Jews converted under the threat or in the midst of persecution. Their conversions usually extended only to external obedience, and they remained *marranos* in their hearts.[29] Others have downplayed the importance of compulsion, suggesting that most Spanish Jews converted out of sincere conviction and because they benefited by becoming Christians. They intended to assimilate. This perspective emphasizes that baptized Jews were subsequently excluded from their former community.[30] A more moderate approach seeks to avoid strict dichotomies. As Gretchen Starr-LeBeau comments, "Not all [Jews] were converted directly by force; some converted out of fear of anti-Jewish violence, while others were genuinely persuaded by the message of Christianity; still others converted to take advantage of business opportunities afforded to Christians."[31] She suggests that "religious identity in late-medieval and early modern Spain was negotiated, rather than emerging from simple either/or categories."[32]

This third approach usefully highlights the complexity of religious practice and identity among New Christians that historians have come to expect from other Spaniards. Juan de Avila, for instance, complained that Sevillano teenagers "ordinarily [went] without mass on Sundays and feast days," and instead gathered together, "playing, and doing other, worse things."[33] Like their Old Christian counterparts, who sometimes skipped Mass in favor of the local tavern, blasphemed, or embraced popular religion and folk magic out of step with church dogma, *judeoconversos* dwelt in a complex religious universe. Some eagerly embraced their new faith. Others, among them, surely, some of the Judaizers tried by the Holy Office, exhibited less zeal, but probably no less than certain of their Old Christian neighbors. They look positively devout compared to Juan Sánchez, the elderly *pícaro* who avoided the confessional for twenty-six years! Indeed, the success with which *judeoconversos* entered into Old Christian society and could be viewed as ethnically and religiously safe often had a great deal to do with their social status *before* converting.[34] Important members of the Jewish community sometimes crossed over into equally high or even higher levels of society. Jews of a lower rank found the process more difficult, often experiencing inquisitorial scrutiny and the suspicion of their neighbors.[35]

Because distinguishing Jews from non-Jews in early modern Spain has proved notoriously difficult, historians know little about the confessional lives of most *judeoconversos*. Stories about the foul smell they gave off circulated popularly, but in practice no physical characteristics (olfactory or otherwise) distinguished them from their neighbors. Certainly, by the middle of the seventeenth century most lived lives indistinguishable from their Old Christian counterparts. Their ancestors had adopted names that bore no trace of Jewish lineage and moved to cities where no one knew their past. Indeed, the fact that the typical occupations of Jews tied them less closely to the land than *moriscos* allowed for relocation and, potentially, escape from their family history.[36] Thus the Bernuy family, whose patriarch the Holy Office condemned for Judaizing in the late fifteenth century, could amass a fortune in the sixteenth century, hold political office, become devout Roman Catholics, and fashion a new family history. By the seventeenth century one Bernuy had become the bishop of Jaén and another the Marquis of Benamejí. In the eighteenth century, the marquis was elevated to the rank of grandee. Indisputably, the Bernuys had become Old Christians.[37]

For those whose community did remember their lineage, the transition proved more difficult. The suspicion of neighbors and the Holy Office dogged them. *Judeoconversos* may have identified themselves as devout Christians or as *marranos*. Or they may have adopted a more flexible attitude that permitted them to move back and forth between Judaism and Christianity. Whatever the case, mainstream culture assumed that bad blood bred heresy. Even in 1593, Judaizing still worried the Tribunal of Granada, particularly after it discovered and executed a group of women who held to the law of Moses. Afterward, a memorandum circulated explaining that the women had denied "that confessors have any power to pardon sins and for that reason they only confessed minor things in order to make a joke out of confession and for fear of the Inquisition."[38] So the specter of the deceitful Jew remained, even for those whose ancestors had been baptized long ago. Nevertheless, the history of most *judeoconverso* families was one of assimilation. They disappeared into mainstream Spanish culture, their pasts only occasionally, if ever, remembered.


## The Gypsy Problem

Historians often exclude the gypsies of early modern Spain from discussions about *nuevos cristianos,* but contemporaries frequently lumped them together with *judeoconversos* and *moriscos* when discussing undesirable elements in society. Moreover, gypsies had a complicated relationship with confession that provides important opportunities for comparison. The state, church, and many Old Christians viewed gypsies as prone to thievery, laziness, and rough living, and as only marginally integrated into mainstream society. Their religious behavior was equally troubling. Documenting their activities, however, is notoriously difficult, since they produced no written history, literature, or bureaucracy of their own.[39] For the most part, only the observations of outsiders remain—trials records, literary descriptions, government policy papers, and so forth.

Many people accused gypsies of failing to make good use of the sacrament of penance. But they rarely complained that gypsies made false confessions, mostly because they seem seldom to have confessed at all. In 1594, for instance, two delegates from Burgos to the Cortes of Castile complained that gypsies did not marry in the form prescribed by the church and that no one ever saw them "confessing, receiving the Most Holy Sacrament [of the Eucharist], or attending mass." The delegates could only hope that God's punishment would not fall upon their own heads for having allowed such public sinfulness to go unchecked.[40]

In 1618 the historian and priest Pedro Salazar de Mendoza (1549–1629) addressed Philip III (r. 1598–1621) on the gypsy problem. For Salazar, the gypsies were more useless and a greater waste than the *moriscos,* who at least had "cultivated the ground, engaged in commerce, the mechanical arts, and occupations." *Gitanos* interacted with outsiders only "in order to rob and kill." They attended church, heard Mass, confessed, and carried dispensations for their marriages only in order to avoid punishment. Gypsies "do not know what the church is, and they enter one only in order to commit sacrilege." True, *moriscos,* having received baptism, had apostatized. But who, asked Salazar, knew if the gypsies had ever even received that sacrament? Yes, they claimed to have been baptized, but could they be trusted? Gypsies slipped easily between Muslim, Protestant, and Roman Catholic lands, accommodating themselves to the religion of each nation. The priest concluded that *gitanos* had probably become spies already. And if not, they soon would.[41]

In fact, many regarded the easy mobility of the gypsies to be the root of the problem. Their nomadic lifestyle frustrated civil attempts to rein in criminality. Ecclesiastically, parish churches could not instruct, guide, or correct them effectively. At the beginning of the seventeenth century the Franciscan Melchor de Huélamo claimed a connection between the gypsies and the *alumbrado* heresy. Both refused to abide within the parish structure and as a result lived "very suspicious lives." "The gypsies' free living [*libertada vivienda*]," he explained, "not having a *cura* nearby nor [belonging to] any diocese (since today they are here and tomorrow in France) results in a thousand disadvantages. Because no one is charged to ask them how they live or if they have confessed, nor [to tell them] which days they must keep [holy] nor on which they should fast, they live as heathens and publicans."[42] Without oversight from the church, how could gypsies be expected to behave like Christians? And how could churches keep an eye on these rascals unless they settled down?

The Holy Office faced a similar set of problems, as indicated by the case of one Torralva the gypsy, denounced as a *luterano* in March 1593. Torralva had taken part in a discussion about confession with a group of Old Christians.

When the conversation turned to the irreverent sacramental behavior of gypsies, he retorted, "Among you all there are many who confess and don't tell the truth in confession." *Gitanos,* he suggested, "didn't confess with any priest because they only did that with God."[43] While the Inquisition went through the motions, gathering statements and informing its superiors of the situation, Torralva left town, moving on to the village of Rejuenco, where he stayed for a short time. Later, a witness caught sight of him walking in the Val de Viana. And then nothing. His speed and transient lifestyle outpaced inquisitorial justice. Despite the Holy Office's desire to bring gypsies to heel, their mobility proved an effective countermeasure.

The church, to be sure, attempted to bring the same bureaucratic structures to bear on them that it did upon the more stable elements of society. In 1601, for example, Archbishop Sandoval y Rojas of Toledo instructed ecclesiastical judges and parish priests to make sure that the gypsies under their jurisdiction had been baptized.[44] In 1602 the diocesan synod convened by Bishop Pacheco of Cuenca commanded that priests should take special care to see that both *moriscos* and *gitanos* received the sacraments of baptism, confirmation, marriage, extreme unction, and penance "in the form prescribed by our holy mother Church." And with regard to the Eucharist, he ordered priests to refuse it to gypsies unless an explanation could be offered as to why they should receive the body of Christ.[45]

These sorts of approaches, however, proved to be inherently unworkable because ecclesiastical discipline required social stability. Yet normal disciplinary procedures had no impact on gypsies, and even extreme measures failed to produce results. According to Melchor de Huélamo, whipping a gypsy did no good; exile did even less.[46] Like Torralva, gypsies could pack up and leave all too easily, fading into the countryside and popping up in another town, while episcopal and inquisitorial bureaucracies slowly went about their business. Gypsies clearly had to be domesticated. In 1609 Alonso de Ulloa proposed resettling them in villages, forcing them to learn trades and stay put. He proposed that civil and ecclesiastical authorities join forces to "investigate the gypsies' marital status and ensure that they confessed, received the sacraments, and baptized their children."[47]

Into the eighteenth century, the Crown sought to regulate the itinerancy of gypsies by mandating various policies, the vast majority of which floundered at the local level, where they were rarely implemented. Indeed, even the church worked at cross-purposes with the civil authorities by asserting its right to grant sanctuary to gypsies whom the king's forces sought to arrest.[48] By the

1720s the state had achieved a modicum of success: a commission organized by Philip V (r. 1700–1724) allowed that "some gypsies, especially those who had been granted *vecinidades* [citizenship], had nominally accepted the Church's teachings, even if only to the extent of baptizing their children."[49] Yet the combined pressure of government and church accomplished little else, and most gypsies continued to live outside the boundaries of civil and ecclesiastical law. The *gitano* communities weathered the storms of the early modern period and finally achieved a degree of tolerance at the end of the eighteenth century. They had been threatened with exile, stints in the galleys, and deportation to the Americas. One scheme even proposed separating male *gitanos* from female and breeding them out of existence. But if the goal was corporate survival, the ephemeral nature of the gypsy lifestyle proved a successful strategy.

In early modern Spain confessional practice was regulated through a variety of mechanisms. The parish structure acted as the first line of attack, but when that failed the Inquisition could be called upon. Most people found ways to live within the strictures of that stabilizing environment, relying on loopholes, gray areas, and personal connections to soften the hard edges of episcopal legislation. The gypsies, however, present an interesting alternative, a wholesale refusal to engage in confessional negotiation. Their success brings into sharp relief the church's failure to realize local religious changes by using confession as a reforming mechanism. In the absence of social stability, civil and ecclesiastical pressure could be brought to bear only in fits and starts and proved incapable of transforming a closed, mobile society as long as that society maintained a strong corporate identity.

## The *Morisco* Problem

Many Spaniards recognized *judeoconversos'* and gypsies' problematic relationships with the sacrament of penance. However, in spite of the profiling that set them apart in the eyes of the church, the state, and their neighbors, many members of these groups succeeded in weathering the storm of episcopal legislation, inquisitorial attention, and the policies of the secular arm. Most converted Jews chose a strategy of assimilation, while gypsies closed ranks and embraced the periphery. Neither strategy succeeded perfectly. In times of trouble, neighbors might still remember *judeoconversos'* ancestry, and *gitanos* endured decades of harsh persecution. But their strategies at least provided avenues for survival.

The *moriscos* (and the Spanish church and state that sought to Christianize them) found it more difficult to devise a strategy that allowed them to remain in Spain. Indeed, for the vast majority of *moriscos,* exile from the peninsula between 1609 and 1614 foreclosed all other possibilities. Significantly, confessional behavior played an important part in the complex process by which the authorities ultimately decided upon this solution. And the end to the drama amounted to a recognition that the sacrament had failed to bring about the widespread assimilation of *moriscos* to Christianity.

Like the Jews, *moriscos* had converted under pressure, and, consequently, their reasons for receiving baptism, and the degree to which Christianity became a matter of sincere belief rather than merely external compliance, varied dramatically. When Charles V ended the legal toleration of Islam in 1526, the result was the creation of large *morisco* communities in Granada, Aragon, Valencia, and Castile, as well as smaller ones in Catalonia, the Basque lands, Murcia, and the Canary Islands. Recognizing the unusual nature of their conversion experience, the king negotiated a forty-year grace period with two of the largest *moriscos* communities, those of Granada and Valencia. In exchange for a considerable financial contribution, Charles promised leniency from the Holy Office and the same liberties enjoyed by other Christians. This period of grace would, he hoped, afford the converts adequate time to ease into their new religion and undergo proper catechesis.[50]

Castilian *moriscos,* some of whom converted before 1526, often lived in smaller communities alongside Old Christian neighbors, and they appear to have been losing touch with their Muslim identity.[51] While some Castilian *moriscos* continued to engage in Islamic practices, they rarely understood the significance of their actions, and most had embarked upon a process of assimilation.[52] Indeed, one of the great concerns about these *moriscos* during their expulsion was that they might easily slip through the net, since they were so *ladino* (meaning Spanish-speaking, but taking on the added implication of sly). Many had become indistinguishable from Old Christians.[53]

Their assimilation hit a snag in 1570 because of events that occurred in Granada. When Philip II came to the throne in 1556, he adopted a more rigid approach to the *moriscos* than had his father. Philip saw them as a challenge to the religious identity and integrity of his realm, part of a broader offensive against the true faith that had already infiltrated his northern lands and that now, in a different guise, threatened his Mediterranean holdings.[54] When the forty years of grace granted to the *moriscos* of Granada (*moriscos granadinos*) came to an end, he did not renew it. In 1566 the Junta of Madrid commanded *moriscos* to give up their traditional customs and begin acting like Spaniards within three years.[55] Women were forbidden to wear veils or apply henna dye to their bodies. Private patios in *morisco* dwellings were forbidden. Christian names were to replace Muslim ones, baths were to be destroyed, and Arabic was prohibited.

The 1565 episcopal synod convened by Archbishop Pedro Guerrero in Granada similarly allowed the new converts much less leniency. It focused particularly on *moriscos'* confessional behavior. Earlier in his tenure Guerrero had approached them with a sort of "benign neglect," believing that, lacking well-trained and dedicated priests, any attempt at rapid assimilation was doomed to fail. Remarkably, he even attempted to grant all confessors in his archdiocese authority to absolve heresy, even Islamic activities, without remitting cases to himself or the Holy Office.[56] By the 1560s, however, having weathered two sessions at Trent and numerous local crises, Guerrero was less optimistic.[57] In part, he manifested this attitude by taking a harder line toward New Christians and demanding that they conform to proper confessional behavior. Lamenting *morisco* familiarity with and devotion to penance, Guerrero announced that he would no longer countenance lackadaisical behavior, whether from the *granadinos* or their confessors.

The archbishop sought to restore awe and respect to the sacrament. He forbade *moriscas* to bring snacks with them when they came to church for confession and complained that many people, especially the New Christians, "whether because of their youth or coarseness and ignorance," did not even know how to confess properly. Thus he proscribed allowing *moriscos* to "pass lightly" through the encounter, urging priests to "detain them and inform them and teach them how they should accuse themselves, and ask them about their *estado* and [the *estados*] of those with whom they have dealings and with whom they converse." He wanted to know "what prayers and devotions they undertake and other particular questions that seem to pertain" to *morisco* penitents.[58] He ordered priests to explain to confessants their obligation in and the sacramental character of confession so that "they might become fond of it and know how they have to behave in it."[59] This, Guerrero explained, was what it meant "to carry out the office of confessor and curate."[60]

As a result of this assault on the culture and traditions of the *moriscos granadinos,* by the late 1560s Granada was in an uproar.[61] In late 1568 *moriscos* rose in the Second Revolt of the Alpujarras. They held out until the autumn of 1570, hoping for Ottoman reinforcements that never arrived. Subsequently, all *moriscos granadinos* were relocated to Castile so as to neutralize the threat they posed and facilitate their eventual assimilation. The opposite occurred, however, as *granadinos* exerted a proselytizing influence on Castilian *moriscos,* teaching them the Koran and the articles of their faith. Certainly, this did not reverse all of the assimilation that had occurred, but the threat of contamination was real.

In Aragon and Valencia, a different but no less complicated story played out. In these regions *moriscos* typically lived in rural locales, laboring as servile farmers on the lands of powerful nobles. The relationship between those nobles and their New Christian vassals entailed the former's protecting the latter from abuse by external forces. The landholders exhibited a proprietary attitude toward the *moriscos* who worked their fields and whose cheap labor made them wealthy. Local nobles were reluctant to see other institutions— the episcopacy and the Inquisition—interfere with their *moriscos.* Some nobles promised to implement Christianizing programs, but these rarely materialized, hampering Christianization efforts.[62]

In Aragon, where *moriscos* made up about one-fifth of the population, the process of assimilation was in certain respects successful. These *moriscos* were much more likely than their Valencian counterparts to live among Old Christians and to work in artisanal trades that required interaction with the broader community.[63] By and large, knowledge of Arabic disappeared, and they adopted Christian names, abandoned traditional garb, used the Christian calendar, and saw their children baptized. The parish registers of the village of Burbaguena (Zaragoza) indicate that both Old and New Christians in the village confessed for the Easter duty and on their deathbeds in the middle of the sixteenth century.[64] Aragonese bishops rarely singled out *moriscos* for instruction in doctrine or practice. Instead, they addressed the entire community, including the newly converted.[65]

But if cultural assimilation occurred in Aragon, *moriscos* still remained attached to their Islamic identity, even if it had lost some of its coherence. Although they did not know Arabic, most of the Islamic literature preserved in Spain comes from this region. In the second half of the sixteenth century, when the Inquisition turned its attention to *morisco* communities, Aragon bore its severest scrutiny; more than 90 percent of the *morisco* settlements there had neighbors not merely tried by the Holy Office but exhibited at an auto-da-fé.[66]

The *moriscos* of Valencia differed from those in Aragon. For one thing, there were more of them, one-third of the total population rather than one-fifth. And they tended to live in isolated rural communities composed overwhelmingly of other *moriscos,* not in mixed communities.[67] These *valencianos* tended to enjoy greater protection from local nobles than did the Aragonese. Valencian nobles wanted outsiders to stay out of their business. This was especially true for the Inquisition, which they believed would scare away their cheap labor force.[68] The Inquisition granted the *valencianos* forty years of grace in the 1520s and another concession from the mid-1570s to the mid-1580s. And when the Holy Office did strike, it focused its attention on the few communities where *moriscos* lived alongside Old Christians, leaving most areas untouched. As a consequence, Valencian *moriscos* maintained a strong Islamic identity. They spoke Arabic, and in some remote areas nothing else. They circumcised their sons, supported *alfaquís* (religious leaders), and maintained relations with Muslims outside Spain. Crypto- (and sometimes overt) Islam flourished. This was the reality that confronted Juan de Ribera when he became archbishop of Valencia in 1568.

## *Moriscos* and Confessional Failure

During his tenure, Ribera underwent a dramatic transition in his attitude toward the *moriscos* in his diocese. In 1571 he secured limited immunity from the Inquisition for many New Christians. He personally bore much of the financial burden of supporting new parishes and priests in *morisco* neighborhoods and encouraged an aggressive preaching campaign. However, the early programs of this model Tridentine bishop failed to produce the expected results.[69] *Morisco* obstinacy and the foot dragging of local priests so frustrated Ribera's plans that by the 1580s he had become one of the strongest proponents of expulsion.

In fact, as was the case for most of the plans formulated to deal with *moriscos,* there was more than enough blame to go around for the failure of Ribera's program of assimilation. Reforming bishops, inquisitors, regular missionaries, and even some local priests labored for the sincere conversion of the New Christians and pursued schemes, often at great personal cost, that they hoped would make the difference. Yet these schemes often proved misguided and poorly planned. Many *moriscos* had little interest in actually submitting to them. They saw the situation differently, viewing the immense sums they paid to the Crown as the price for practicing Islam covertly. Between reforming intent and *morisco* obstinacy very often stood the failure to realize grand plans and legislation effectively at the local level.

Sometimes the obstruction of local nobles, to whom the status quo appealed, was the source of failure, but often the requests of reforming bishops simply went unheeded. In 1573 Ribera convened his suffragans to endorse his plan for creating twenty-two new *morisco* parishes. He even earmarked substantial episcopal and personal funds toward that end, but he found little enthusiasm for the project among local clergy, whom he expected to carry out the work on the front lines.[70] There seemed to be a real opportunity here, and even a sense of confidence that the new converts could be reached. Yet dramatic changes failed to materialize. As one observer commented, "I do not know why it is that we are so blind . . . that we go off to convert the infidels of Japan, China and other remote parts . . . rather as if someone had his house full of snakes and scorpions yet took no care to clean it, but went to hunt for lions or ostriches in Africa."[71]

Local priests' negative attitude toward the *nuevos cristianos de moros* appears to have been widespread in Spain, and secular clerics demonstrated little willingness to live among or waste their lives serving such disagreeable flocks. Repeatedly, *moriscos* were viewed and treated as distinct, different, problematic, and undeserving. In December 1526, shortly after conceding the forty years of grace, Charles V wrote to Pedro Ramírez de Alba, archbishop-elect of Granada (r. 1526–28), expressing his concerns about the behavior of priests toward *moriscos granadinos*. The king had learned that priests were rounding up the new converts and forcing them to attend Mass, receive the sacraments, and make offerings. After all this, the priests then reproached the *moriscos* for their behavior. For the time being, Charles desired a gentler approach. He did not want Archbishop Alba to neglect the religious comportment of the *granadinos*: they should attend Mass, hear sermons, and confess and commune each year. But in this they were to be treated like all Christians, "Old as well as New." The king urged *curas* to see that *moriscos* attended Mass, but he did not want priests to "make any difference in the penalty imposed on the one group as opposed to the other." Even in the midst of this seemingly egalitarian decree, however, Charles could not help but urge the priests "especially" to "take great care in confessing [*nuevos cristianos*]."[72]

In the wake of Trent, when Pedro Guerrero summoned his suffragan bishoprics of Almería and Guadix to a provincial council, he attempted to push through a harsher but coherent program for reforming *morisco* behavior. Flexing his archiepiscopal muscles, Guerrero banned proposals from anyone but himself and refused to hear dissenting opinions. The cathedral chapter of Granada protested, filing a lawsuit against its archbishop, and the city's municipal councilors declared their right to review and protest "any provisions of the council that negatively affected city residents."[73] Yet another reforming program failed to materialize.

After the Second Revolt of the Alpujarras and the forced relocation of the *granadinos*, Valladolid boasted one of the largest communities of *moriscos* in Castile—1,470 in the city itself and around twenty-four hundred in the diocese. It also produced the most ambitious and comprehensive episcopal plan for assimilating New Christians. Bishop Juan Bautista de Acevedo (r. 1601–6) convened Valladolid's first diocesan synod in 1606 and devoted, in the form of a letter to his *curas*, ten folio pages of the synodal constitutions to this strategic plan for reaching "the newly converted *granadinos*."[74] As this suggests, the bishop focused on achieving a true conversion of those *moriscos* who had been relocated to the region in the early 1570s. The more assimilated *moriscos*, whose families had dwelt in Castile for generations, apparently did not demand the same attention.

Acevedo's plan reiterated many of the proposals and concerns formulated by earlier synods. He established the parish as the primary point of contact between the church and the *moriscos*, ordering *curas* to draw up registers of their New Christian parishioners listing their full names, ages, addresses, and occupations. He wanted *moriscos* baptized and confirmed, attending Mass, learning Christian doctrine, marrying in and being buried by the church, and prepared to receive the Eucharist. However, Acevedo particularly focused on confession as "the principal means and remedy" by which the souls of this people would be won.[75]

Acevedo's plan recommended that priests neither allow *moriscos* to flout their Easter duty nor force them to observe it. Rather, he exhorted confessors to exercise "particular care and vigilance in administering [the sacrament] to [*moriscos*] with punctuality and with prudence." After confessions, priests were to detain the New Christians in order "to teach and instruct them in those things that seem most necessary to [the *cura*] for eradicating from their hearts any subterfuge and directing them toward true knowledge." If the *cura* could manage the *moriscos* in a given parish on his own, he should confess them himself, recording their names, ages, and other pertinent information and giving them a *cédula de confesión*. These *cédulas* were later to be compared against the *padrón* of confessants in the parish. If too many *moriscos* resided in a parish for the *cura* to handle, the bishop himself would appoint one or two more confessors "of good zeal and doctrine."[76]

The episcopal nomination of specific parochial confessors for *moriscos* is something of an innovation. Normally, bishops left such appointments to the discretion of *curas*, who might well have asked other clergy attached to the church, the priests of neighboring parishes, or local regulars to help deal with the glut of confessants around Easter. Bishop Acevedo, however, went even further. He commanded not only that the *granadinos* comply with the Lateran precept of annual confession but also that parish clergy regard only those *moriscos* who confessed with their *cura,* or with Acevedo's episcopally appointed confessors, as having fulfilled their Easter duty.[77]

This legislation, at least in theory, made confession much less flexible for *moriscos.* By relying upon loopholes like the *bula de la cruzada,* most Old Christians sidestepped the obligation to confess to their parish priest at Easter. Acevedo meant for the *granadinos* in the diocese of Valladolid to feel the full weight of *Omnis utriusque sexus. Nuevos cristianos* who failed to reconcile with their *cura* or an episcopal confessor were subject to a substantial fine: three *reales* for anyone under fifteen years of age and eight *reales* for everyone else.[78]

This was harsh legislation, especially since early modern Spaniards considered it important to have a say in determining with whom they confessed. Indeed, it may well have exceeded Acevedo's powers, since he had no authority to nullify a papal indulgence like the *cruzada.* But unlike the disputes over sacramental jurisdiction that raged in early modern Córdoba and Seville, no jurisdictional conflict between regular and secular clergy developed, perhaps because Acevedo's plan seems to have gone unimplemented.

As with so much else in confession, episcopal legislation did not have the last word; the execution of legislation at the local level often told a different story. The evidence suggests that parish priests simply did not attempt to implement Acevedo's plan.[79] In any case, the bishop resigned shortly after the conclusion of the synod (and before the publication of the constitutions). Even if his successor, Juan Vigil de Quiñones y Labiada (r. 1607–16), had adopted Acevedo's plan for reaching New Christians, it would have had precious little time to succeed before the expulsion of Castilian *moriscos* began in early 1610.

If parochial enforcement failed to correspond to episcopal legislation, the regular orders provided an alternative that occasionally produced results. Early in the sixteenth century this meant the mendicants, especially Franciscans and Dominicans. The former, for example, labored as preachers and teachers among the *moriscos granadinos.*[80] In the second half of the sixteenth century, however, the Society of Jesus entered the fray. These regular orders sometimes provided an effective means of overcoming the disjuncture between episcopal decrees and local implementation.

After receiving papal confirmation in 1540, Jesuits rapidly established houses in cities throughout the Iberian Peninsula, awakening devotion through preaching, confession, and teaching. Although this was not its main focus, the Society also worked with several *morisco* communities. Uniquely among the religious orders in Spain, the Jesuits avoided implementing purity-of-blood statutes for membership until 1593, which bolstered their ability to engage New Christians. Even Diego Laínez, the Society's second general, had *judeoconverso* ancestry.[81]

The Jesuits arrived in Archbishop Guerrero's Granada in the 1550s and established the Casa de Doctrina in the heart of the Albaicín neighborhood. It became the city's most successful school for religious instruction of *morisco* youths. At the helm stood Juan de Albotodo (1527–1578), a native Granadan and New Christian. He preached in Arabic in the streets of the Moorish quarter and surrounding regions and confessed *moriscos*. More than merely making inroads with a small group of collaborators, the ministry flourished.[82] In the generations between the mass baptisms of 1500 and the deportations of the early 1570s, many *granadinos* began assimilating to Christianity.[83]

In Avila, Ignacio de las Casas (1550–1608), another *morisco* Jesuit, formed the Congregation of the Annunciation, which taught *moriscos* doctrine, customs, the obligations of their *estado,* and how to confess. He too hoped that the indoctrination of the youth would be the key to long-term success.[84] To the south, in Oropesa, Count Francisco de Toledo bequeathed funds for a Jesuit house at the end of the sixteenth century. The work there focused on training young men at a local academy, but some of the Jesuits also worked with New Christians. Francisco López, a member of the Society, served as confessor for a number of *moriscas.* After four years of work, he described them as "so well instructed in the faith that if they did not declare themselves to be of that nation, no one would imagine them to be so because they know Christian doctrine and show themselves greatly attached to it."[85]

Despite these successes, the overall picture of *morisco* assimilation to Christianity does not suggest widespread Christianization. One description of the situation, probably from the early seventeenth century, lamented the mistakes made in failing to evangelize the *moriscos* effectively, suggesting that true conversions had not materialized "because of the incompetence of those charged with the task." It concluded that missionary work should not be abandoned but that programs of assimilation clearly demanded "much more efficacious measures." Harkening back to a plan that Archbishop Guerrero had attempted to implement, the author requested permission for missionary confessors to absolve *moriscos* of Islamic behavior without having to report them to the Inquisition.[86]

One of the impediments to progress lay in the difficulty of determining what it meant to reform the *moriscos*. How did one quantify good Christian behavior?

Gerónimo González de Herrera, who investigated the religious behavior of *moriscos* in the Diocese of Avila, suggested nine qualities that demonstrated true belief: frequenting the sacraments, attending Mass, participating in religious processions, contributing to the pious works of the church, joining confraternities, living exemplary lives, eating pork, drinking wine, and living as Old Christians in all things.[87] Philip III's confessor, Fray Luis de Aliaga, suggested that New Christians needed to demonstrate they had "forsaken the evil sect" by doing things that directly contravened Islamic practice.[88] Thus eating pork and drinking wine became particularly important. Ultimately, he admitted, the local community's opinion of *moriscos* would have to serve as the benchmark for assessing their Christian bona fides. But even this sort of approach had limitations.

In the spring of 1612, for example, Philip III sent the Dominican Juan de Pereda to investigate the *moriscos* in Murcia's Val de Ricote, where the envoy received a mixed report. The eldest among the New Christians still spoke Arabic, avoided pork, and discouraged intermarriage with Old Christians. That many immediately departed for Muslim lands upon hearing rumors of the expulsion further tarnished the community's reputation. Some witnesses reported that the *moriscos* denied the efficacy of penance and that, when confessing, they never disclosed mortal sins.[89] On the other hand, many of their neighbors regarded them as good Christians—in fact, it was widely acknowledged that the Catholic Monarchs had made all *moriscos* in Murcia Old Christians.[90] The Inquisition had not bothered them in more than forty years. Some had become priests, and they even boasted a missionary martyr slain in North Africa.

Pereda concluded that they "generally" ate pork and drank wine, and that the younger generations did not speak Arabic. They supported local religious institutions and exhibited Christian devotion. Despite some testimony claiming poor confessional behavior, more than fifty confessors informed Pereda that their *moriscos* made good use of the sacrament; they earnestly espoused a belief in these confessants' good Christianity.[91] Pereda himself confessed several Murcian *moriscos* and approved of their "simplicity, honesty and knowledge of Christian doctrine."[92] But their expulsion went forward in any case.

The *moriscos* of Murcia may have deceived Pereda. Several detractors offered this complaint to the king. Even if valid, Pereda's conclusions do not indicate that all *moriscos* were good Christians whom government and society unjustly viewed as false converts. The general evidence of participation in Islamic rites is too overwhelming to support such a conclusion. Where Old and

New Christians lived cheek by jowl, as in many parts of Castile, assimilation was sometimes more complete. Nevertheless, even in the most favorable of circumstances, fully integrating *moriscos* into Christian society proved elusive.

Unlike *judeoconversos,* who could move about easily, change their names, and bury their past, *moriscos* often remained tied to the land and too closely monitored to reinvent themselves, even if they wanted to assimilate. Those with swarthy complexions and those who retained the distinctive dress of *moriscos* were easily identifiable. Unlike gypsies, they lived in sedentary communities, which allowed the Holy Office, diocesan representative, and secular authorities to keep watch and execute justice. But the Inquisition lacked the ability either to convert *moriscos* or to change their behavior. More so than the mobile *gitanos* or the assimilating *judeoconversos, moriscos* whom their community identified as untrustworthy and dangerous had no means of escape. Even the successful completion of a sentence of public penance did not reintegrate them; it only further stigmatized the *penitenciados* and their families.[93]

In many regions, even when they moved toward assimilation, *moriscos* continued to be viewed as problematic simply because they were *moriscos.* Many Spaniards believed that they lied about their true religious beliefs, using the principle of *taqiyya,* which permitted Muslims threatened with death to feign conversion. Outwardly compliant, they adhered inwardly to Islam. Surely, when no one else was looking, these false converts showed their true colors by scorning Christian prayers, fasting during Ramadan, and working on Sundays. They washed the chrism off their children after baptism, did not revere the consecrated host, and attended Mass only when compelled. As one catechism written especially for *moriscos* chided, they seemed to know when to sit down in church but not when to stand or kneel.[94]

This deceptiveness was of particular concern in the confessional, where, as in Murcia's Val de Ricote, many believed *moriscos* used *taqiyya* during the sacramental encounter. Thus Philip III warned the bishop of Avila that good Christian status could be determined only "by positive acts [of Christian behavior] against the sect of Moors." "It is not enough," he explained, "that they frequent the sacraments, because they might do this for their own preservation, incurring even greater apostasy."[95] When the Inquisition tried Isabel de Liñán, a *morisca* from Deza (Sigüenza), in 1608, the prosecuting attorney accused her of having "committed a great number of sacrileges every time she had communed and confessed in order to comply with the parish each year, completing her confessions and communions merely for external compliance and to excuse her apostasy by appearing to be Christian."[96]

Dissimulation in confession may indeed have been the outworking of *taqiyya*, but *moriscos* had good reasons to withhold sins. Confession, after all, presented them with a frightening prospect. They knew what would happen if they admitted to fasting during Ramadan or performing ablutions. The Holy Office equated Islamic behavior with heretical conduct. Even if a confessor believed that his *morisco* penitent ought to be granted absolution, he might well feel obliged to report reserved sins to appropriate authorities. Archbishop Gaspar de Avalos of Granada put his finger on the issue. Writing around 1530, he commented, "They [the *moriscos*] also err in the sacrament of penance in that they take confession to be a joking matter, and so . . . it is a miracle when a man among them confesses a sin. [The reasons are,] first, because they do not think that they are obliged to do this, and second, because they do not believe that [their confessions] will be kept secret by the priests."[97]

In spite of inquisitorial opposition, Archbishop Guerrero had attempted to allay these concerns by permitting his confessors to absolve cases of heresy without referring them to a higher authority. Jesuits sought a similar concession, and in 1552 Julius III granted it, even going so far as to forbid bishops to interfere with Jesuits when they exercised the privilege. In November 1555 Miguel de Torres wrote to Ignatius Loyola, asserting "the necessity that we have here [in Granada] for the ability to absolve cases of heresy." Without it, souls were "placed in great and very probable risk."[98]

By contrast, the Inquisition believed that such leniency only allowed Islam to flourish. Indeed, the Holy Office believed that it could solve the problem that bedeviled the religious orders and diocesan authorities. Utilizing a carrot-and-stick approach that offset trials and autos-da-fé with periodic edicts of grace, inquisitors sought to improve upon the limited success of reforming bishops and missionizing regulars. To this end, regional tribunals stepped up efforts to deal with *moriscos,* especially after the forty years of grace expired in the 1560s. In Aragon and parts of Castile, where no such privilege had been granted, the Holy Office went to work even earlier. In Valencia the local tribunal of the Inquisition brought only eighty-two *moriscos* to trial between 1540 and 1559, but between 1560 and 1614 it tried around twenty-five hundred individuals for following the law of Muhammad.[99]

Nevertheless, the Holy Office proved more capable of containing *moriscos* than reforming them. If New Christians fretted over being judged in the confessional, they abhorred confessing their sins before representatives of the Inquisition. Ahmad Ibn Qasim al-Hajari, a *morisco* called upon to translate the famous *plomos* of Granada, described the fear that the Holy Office could instill.[100] While in Granada he encountered a group of *moriscos* from his hometown and attempted to befriend them. But when they learned about al-Hajari's work, they assumed that his days were numbered and feared being implicated in his trial: "They only spoke about religious matters with someone who was 'safe,' that is, someone who could be trusted completely. Many of them were afraid of one another. . . . Thus, when the [*moriscos*] saw in what situation I found myself, they used to say to each other: 'He will certainly fall into the hands of the Inquisitors!'"[101]

The Holy Office intended occasionally publicized edicts of grace to lure *moriscos* in by offering them absolution for previous heretical behavior. There was, of course, a catch. Once reconciled, a defendant forever remained under suspicion and, if convicted a second time, could be condemned as a relapsed heretic and relaxed to the secular arm. Consequently, fewer and fewer people made use of the edicts. The Marquis of Mondejar explained this decline: "Since they are an ignorant people, they think that [the edict of grace] is a deception and it seems to them that relying on fortune puts them in a better position than being reconciled [by the Inquisition] whereby they would incur the punishment of relapsing if they return to their sins."[102]

Ultimately, neither reforming bishops, nor missionary regulars, nor the efforts of the Holy Office succeeded in fully Christianizing the *moriscos*. Even if they began embracing their new religion enthusiastically, this probably would not have forestalled the resolution enacted by the Crown between 1609 and 1614. As early as 1581 the king and his counselors began to discuss ridding themselves of these New Christians.[103] Both Philip II and Philip III believed that *moriscos* represented a dangerous fifth column, ready to join forces with Turks or Protestants to bring Roman Catholic Spain to its knees. Given that conviction, could anything have persuaded the Crown to trust the *nuevos cristianos*?

While some bishops and local nobles continued to press for programs of assimilation up to the eve of the expulsion, many viewed expulsion as a necessity. Even Archbishop Ribera of Valencia, once an enthusiastic supporter of assimilation, reversed course. He wrote to Philip III in January 1602: if they did not expel the *moriscos,* they risked losing Spain to "heretics and traitors." Pedro de Valencia, Philip's chronicler, disagreed strongly. In 1606 he proposed yet another scheme for integrating *moriscos* into Christian society without the use of force. In November 1608, at the request of Pope Paul V, a number of important theologians and churchmen from the ecclesiastical province of Valencia met to consider the matter. The bishops of Orihuela, Tortosa, and Segorbe (but not the archbishop of Valencia!) advocated conciliation rather than expulsion for the *moriscos,* who, after all, had been baptized into the Catholic Church. By this point, however, the die was cast, and the Royal Council viewed the expulsion as a fait accompli.[104]

In September of the following year the deportation of Valencian *moriscos* to North Africa commenced. Although the Crown made occasional allowances for devout *moriscos* to demonstrate their good Christian status, it ultimately permitted very few to remain.[105] The king feared that the process would become intractably snarled if he began granting exceptions. We can only guess at what might have happened had a reprieve been granted. The Crown and much of the ecclesiastical hierarchy doubted that further efforts would make the difference. The perceived military threat posed by *moriscos,* and their obstinate unwillingness to sincerely embrace the Catholic faith, outweighed other considerations. Bishop Acevedo's "principal means and remedy" had failed. The possibility of confessional negotiation collapsed under the crush of political expediency.

## Conclusions

Jews, gypsies, and *moriscos* engaged sacramental confession with distinct strategies, and the impact of social and cultural exigencies resulted in a series of unique settlements. Many baptized Jews, who were often able to relocate because of their ties to artisanal and mercantile urban life, found themselves able to bury their past and assimilate to the dominant religious culture. By the middle of the seventeenth century, most *judeoconversos* had disappeared among Old Christians and could no longer be identified as problematic by the Holy Office. Only in exceptional moments of tension did they reemerge. Their confessional life became largely indistinguishable from that of the rest of the population. A minority, like Teresa of Avila, made the sacrament a central part of their lives. Others, like some Old Christians, endured it as an annual inconvenience.

Gypsies embraced a contrasting strategy, based on a withdrawal to the margins of the dominant society. Relying on flexibility and mobility, they shunned the protection and stability granted by church and state and often succeeded in avoiding bureaucratic attempts to restrict their freedom. Neither the Crown, nor local nobles, nor the parish system, nor the Inquisition could control them. Although gypsies refused to be reformed, the king did not execute a final solution in their case. Instead, Spain embraced them—the official line held that "gypsies were to be regarded as Spaniards, wayward, ruinous, and of the lowest

sort, naturally, but Spaniards nonetheless."[106] Ironically, their confessional obedience was probably the worst of the three groups.

King Philip III, his royal counselors, and many nobles and church leaders
judged that the *moriscos* had played the game of confessional negotiation falsely
and barred them from sitting at the table. Many had hoped for a better outcome. Often, bishops saw confessional transformation and catechization as the
preferred means of making good Christians of baptized Muslims and their descendants. No one wanted to expel the *moriscos*—not exactly. But it happened
anyway. Bishops and local priests routinely neglected opportunities for instruction and pastoral oversight. Inquisitorial methods only further alienated the
marginalized communities from the rest of society, yet the hard-nosed policies
of the Holy Office became standard procedure. The government, and sometimes the church, failed to distinguish between those who were assimilating
and their more stubborn counterparts.

The *moriscos* languished between the strategies of *judeoconversos* and *gitanos,*
and most failed to assimilate into the dominant culture. This was partly due
to their being so closely tied to the land, partly because they looked different,
and partly because repeated inquisitorial and civil census taking, parochial list
making, and frequent visits from the Holy Office made assimilation impossible. Partly it was because so many of them treasured components of Islamic
practice. Because the Crown viewed these New Christians as a military threat,
integrating them into Spanish society became out of the question. *Moriscos* also
failed to take their cue from the gypsies, who outsmarted inquisitors and royal
bureaucrats by moving about as the winds carried them. Like the gypsies,
many *moriscos* lived in separate communities, but they were easy to recognize
and locate, and their communities were likely to fracture when pressure was
brought to bear. For some three hundred thousand *moriscos,* the consequence
was expulsion to other regions of Europe or North Africa, where assimilation
generally proved to be no easier than it had been at home.

# CONCLUSION

[Sebastian] used to spend such time in the confessional that I would wonder what he had to say because he never did anything wrong; never *quite*. At least, he never got punished. Perhaps he was just being charming through the grille.
—EVELYN WAUGH

In 1584 Juan Rodríguez, an old cooper, found himself before the Holy Office for the second time in his life. Eleven years earlier he had endured public penance for blasphemy and for failing to fulfill his Easter duty. Now eighty years old and living in Santiago de Compostela, he still had trouble complying with the demands of the church. Witnesses testified that the parish priest had recently challenged Juan about his reluctance to confess. During the exchange, the cooper denied believing in God and claimed that neither the bishop nor the pope could excommunicate him. The old man seemed to call the entire structure of sacramental confession and priestly absolution into question, for when the *cura* confronted him, Juan declared that he preferred confessing to an oak than to a priest and claimed not to have confessed in three years.[1]

When summoned by the Inquisition, Juan defended himself against the accusations. While he could do little to explain away the irreverent and blasphemous statements about God, the pope, and bishops, they had probably slipped out in an angry moment. As for his confessional behavior, he believed that it was altogether justified. The witnesses, Juan explained, had gotten the story all wrong. In fact, the impoverished cooper spent his days wandering the streets of Santiago de Compostela and begging for alms. While doing so, he had completed his Easter duty, although not at his home parish of Santa María Magdalena de Dios. As for shriving to a tree, yes, he had made the comment, but

The epigraph to this chapter comes from Waugh's *Brideshead Revisited*, 62.

the inquisitors needed to consider the context. What Juan had actually said was that he preferred to confess to an oak than to *his* priest at La Magdalena. This was less a case of refusing to comply with the demands of the church than a matter of honor. The priest in question had, years before, taken Juan's daughter to his bed, and was still cohabiting with her. This shameless priest was the very one who had recently confronted Juan about his Lenten compliance.

The poor old cooper resented this treatment and probably found satisfaction in giving a piece of his mind to the priest who had first dishonored Juan's family and then, adding insult to injury, proceeded to rebuke the layman publicly for not confessing at his parish church. Juan appears to have uttered the blasphemous curse *Niego Dios* (I deny God) in the midst of that row. How could anyone expect him to reveal his sins to such a priest, to kneel before him in humble submission, call him father, and hear the words of absolution pronounced through his offending lips?

> I, a sinner, confess to God almighty, and to the blessed ever-virgin Mary, and to the blessed Saint Michael the Archangel, Saint John the Baptist, and to the holy Apostles Saint Peter and Saint Paul, and to all the saints, *and to you, father,* that I sinned gravely in thought, word, and deed through my sin, my sin, my very great sin. For this I beg [all the saints] *and you, father,* that you intercede on my behalf with God our Lord. (Emphasis added.)[2]

Penitents recited these or similar words when they begged for the forgiveness of their sins. The appeal to clerical intercession must have rung hollow in Juan's ears. The old man believed that in this matter he knew better than the priest or the church hierarchy. He did not accept their ability to excommunicate him; he maintained the appropriateness of his extraparochial confessions.

Like Juan Rodríguez, Spanish laypeople refused simply to have confessional practice dictated to them. To be sure, the sacred space and ritual components emphasized the confessor's role as God's representative. In spite of Juan's protests, the shriving priest and his ecclesiastical superiors, not the penitent, reserved to themselves the power of binding and loosing, of pronouncing absolution and excommunication. But laypeople seem seldom to have understood that this meant they should participate only passively in the encounter. On the contrary, they regarded it as their privilege to ferret out ways to exert their own influence on the sacrament.

This rarely meant giving up on formal religion. On the contrary, their confessional piety remained churchy; it simply became less tied to the parish. The vast majority of early modern Spaniards learned to work within the institutional penitential system, using loopholes and gray areas to facilitate confessional practice. While hardly rebels, they did sometimes behave in rascally ways—they might well have described their own behavior as *picaresco*. They procured the affection of local priests with gifts, avoided disagreeable confessors, played ignorant when it was useful, and took advantage of rivalries between secular and regular clerics. They discussed confession in the streets, churches, and homes with friends, neighbors, and family members. The literate consumed devotional treatises, manuals of confession, and saints' *vitae* and communicated to others the lessons they learned. These works taught them how to behave with respect to the sacrament, what to expect from it, and how to make the encounter meet their needs. Even when their actions pushed the boundaries of propriety, laypeople rarely suffered any formal punishment.

The clergy, too, learned to adapt. The rigid legislation enacted by bishops and synods only occasionally matched the parish reality. The growing ranks of regular priests, the proliferation of contradictory confessional how-to manuals, and the Crown's financial needs wore away at the strict enforcement of diocesan programs, which saw confession, particularly during Lent, as rooted in and regulated by the parish church. Given the impracticality of those programs, priests on the front lines—parish clergy, regular clerics, and missionary confessors—often learned to negotiate the sacramental encounter in dialogue with their penitents. Manual authors and reforming bishops encouraged priests to secure penitents' confessional confidence by conspicuously behaving in ways that would attract laypeople and inspire devotion.

Not everyone found it easy to arrive at a mutually satisfying confessional modus vivendi. Sometimes this failure stemmed from ecclesiastical, secular, or popular assumptions (valid or not) about penitents' religious behavior. At other times confession failed because priests behaved inappropriately or lackadaisically toward the faithful. Some *curas* exerted their power by soliciting congregants sexually; others broke the confessional seal. Some women were treated as second-class confessants. In yet other cases the fault lay more immediately with penitents who refused to bow to the demands of the church or to live within the confines of the confessional system.

Yet the same laxity that undercut episcopal legislation, enabled soliciting priests, and permitted penitents to flout their obligations created an environment in which laypeople could more easily participate in the sacrament. Most Spaniards fell somewhere between the extremes of the devout *beata,* whose life revolved around daily encounters with a spiritual director, and the *pícaro* who avoided confession for decades. They participated in the sacrament dozens, if not hundreds, of times over the course of their lives, and they knew their confessors to be imperfect men. They steered clear of shame and dishonor, gossiped about neighbors, engaged in illicit relationships, and occasionally blasphemed. Living and dying within the church mattered, but the demands of the confessional had to be balanced against the other pressures of daily life. They lived this facet of their religion imperfectly. But by the mid-seventeenth century, more so than had been the case even a century earlier, confession had become a facet of the laity's religious life.

Local realities that complicated reforming programs, infighting between priestly factions, and the spread of the *cruzada* indulgence enabled laypeople to determine when and with whom they would confess. Although largely excluded from the theological and political debates that took place among the intellectual, social, and religious elites, common Spaniards nevertheless exerted a tremendous influence on sacramental practice at the grassroots level. That influence percolated upward, affecting the tenor of those debates, even as synodal constitutions, royal and episcopal decrees, and inquisitorial scrutiny trickled down, limiting the range of penitential options available to laypeople.

The implications of this story extend beyond confessional practice. The processes at work in confession opened up new ways and places for people to worship by facilitating the development of spiritual direction, frequent confession and communion, private oratories, new forms of devotional literature, the boom in indulgences and masses for the dead, and the spectacle of itinerant missionary confessors and *cruzada* preachers. Furthermore, they changed the way that women expressed their religiosity, altered the process of clerical formation, and transformed the relationship between parish priests and their flocks, as well as the expectations those flocks had of the priests with whom they interacted. They provided regular orders with new inroads for engaging the religious lives of the people, thereby encouraging the blossoming that those orders experienced in early modern Spain. These developments are by no means incidental to Spanish religiosity; indeed, they lie close to its heart.

More broadly still, the transformation of early modern confession was deeply connected to the rise of the Spanish state. The sacrament of penance proved too unwieldy to be a means of social control, strictly speaking, but it did become an avenue by which monarchs attempted to safeguard the orthodoxy (and loyalty) of subjects. It was supposed to keep heretics out and everyone else obedient to the dictates of the Holy Mother Church and her great defender, the Spanish monarch.

We see this trend at work in Philip II's effort to control the implementation of Tridentine decrees in his realms. The king urged peninsular archbishops to convene councils immediately after the conclusion of Trent in part because this seemed the best course for directing how reform came upon Spain. The approaches taken in these provincial councils were subsequently brought to bear upon the locales through the constitutions adopted by episcopal synods at the diocesan level. The king pressured conciliar and synodal authorities to fol-low his lead in interpreting and applying the spirit of Trent, not without some reluctance on their part.[3] The *patronato* that the Crown exercised over high church offices, and its influence over ecclesiastical affairs, including the Inqui-sition, afforded it a prominent role in programs to reform confession. Likewise, the Crown took direct action in ordering the establishment of confessionals in churches, attacking the problem of confessional solicitation, adjudicating jurisdictional disputes between regular and secular clergy, and overseeing the reform of religious orders.[4] Thus the changing face of confessional practice and the bureaucratization of the sacrament formed part of a larger process of rationalizing the way in which rulers related to those they ruled.

Nowhere, perhaps, is this process clearer than in the handling of *moriscos'* penitential behavior. Like Bishop Acevedo of Valladolid, the state treated con-fession as "the principal means and remedy" for turning false Christians into real ones and subjects of dubious loyalty into true Spaniards. While Philip III and many of his advisors ultimately concluded that this program had failed, that very failure fed a vision of Spain that emphasized purity of blood and reli-gious uniformity. The same vision sharpened Spanish resolve, which became aggressively expansive in defending the faith, not only in Iberia but in opposi-tion to the Islamic threat in the Mediterranean, the Protestant menace in greater Europe, and among the idolatrous native inhabitants of the New World, the Philippines, and other lands encompassed by the empire. Here we cross paths with the budding notion of Spanish national identity and mission.

One of the ways in which that mission reconnects with the story of confes-sional practice is through the dissemination of the bull of crusade, not only in mainland Spain but also in its southern Italian holdings (Sicily and Sardinia), the New World, and the Philippines. This indulgence had both immediate and long-term effects upon the practice of confession, but it also became, as we have seen, an important tool in the state-building enterprise. It served as a stable rev-enue stream during a period of great economic uncertainty and supported the rise of Spanish military power, which dominated Europe for a century, even as the crusade bull compromised episcopal legislation. The evolution of and controversies associated with confession were intimately connected to the new ways in which the state fashioned itself and expounded its raison d'être among its early modern subjects and in the wider world.

As all of this suggests, another broad implication of the trends explored in this book is the formation of Spanish identity. *España,* we are often told, *es diferente.* The changes in confessional practice and their subsequent impact on devotion and religious life helped create a sense of distinctiveness among Spaniards. Their awareness that confession was under attack in Spain was not understood to mean that they had turned against the sacrament.[5] Rather, it was foreigners—German Lutherans, French Huguenots, Dutch rebels, false Jewish and *morisco* converts, and, lurking behind it all, that great interloper, the Devil—who sought to undermine the sacrament.

A comparison with other Roman Catholic lands is instructive, for they too found it difficult to reform the practice of confession in the early modern era. Like Spain, Milan, the Southern Netherlands, and many of the Roman Catholic Germanic lands saw an intense focus on confessional practice, but often the attempts to implement reforms proved frustrating. The Southern Netherlands, with their close ties to Spain, were one of the most successfully re-Catholicized regions of Europe. And yet even as penitential symbolism came to form a key part of post-Tridentine church architecture there, the Jansenist controversy split the church.[6] In Milan, Carlo Borromeo labored to make confession an integral part of lay devotion, with some success.[7] And although historians of Italy have emphasized confession's usefulness as a means of social control, frequent confession often overtaxed busy clerics, as in Spain, sometimes causing the quality of confessions to decrease.[8]

The eastern Hapsburg lands and Roman Catholic Bavaria saw church and state coordinate their efforts to impose proper confessional practice in the countryside. In one extreme example, the Count of Bavaria sent armed troops, accompanied by priests, to determine whether his subjects had completed their Lenten confessions.[9] Attempts to use confessional receipts (*Beichtzettel*) in Bavaria resulted in a "lively trade" in counterfeits, and perfunctory confessions and absolutions became common.[10] The parishioners in Aufkirchen, "all catholic and diligent in worship," simply refused to disclose specific sins despite their confessors' efforts.[11] By the late eighteenth century the Roman Catholic Hapsburg Empire saw imperial minister Joseph Eybel pen *What Is an Indulgence?* (1782) and *What Do the Sources of Ancient Christianity Say About Auricular Confession?* (1784). Both scrutinized the sacrament of penance and raised disconcerting questions about its historical origins. Eybel emphasized the insufficient training of priests to carry out their task effectively and doubted confession's ability to produce true contrition. The Vatican condemned the tracts, but Emperor Joseph II retained Eybel's services.[12]

In southwestern Germany the state played an earlier and more direct role in undermining the church's attempts to regulate confession at the parish level. In the bishopric of Speyer, for instance, while villagers displayed a strong loyalty to Roman Catholicism, they ignored or resisted innovations such as additional confessions. In Burkheim, late sixteenth-century Austrian officials enforced attendance at Mass and payment of tithes but cared little about to whom laypeople confessed, especially when the parish priest appealed to his bishop rather than to secular leaders for support. In 1586 the Burkheimers forced their local *pfarrer* to let them confess and commune with other priests at Easter in exchange for promising to pay their tithe and fees. Confession became more frequent in the eighteenth century, but not as a discreet expression of personal devotion. Instead, in preparation for receiving the Eucharist, laypeople confessed when celebrating important holy days.[13]

French proponents of confessional piety found themselves struggling not only against Huguenots but also against Jansenists, who denounced the frequent confession promoted by Jesuits. Jansenists demanded extremely rigorous confessions, which may have safeguarded the sacrament's sanctity but failed to motivate most people to live sufficiently holy lives to receive absolution. In some areas where rigorist approaches held sway, participation in Easter communion fell to between 50 and 20 percent. In one parish of seven hundred inhabitants, only eighty received the Eucharist.[14] Although the same sacramental practices that had, not without complaints, been implemented in much of Italy and Spain spread in France, some laypeople refused to accept innovations like parish confessionals. At the end of the seventeenth century, parishioners in rural Sennely-en-Sologne simply refused to use them.[15] Even the Easter duty was not widely fulfilled before 1600.[16] Although both confessionals and the practice of frequent confession spread in the seventeenth century, by the eve of the French Revolution, some devotees excepted, the sacrament of penance had become a toothless and ineffective institution in France.[17]

Roman Catholics in Protestant lands who worshipped secretly (England and the Celtic lands) or as members of a tolerated minority confessional community (the Dutch Republic) experienced a dearth of ordained priests, which limited their access to confession. In the Netherlands, the collapse of the diocesan structure cleared away entrenched practices and habits, enabling missionary Jesuits and seminary priests to bring the "cutting edges" of the Counter-Reformation to the laity. Confession and priestly absolution became increasingly important, but the strict neo-Augustinian approach of the Holland Mission's secular priests drove laypeople into the arms of Jesuits, who focused less on external demonstrations of contrition than on developing a moral conscience.[18]

In England, by contrast, many recusants embraced devotional practices that did not require clerical intercession. In 1617, for example, William Stanley's *Treatise on penance* argued that, in lieu of sacramental confession and communion, devotees could examine their consciences privately and foster within themselves "a fervent desire, to receive spiritually their Sweet Savior, in the Holy Sacrament of the Altar." This would provide as much merit as if they had received the body and blood of Christ in the host.[19] In an emergency, Christ could grant absolution to a contrite penitent directly, without priestly intercession.[20] Both the British and the Dutch communities suffered their own brand of persecution and, for all their vitality, remained numerically stunted.

Many of these same problems existed in Spain. In the Diocese of Ourense, for example, parishioners regularly failed to confess annually even at the end of the seventeenth century.[21] But what was different—both for many inside and for those looking in from the outside—was a sense that Spanish life was differentiated by adherence to an intense confessional piety, which was absent or had been less perfectly brought to bear in other regions. Both commoners and inquisitors expected foreigners to hold heterodox views on confession. Thus the distinction that saved gypsies from exile (in spite of their abominable confessional behavior) but damned the *moriscos* was the fact that the former could be viewed as Spaniards while the latter could not.[22] And as Vicente Ramon reminded the inquisitors, his brother-in-law, the French tailor Guillermo Bononel (who shirked his confessional duties, mocked the bull of crusade, and threw a crucifix at his Spanish wife), was a *"lombardo frances* from the land of heretics"— damning testimony indeed.[23]

The eighteenth century and the waves of the Enlightenment that buffeted much of ancien régime Europe had a more limited impact on Spain thanks to the filtering work of the Inquisition and its index of prohibited books. But elsewhere confession came under heavier attack than ever before, as notions of improving humanity through social engineering and psychological conditioning began to erode the seriousness, and even the concept, of sin.[24] Joseph Eybel's tracts mingled with Voltaire's attacks on auricular confession.[25] The philosophes tended to regard the act of confession as useful for "psychological release" but maligned absolution as the superstitious invention of priests. The anticlerical wing of the Enlightenment subjected the sacrament, a proof of humanity's self-imposed immaturity, to direct mockery and derision; less abrasive authors depicted confessors as unctuous showpieces, good for soothing headaches, flattering women, and advising on etiquette, but little else.[26]

Things were different in Spain, at least for those looking in from the outside. By the nineteenth century, the critiques of confession by Protestants and philosophes had created an image of Spain that showcased an utterly devout and hopelessly orthodox confessional piety. As with the continued existence of the Inquisition, the apparatus of sacramental penance became proof of the peculiar backwardness of the Spanish.[27] Thus an 1821 issue of the *New Monthly Magazine and Literary Journal* offered a letter purportedly penned by Leucadio Doblado of Seville. He claimed to have received from a young Spanish cleric a manuscript titled "A Few Facts Connected with the Formation of the Intellectual and Moral Character of a Spanish Clergyman," which assured its readers that they could not expect "to be acquainted with Spain without a sufficient knowledge of the powerful moral engines at work in that country." Those moral engines were the product of sacramental confession, the effects of which "upon young minds are generally unfavourable to their future peace and virtue." The priest's screed described a terrifying first confession and years of lingering guilt, the early consequences of a corrupt system.[28]

In 1845 the Englishman John Dowling suggested that the "horrible disorders, seductions, adulteries, and abominations of every kind that have sprung from this practice of auricular confession, especially in Spain and other popish countries, are familiar to all acquainted with the history of Popery."[29] The anonymous (but purportedly Spanish) author of *Roman Catholicism in Spain* (1855) claimed that the practice of confession had only recently begun to fall off among city dwellers; nowadays, he explained, priests who demanded *cédulas* of urban parishioners were "exposed to mortification and rebuke." And yet, so strong was the traditional hold of the sacrament upon laypeople that priests could still force "the inferior classes of society" to participate. The author concluded that "auricular confession may be considered as the most tyrannical, odious, and immoral institution, which superstition, leagued with sordid interests, could ever have invented."[30] William MacKray claimed in 1859 that "the unbounded influence which the clerical orders possessed over the minds of [Roman Catholic] people" could nowhere be more clearly illustrated than in "the prevalence of the practice of auricular confession." As a consequence, domestic life became, "to a very great extent, the scene of jealousy, and suffering, and misery." MacKray's primary illustration was, of course, Spain.[31]

These examples merely gesture toward the impact that confessional practice had on foreign perceptions of Spain; a full analysis of this phenomenon would require its own detailed study. Surely such works drew upon the strident critiques of sacramental confession offered by Luther and other early Protestants. But the hyperbolic disgust with which nineteenth-century writers regarded Spanish penitential practice was specific, not general; one can often hear distorted echoes of the system that peninsular bishops attempted to realize. Authors mocked confessional receipts, the *padrón*, parochial jurisdiction, the Easter duty, sexual advances in the confessional, the *bula de la cruzada*, the seal of confession, reserved sins, penitential manuals, and incomplete confessions. Such trappings, these works suggested, had become all too characteristic of the backward and misguided society to which Spaniards belonged.

Yet, ironically, while nineteenth-century authors depicted confession as impeding progress—religious, social, and cultural—more recent commentators have described it as an institution that fostered the modern notion of the individual, with its sense of interiority and subjectivity.[32] Some describe the sacrament as a mechanism that enabled individuals to satisfy deep compulsions to confess, arguing that by the end of the early modern period the mandate to do so had been internalized, becoming a component of the Western psyche still discernible today in psychoanalysis, autobiography, medical inquiry, daytime television talk shows, and Internet blogs.[33] Others suggest that people resisted the command to confess as a surprising and novel demand. Rather than a vehicle for truth telling, confession in this view becomes a means of self-fashioning, "a privileged form of subject formation."[34] In either reading, early modern confession becomes a watershed wherein scholars claim to uncover something of the modern, or perhaps even the postmodern.

We must be cautious, however, about overemphasizing the scrutinizing power of the confessor or the ability of the penitential system—ostensibly, a terribly intrusive apparatus—to correct and control. Laypeople experienced some freedom to move about within this system and manipulate it. Consequently, their need to flee from confession, or to remake themselves in the midst of it rather than disclose their sins, may not have been as dramatic an impulse as literary critics, psychologists, and sociologists have suggested.

But this does not mean that confession played no role in the creation of the modern self. In fact, the complex tensions at work in the confessional system in Spain (and similar forces seem to have been active in other contexts) allowed laypeople to exercise agency in their religious lives. Their ability to confess when and with whom they chose, their tendency to turn away from the parish and toward regular priests, the possibility (at least in more urban settings) of making serial visits to confessors in search of an obliging priest—in effect, the implementation of a navigable bureaucracy—meant that penitents could lay claim to a degree of anonymity and freedom that smacks of modernity. This latitude, a function of the processes that I have been at pains to expose in this book, ultimately undermined the disciplinary oversight that monarchs, bishops, and inquisitors had sought to realize by reforming and regulating confession.

In Spain it took longer for this post-Tridentine system of regulated, frequent confession to unravel than it did in many other parts of Europe. Ironically, the sacrament's relative stability in the peninsula had much to do with the fact that the loopholes in bureaucratic oversight allowed for substantial flexibility; confessional legislation never functioned as efficiently as its authors had intended. But even in Spain, the system eventually entered into decline.[35]

In the post–Vatican II era, the new *Ordo paenitentiae* (1974), the subsequent focus on reconciliation rather than penance, and frequent papal calls for Roman Catholics to rediscover confession may all be seen as attempts to revive the sacrament's flagging popularity. Nowadays, most Spaniards, particularly those raised in a post-Franco world, view confession with derision as something in which they were obliged to participate as children but that no longer has a claim upon them. Only 27 percent believe in the existence of a single true religion, and Spaniards find themselves increasingly disconnected from Christian morality as described by Rome. As Nancy Ammerman observes, "priests have lost their authoritative role as confessors, and the Church has lost the loyal moral obedience of its members."[36]

If changes in confessional behavior have broader implications for religious practice, state building, identity formation, and the onset of modernity, we must also note that these transformations were not restricted to Iberia alone. Tracing Spanish influence upon confession as practiced elsewhere in Roman Catholic Europe, let alone the world, would be a vast project. But such connections do exist, for Spain's rise to world prominence coincided with its golden age of sacramental confession. As James Amelang has noted, late medieval Spaniards looked to Italian models of piety, but by the second half of the sixteenth century, Italians had begun looking west.[37] Spain's close ties to its Austrian Hapsburg cousins, its proximity to France and Portugal, its claim to the Low Countries and Franche-Comté, its anti-English alliance with Ireland, its presence on the Spanish Road through the heart of Europe, even its sponsorship of seminaries for training priests from Protestant countries incline one to expect that much of Roman Catholic Europe knew something of Spanish confession.

Certainly, the penitential printing boom facilitated the dissemination abroad of Spanish confessional practice. Seminaries across Europe adopted Azpilcueta's *Manual*, which became a widely recognized and highly regarded voice in Roman Catholic moral theology. Italian priests in seventeenth-century Fiesole were formed by studying Latin editions; English seminarians at Douai-Rheims and English recusants at home read and discussed it.[38] By 1600 editions had been printed in Antwerp, Cologne, Paris, Würzburg, Venice, Lyon, Rome, Turin, and Genoa. In one fascinating example of the multinational use to which the Navarese doctor was put, the English Benedictine Gregory Sayers reworked Azpilcueta's ideas and published them in Latin as *Flores decisionum* in Venice in 1601. Titles such as Juan Polanco's *Breve directorium* (Rome, 1554), Pedro de Soto's *Defensio catholicae confessionis* (Antwerp, 1557), Francisco de Toledo's *Instructio sacerdotum ac poenitentium* (Venice, 1596), and Juan de Maldonado's *Lu somme des cas de conscience* (Rouen, 1614), which passed directly from a Latin edition published in Lyon into French without ever appearing in Castilian, give a sense of the cosmopolitan confidence of Spanish authorities.[39]

Of course, such influences did not move only in one direction. Azpilcueta wrote his *Manual de confessores y penitentes* while teaching at the University of Coimbra. The Portuguese Manuel Sa's *Aphorismi confessariorum* was printed in Madrid in 1600. The Jesuit Hermann Busenbaum's *Medulla theologiae moralis* was frequently published in Castilian in Zaragoza beginning in 1664, with a special addendum for his Spanish audience: an eighty-page appendix on the bull of crusade. In 1695 the Italian Paolo Segneri's trilogy of guidebooks appeared posthumously in Madrid as *El confesor instruido, El penitente instruido,* and *El cura instruido*. And in the eighteenth century the works of Alfonso Liguori, whom Pius XII named patron saint of confessors and moralists in 1950, found a place in the Iberian market.

Many of the authors mentioned above (Toledo, Maldonado, Polanco, Sa, Busenbaum, Segneri) were Jesuits; all of them were regulars. And in addition to spreading their approach to confession through the written word, they carried it abroad as missionaries. Members of the Society of Jesus not only helped popularize frequent confession among Spaniards but also facilitated the exportation of Spanish modes of piety to the rest of Roman Catholic Europe and beyond, sometimes far beyond. While Jesuits carried their faith and practice to India, China, and Japan, Franciscans took Roman Catholic Christianity to Portuguese Africa, which Spain claimed as part of its empire from 1580 to 1668.

Outside of the Portuguese holdings, of course, those regions of the world that constituted the Spanish Empire proper also called to zealous priests. The

# FLORES
# DECISIONVM
## SIVE
## CASVVM CONSCIENTIAE.

Ex Doctrina Confiliorum Martini ab Azpilcueta Doctoris Nauarri
collecti, & iuxta librorum iuris Canonici difpofitionem
in fuos Titulos diftributi.

*Cum annotationibus, quibus ob recentiores quafdam Summorum Pontificum Bullas,
Authoris opinio in multis, vel confirmata, vel refutata eft,
fummo ftudio & diligentia explicatur.*

Authore R. P. D. GREGORIO SAYRO Anglo, Ordinis D. Benedicti
Congregationis Cafinenfis, aliàs S. Iuftinæ de Padua Monacho,
& Sacri Monafterij Cafinenfis profeffo.

*Propter varias autem Editiones, ad maiorem lectoris vtilitatem, qualiter editio prima
& propria Authoris, cum altera recentiori, & Confilijs penè trecentis aucta
conueniat, & ab ea diffentiat, in principio cuiufque
Decifionis oftenditur.*

ACCESSERVNT INSVPER SEX INDICES.

Primus Titulorum iuris Canonici cum
   numero Decifionum;
Secundus Locorum Sacri Concilij Tridentini.
Tertius Bullarum Summorum Pontificum;
Quartus Concordantiarum primæ editionis

cum fecunda.
Quintus econtra Concordantiarum editionis fecundæ cum prima.
Sextus Rerum, & materiarum notatu di-
   gniffimarum.

*Quorum Tres priores in principio, tres vero pofteriores in fine libri appofuimus.*

Cum licentia Superiorum, & Priuilegijs.

# VENETIIS. MDCI.

*Apud Baretium Baretium, & Socios.*

Fig. 5 Gregory Sayers, *Flores decisionum* (Venice, 1601). Courtesy of Saint Louis
University Libraries, Special Collections.

first Spanish missionaries arrived in the Philippines in 1565, and by the early seventeenth century Augustinians, Franciscans, Jesuits, and Recoletos were hard at work.[40] The adaptation of Spanish religion to the region and, especially, the introduction of confessional practice proved a complicated and trying task for the missionaries (as it certainly was for the natives), but one that was viewed as indispensable.[41] In the New World, too, bringing confession to bear upon the lives of indigenous converts became essential to evangelization.[42]

Those who remained at home reminded missionaries that the fields of Spain were also ripe for harvest. In 1564 the general of the Society of Jesus, Diego Laínez, was exhorted to allow his Jesuits to go abroad only rarely, "for here [in Spain] we have real Indies and the labourers are few."[43] Indeed, in the Indies of Spain much work remained to be done, and the ongoing mission at home demanded a continual and massive allocation of resources. While we may be inclined to remember the scandalous examples of soliciting priests or obstinate penitents, more remarkable is the vast amount of valuable time and energy (physical, emotional, devotional, and bureaucratic) that Spaniards expended in making confession a central component of peninsular religious life.

A visit to virtually any of the great churches of Spain affords a physical manifestation of the degree to which the work of religion there has consisted of continuous labor, the building of new upon old. Invariably, a ring of chantries encircles the main altar, broken only by the occasional doorway or confessional. The chantries, as we find them now, have undergone centuries of modification and accretion. While a first generation endowed the chapel and masses to be said for the dead, it was left to later generations to outfit the altar with costly vessels and linens, to place a baroque triptych atop that altar, or to procure a polychrome statue of the Virgin to stand watch. Church building is never done—just ask the laborers at Barcelona's Sagrada Família, now in its thirteenth decade of construction. It was the same with the sacrament of penance in Spain. The forgiveness of sins demanded a constant outlay of human and economic resources to train up confessors, draw in penitents, and lay the foundation for subsequent generations. The people of early modern Spain, both lay and religious, negotiated the development of that system, participated in it, and paid the heavy price it demanded.

# NOTES

## Introduction

1. AHN, Inq., leg. 69, exp. 25 (20 August 1581).

2. Ibid. (13 September 1581). "Dixo que luego pantaleon llego a este declarante y le dixo que se queria confesar con el y esta me hincado de rodillas este declarante le preg[un]to quanto tiempo avia que se avia confesado el qual le respondio que este ano no se avia confesado ni cumplido con el precepto de la madre s[an]ta iglesia y que los mas anos se avia confesado. Y preg[unta]do con que confesores se avia confesado no le dixo con quien y que la causa por que este ano no se confesava hera por que le avia mandado el visitador que so pena de ex[comuni]on echase de su casa una muger que thenia el qual no la echo, y por eso no se confeso y que luego avia salido de alli de los sauzes . . . y que esperava cierto recaudo muy presto para irse a espana y dexarse esta ysla." All translations are my own unless otherwise noted.

3. Ibid. (6 December 1581). "Sospechoso de herege por aver tanto tiempo q[ue] se a apartado de los sacramentos de la penitençia y eucharistia."

4. *Canons and Decrees of the Council of Trent*, 91.

5. For overviews of the history of penance, see McNeill, *History of the Cure of Souls;* and Kidder, *Making Confession, Hearing Confessions.*

6. *Canons and Decrees of the Council of Trent*, 89–90.

7. Luther described confession as "one of the greatest plagues on earth whereby you have confused the conscience of the whole world, caused so many souls to despair, and have weakened and quenched all men's faith in Christ." "Exhortation to All Clergy," 71. See also Calvin, *Institutes of the Christian Religion*, 1:645.

8. Kamen, *Phoenix and the Flame*, 123–24.

9. Thomas, *Religion and the Decline of Magic*, 155.

10. Foucault, *Discipline and Punish*, 27.

11. Tentler, "Summa of Confessors," 109.

12. Hepworth and Turner, *Confession*, 169–70.

13. On Roman Catholic Europe, see Myers, *"Poor Sinning Folk";* Prosperi, *Tribunali della conscienza;* de Boer, *Conquest of the Soul;* Briggs, *Communities of Belief*, esp. 277–338; Haliczer, *Sexuality in the Confessional;* and Bilinkoff, *Related Lives.* On the mission fields, see Rafael, "Confession, Conversion, and Reciprocity"; Martínez Ferrer, *Penitencia en la primera evangelización;* Pardo, *Origins of Mexican Catholicism;* and Standaert and Dudink, *Forgive Us Our Sins.* On Orthodox Russia, see Kizenko, "Written Confession." On Protestant Europe, see Rittgers, *Reformation of the Keys;* and Parker, "Pilgrims' Progress." On cross-confessional studies, see Lualdi and Thayer, *Penitence in the Age of the Reformations;* and Firey, *New History of Penance.*

14. Bossy, "Social History of Confession," 21.

15. Bossy, *Christianity in the West*, 126–39.

16. For example, Simplicio, *Peccato, penitenza, perdono.*

17. Barnes, "Social Transformation of the French Parish Clergy," 141. See also Hoffman, *Church and Community.*

18. Forster, *Catholic Revival in the Age of the Baroque;* and Poska, *Regulating the People.*

19. But see Nalle, *God in La Mancha;* Fernández Terricabras, *Felipe II y el clero secular;* and Melvin, "Fathers as Brothers in Early Modern Catholicism."

20. See the following works of Kathleen Comerford: *Ordaining the Catholic Reformation;* "'Care of souls'"; and *Reforming Priests and Parishes.* For Spain, see Nalle, *God in La Mancha,* 70–103; and Rawlings, *Church, Religion, and Society,* 71–73.

21. Oestereich, *Neostoicism and the Early Modern State;* Hsia, *Social Discipline in the Reformation;* Reinhard, "Reformation, Counter-Reformation, and the Early Modern State"; Schilling, *Religion, Political Culture, and the Emergence of Early Modern Society,* 205–45. For an application of these paradigms to confession, see Tentler, *Sin and Confession.*

22. See Poska, "Confessionalization and Social Discipline," 308–19.

23. Tentler, "Summa of Confessors," 136–37.

24. Foucault, *Abnormal,* 177.

25. Foucault, *History of Sexuality,* 61.

26. Foucault, *Abnormal,* 178.

27. De Boer, *Conquest of the Soul;* Briggs, *Communities of Belief;* Forster, *Catholic Revival in the Age of the Baroque.*

28. Briggs, *Communities of Belief,* 336.

29. See the following works by Jodi Bilinkoff: "Confessors, Penitents, and the Construction of Identities"; "Confession, Gender, Life-Writing"; and *Related Lives.*

30. On sexual solicitation in the confessional, see Sarrión Mora, *Sexualidad y confesión;* Alejandre, *Veneno de Dios;* and Haliczer, *Sexuality in the Confessional.*

31. Cf. Ozment, *When Fathers Ruled;* and Roper, *Holy Household.*

32. Weber, *Teresa of Avila and the Rhetoric of Femininity;* Ranft, "Key to Counter-Reformation Women's Activism"; Bilinkoff, *Related Lives;* and Leonard, *Nails in the Wall.*

33. See Poska, *Women and Authority.*

34. See Monter, *Frontiers of Heresy;* Tueller, *Good and Faithful Christians;* Starr-LeBeau, *In the Shadow of the Virgin;* Perry, *Handless Maiden;* and Pym, *Gypsies of Early Modern Spain.*

35. Bossy, "Moral Arithmetic," and *Christianity in the West,* 45–50, 127–28, 132–35.

36. Delumeau, *Sin and Fear,* 244.

37. Brooks, *Troubling Confessions,* 101.

38. Myers, *"Poor Sinning Folk,"* 7–8.

39. Foucault, *Abnormal,* 178.

40. Senior, *In the Grip of Minos,* 85.

41. Brooks, *Troubling Confessions,* 101.

42. De Boer, *Conquest of the Soul,* 86–87.

43. Bilinkoff, *Related Lives,* 32–45.

44. *Vitae* blur the line between prescription and description as they relate actual confessional experiences, but in an idealized and didactic fashion. Bilinkoff, *Related Lives,* 9.

45. See González Povillo, *Gobierno de los otros.*

46. See, for instance, Moore, *Formation of a Persecuting Society.* Jean-Pierre Dedieu provides insight into the profitable use of inquisitorial sources in "Archives of the Holy Office of Toledo." See also Griffin, *Journey-Men Printers,* 24–25.

47. Christian, *Local Religion in Sixteenth-Century Spain,* 5.


*Chapter 1*


1. BAV, Ottobani latini, 495. "Dizen tambien hazerse esto santo sacramento pernicioso, porque da occasion á que no se haga la confesion entera y que se callen en ella muchas faltas, y aun dizen que con tanto perjuicio y daño de sus honrras y famas no les obliga el precepto de la integridad de esto santo sacramento, y que no peccan en dimidiar sus confessiones."

2. Homza, *Religious Authority*, 143. See also Maryks, *Saint Cicero and the Jesuits*, 8.

3. Burke, "How to Become a Counter-Reformation Saint." See also Bilinkoff, *Related Lives*, 32–45.

4. The categories manual writers used to discuss ideal priests were somewhat fluid. The concept of *bonitas* (charitable disposition), for example, sometimes served a function similar to that of prudence. See de Boer, *Conquest of the Soul*, 19.

5. Immediate jurisdiction was also granted to bishops (in their dioceses), abbots (in their monasteries), and the pope (throughout Christendom). On the licensing of confessors in early modern Naples, see Mancino, *Licentia confitendi*.

6. The bull *In coena Domini* contained the normative list of papally reserved sins. It was included in most synodal constitutions, some of which required that confessors possess a copy of the bull. See García-Villoslada, "Felipe II y la Contrarreforma Catolica," 3.1:55–56.

7. Azpilcueta, *Manual de confessores y penitentes*, 422; Ledesma, *Primera parte de la Summa*, 183–90; Fernández de Córdoba, *Instrucion de confessores*, 8–10.

8. Azpilcueta, *Manual de confessores y penitentes*, 38. See also Valtanás, *Confessionario muy cumplido*, fol. 8v; Alva, *Confessionario mayor y menor*, fol. 4v; Ledesma, *Primera parte de la Summa*, 277; Corella, *Practica del confesionario*, introduction.

9. *Constituciones synodales del Obispado de Barbastro*, 70–71. "Y ha de estar el Penitente de rodillas, sin espada, ni otra arma alguna; y las mugeres, con habito y tocado honesto; y tods con las manos conpuestas, y los ojos baxos, mostrando en la verguença del rostro, el sentimiento y dolor interior." See also *Constituciones synodales del obispado de Cuenca*, 283; *Synodo diocessana que su Señoria Don Fray Enrique Henriquez*, fol. 19v; *Constituciones promulgadas por . . . D. Fr. Francisco de Roys y Mendoza*, 253.

10. John O'Malley points out that this practicality was atypical of early Jesuit approaches to confession. *First Jesuits*, 145.

11. Azpilcueta, *Manual de confessores y penitentes*, 16. "El saber del confessor para ser perfecto, y por si solo determinar todo, ha de ser tanto, que incluya Theologia, Canones, y leyes, y aun las constituiciones synodales de la tierra do oye."

12. Teresa of Avila, *Life of Saint Teresa*, 40.

13. Azpilcueta, *Manual de confessores y penitentes*, 19. "Que no pregunte todo lo que puede aver cometido el penitente, sino solo aquello que comunmente los de su qualidad suelen hazer."

14. Fernández de Córdoba, *Instrucion de confessores*, 22–23.

15. Azpilcueta, *Manual de confessores y penitentes*, 391–92. "Parece que es mas seguro y mejor encomendar la missa al sacerdote, que parece bueno, que al que parece malo."

16. Ibid., 392.

17. *Constituciones Synodales del Obispado de Avila*, fols. 99v–100r.

18. Fernández de Córdoba, *Instrucion de confessores*, 144. "No basta ser casto, si no parecerlo."

19. Azpilcueta, *Manual de confessores y penitentes*, 32.

20. Ledesma, *Primera parte de la Summa*, 313. "Porque si el sacerdote no guardasse secreto se destruyria el mismo sacramento, porque nadie se querria confessar."

21. Ibid., 276.

22. Fernández de Córdoba, *Instrucion de confessores*, 24.

23. Ledesma, *Primera parte de la Summa*, 276–77.

24. Azpilcueta, *Manual de confessores y penitentes*, 38. "Recebir al peccador, con alegre grave-dad, y mostrar se le en todo, qual ha de ser dulce y affable, suave, prudente, discreto, manso, piadoso, y benigo, y animelo a descubrir sus llagas, y a esperar salud dellas."

25. Ibid., 40. "Mirar discretamente, si el penitente trae la devida contricion."

26. Ibid., 30; Henriquez, *Summa theologiæ moralis*, 4.24, n. 5; Soto, *Commentarium in IV. sententiarum*, 768, 776–78; Escobar y Mendoza, *Liber theologiae moralis*, 7.4.5, n. 27.

27. Ledesma, *Primera parte de la Summa*, 248.

28. Soto, *Commentarium in IV. sententiarum*, 776.

29. Nalle, *God in La Mancha*, 94.

30. Fonseca Montes, *Clero en Cantabria*, 140–88.

31. Rawlings, *Church, Religion, and Society*, 71–73.

32. Homza, *Religious Authority*, 125, 259n39.

33. O'Malley, *First Jesuits*, 145–46.

34. Arias, *Vida del V.Y.R. Fray Simón de Rojas*, 1:283.

35. Melvin, "Fathers as Brothers in Early Modern Catholicism," 158–59.

36. AHN, Inq., libro 731, fol. 190r.

37. Gómez, *Perfecto examen*.

38. Pérez de Heredia y Valle, *Concilio provincial de Granada*, 459.

39. AHN, Inq., leg. 2022, exp. 77; Contreras, "Aldermen and Judaizers," 109.

40. Theiner, *Die Entwicklung der Moraltheologie*, 97–145.

41. Morgado García, "Pecado y confesión en la España moderna," 119–20.

42. See Homza, *Religious Authority*, 160.

43. In Salamanca in 1579, 1580, 1582, and 1583; Zaragoza in 1583; Toledo in 1585; Barcelona in 1585, 1589, 1596, and 1604; Alcalá in 1591 and 1593; without location in 1612; Lerida in 1615; and Pamplona in 1626.

44. In Salamanca in 1625 and 1627; Valencia in 1628; Barcelona in 1634; Huesca in 1638; Alcalá in 1640; and Madrid in 1643, 1650, 1653, 1664, and 1667.

45. Tejero, "Escritos sobre el Doctor Navarro," 43; Zagorin, *Ways of Lying*, 165.

46. See Dunoyer, *Enchiridion confessariorum de Navarro*.

47. Holmes, *Elizabethan Casuistry*, 1.

48. Leonard, "On the Mexican Book Trade," 32.

49. Leonard, "Best-Sellers of the Lima Book Trade," 27.

50. Nalle, *God in La Mancha*, 86; Comerford, *Ordaining the Catholic Reformation*, 80–81; Melvin, "Fathers as Brothers in Early Modern Catholicism," 226.

51. Nalle, "Literacy and Culture in Early Modern Castile," 21.

52. Pérez de Heredia y Valle, *Concilio provincial de Granada*, 459.

53. *Constituciones Synodales, del Arcobispado de Sanctiago*, fol. 52r–v.

54. *Constituciones Synodales del Obispado de Avila*, fols. 187v–188r.

55. For example, *Constituciones Synodales, del Arcobispado de Sanctiago*, 20r; *Constituciones synodales del Obispado de Barbastro*, 151; and *Constituciones sinodales del Obispado de Orense*, fol. 129v.

56. AHN, Inq., leg. 76, exp. 15 (10 July 1582). "Dixo q[ue] tiene alg[un]os libros de casos de conciencia en romance y q[ue] no ha estudiado ny sabe latin ni ha abierto en su vida libro Latino."

57. AHN, Inq., leg. 231, exp. 3, fol. 26r.

58. AHN, Inq., leg. 227, exp. 2.

59. AHN, Inq., leg. 75, exp. 7 (undated letter of Augustino Sardo to the Holy Office). "Dixe simple e ignorantemente q[ue] la fornicacion simple no era pecado, por q[ue] yo no he estudiado theologia sino solamente un poco de gramatica en mi moçedad, pareciendome q[ue] lo avia leydo en la suma de navarro por q[ue] nunca lo avia oydo dezir lo contrario."

60. Gavarri, *Instrucciones predicables*, and *Noticias singularissimas*.

61. See Maryks, *Saint Cicero and the Jesuits*, 127–43.

62. See Stone, "Scrupulosity and Conscience"; O'Malley, *First Jesuits*, 145; and Maryks, *Saint Cicero and the Jesuits*, 2.

63. Maryks, *Saint Cicero and the Jesuits*, 2.

64. Medina, *Expositiones in primam secundae divi Thomae*, q. 19, a. 6. "Mihi videtur, quod si est opinio probabilis, licitum est eam sequi licet opposita probabilior sit."

65. Morgado García, "Pecado y confesión en la España moderna," 120. See also Vázquez, "Controversias doctrinales postridentinas," 4:461, 464.

66. Pascal, *Provincial Letters*, 129–30.

67. Delumeau, *Confesión y el perdón*, 117–22.

68. Maryks, *Saint Cicero and the Jesuits*, 83–106.

69. O'Malley, *First Jesuits*, 143–44; Lea, *History of Auricular Confession*, 1:302–3.

70. O'Malley, *First Jesuits*, 144.

71. AGS, PRCD, leg. 22, doc. 84, fols. 584r–658v; and doc. 92, esp. fols. 680r–685r.

72. Lea, *History of Auricular Confession*, 1:302–7.

73. AGS, PRCD, leg. 22, doc. 92, fol. 680r. "Y aunque vienen algunos a examinarse, son pocos y los que confiesan muchos."

74. Ibid., fol. 683v.

75. BNM, VE/18/30 and VE/34/21. Pedro de Castro, archbishop of Seville, attempted a similar gambit at about the same time. See Marshall, "Frequent and Daily Communion," 312–13.

76. Madrid, *Bullarium fratrum ordinis minorum*, 5:265–302.

77. Marshall, "Frequent and Daily Communion," 313–15, esp. n. 134.

78. Universidad de Granada, Biblioteca Hospital Real, cajas A-044–112 (16–1) and A-044–124 (27).

79. See Gavarri's comments about "the ignorance of some penitents" in *Noticias singularissimas*, fols. 224r–225r.

80. Dedieu, "'Christianization' in New Castile," 4.

81. *Constituciones Synodales del Arçobispado de Toledo . . . Año de. 1566*, fols. 49v–50r. The same was true, but to little effect, in Galicia. See Poska, *Regulating the People*, 47.

82. Dedieu, "'Christianization' in New Castile," 15; Nalle, *God in La Mancha*, 123.

83. Comerford, "Clerical Education, Catechesis, and Catholic Confessionalism," 255.

84. *Canons and Decrees of the Council of Trent*, 27.

85. Bilinkoff, *Avila of Saint Teresa*, 96–97.

86. See Morán and Andrés-Gallego, "Preacher."

87. Kamen, *Phoenix and the Flame*, 379.

88. Tueller, *Good and Faithful Christians*, 227.

89. Keitt, *Inventing the Sacred*, 99–100.

90. AHN, Inq., leg. 4972, no. 11, fol. 5r. "Y q[ue] no confesase con teatinos q[ue] eran muy escrupulosas por q[ue] no hiziesen algo lo q[ue] no era nada." Contrariwise, some criticized the leniency of Jesuits toward their penitents. See Mathers, "Early Spanish Qualms," 686.

91. Segura, "Teatro en los colegios de los jesuitas," 313.

92. Kallendorf, *Conscience on Stage*, esp. 85–92 and 181–83.

93. Hathaway, "'Music charms the senses,'" 227. José Gavarri provided missionary confessors with *saetas* (processional songs) to be sung as they entered towns and villages. See *Instrucciones predicables*, 370–76.

94. *Constituciones synodales del Obispado de Barbastro*, 98–99. Similarly, see *Constituciones Synodales Fechas . . . Obispado de Valladolid*, fol. 139v.

95. *Constituciones synodales del Obispado de Barbastro*, 73. See also *Concilio provincial de Granada*, 461; *Constituciones Synodales Fechas . . . Obispado de Valladolid*, fol. 158r; *Constituciones synodales del obispado de Coria*, 248; and *Constituciones Synodales del Obispado de Avila*, fol. 189r.

96. Marshall, "Frequent and Daily Communion," 337–484.

97. See Haliczer, *Sexuality in the Confessional*, 22–32.

98. Rouillard, *Historia de la penitencia*, 66–67.

99. *Canons and Decrees of the Council of Trent*, 90–93. See also Blanco, *Historia del confesionario*, 90–92.

100. See, for example, Pérez de Heredia y Valle, *Concilio provincial de Granada,* 465; *Constituciones Synodales del Arçobispo de Toledo,* fol. 83r–v; *Constituciones synodales del Obispado de Barbastro,* 74–75; *Constituciones Synodales Fechas . . . Obispado de Valladolid,* fols. 150v–151v; *Constituciones synodales del obispado de Coria,* 260; and *Constituciones Synodales del Obispado de Avila,* fol. 198v.

101. Tausiet, "Excluded Souls." At the level of the episcopal mandate, see *Constituciones Synodales del Obispado de Avila,* fol. 194r.

102. AHN, Inq., leg. 110, exp. 11, fol. 4r.

103. Tentler, "Summa of Confessors," 103–25; Tentler, *Sin and Confession,* 13, 61, 234–51; Doran and Durstan, *Princes, Pastors, and People,* 185–86; O'Malley, *First Jesuits,* 143.

104. Lea, *History of Auricular Confession,* 1:228.

105. AHN, Inq., leg. 1706, exp. 15, fols. 1r, 6v–12v.

106. AHN, Inq., leg. 1705, exp. 2, fol. 6v.

107. See Bilinkoff, *Related Lives;* and Ranft, "Key to Counter-Reformation Women's Activism."

108. Marshall, "Frequent and Daily Communion," 2.

109. MHSI, *Litterae quadrimestres,* 5:150.

110. AHN, Inq., leg. 40, exp. 4. "Confiesa cada mes q[ue] puede y la ultima vez confeso en el convento de st Fran[cis]co de la villa de Alcacar con un frayle cuyo n[ombr]e no sabe."

111. Real Academia de la Historia, Madrid, Papeles de Jesuitas, vol. 174, item 26.

112. Kagan, *Students and Society,* 5–30; Daddson, "Literacy and Education"; Eamon, *Science and the Secrets of Nature,* 94–96.

113. See Prosperi, *Tribunali della conscienza,* and "Inquisidor como confesor," 61–85.

114. AGS, PRCD, leg. 22, doc. 92, fol. 681r. "No tengo por de tanta ymportancia todos los demas decretos de la reformaçion que se hizieron en el Concilio, como este solo." Cf. *Canons and Decrees of the Council of Trent,* 170.

115. Homza, *Religious Authority,* 150–74.

116. Blanco Sánchez, "Inventario de Juan de Ayala."

117. Whinnom, "Problem of the 'Best-Seller,'" 194.

118. AHN, Inq., leg. 242, exp. 47 (p.a.).

119. Homza, *Religious Authority,* 150.

120. Azpilcueta, *Manual de confessores y penitentes,* 420–21. "Pero, si el confessor no tiene tan clara, & insoluble razon, y solamente la cree por razones provables, o dubda, o vee que el penitente con alguna razon se allega a la opinion de algun doctor notable, develo dexar a su consciencia, y absolverlo."

121. Ledesma, *Primera parte de la Summa,* 276. "Si el penitente es hombre docto, y letrado, de tal fuerte, que puede suplir el defecto de ciencia que ay en el confessor."

122. Fernández de Córdoba, *Instrucion de confessores,* 6–7.

123. Diaz, *Quinze tratados,* 65. "Grandissima miseria es, que no ay peccador por indispuesto que venga a la confession, que no halle en una parte, o en otra, quien lo absuelva. Y que no aya contrato por illicito que sea, que no aya quien lo abone."

124. AHN, Inq., leg. 4972, no. 1.8, fol. 6r. "Pues si un confesor no me absuelve, voy a otro."

## Chapter 2

1. *Canons and Decrees of the Council of Trent,* 39.

2. Ehlers, *Between Christians and Moriscos,* 7–8, 99–101.

3. Toledo, *Instruccion de sacerdotes,* fol. 187v.

4. AHN, Inq., leg. 563, exp. 13, fol. 3r–v.

5. AHN, Inq., leg. 37, exp. 1 (p.a.); leg. 71, exp. 8 (p.a.); leg. 42, exp. 15 (p.a.); leg. 42, exp. 11 (p.a.); leg. 564, exp. 6, fol. 2r; leg. 36, exp. 10 (p.a.).

6. Casey, *Family and Community*, 214.

7. AHN, Inq., leg. 230, exp. 7, fol. 8r.

8. AHN, Inq., leg. 227, exp. 9, fol. 37r.

9. AHN, Inq., leg. 69, exp. 4 (26 February 1697).

10. AHN, Inq., leg., 70, exp. 10 (p.a.).

11. AHN, Inq., leg 76, exp. 10 (13 May 1561).

12. Román, *Tratado historial y moral;* and Sensi, *Perdono di Assisi.*

13. Lea, *History of Auricular Confession*, 3:244.

14. AHN, Inq., leg. 44, exp. 11 (p.a.).

15. AHN, Inq., leg. 37, exp. 22 (p.a.).

16. AHN, Inq., leg. 40, exp. 36 (p.a.).

17. AHN, Inq., leg. 201, exp. 44 (p.a.).

18. Alcozer, *Confesionario breve*, fol. 5v.

19. Diaz de Luco, *Aviso de curas*, fol. 81r–v; Pérez de Heredia y Valle, *Concilio provincial de Granada*, 458; Machado de Chávez, *Perfecto confesor*, 1:374.

20. See, for example, Arias, "Del buen uso de los Sacramentos"; and Granada, *Guia de pecadores.*

21. Gavarri, *Noticias singularissimas*, fol. 1r. "Y todo sirvirá tambien, para que los que no son Confessores, sepan como se han de examinar sus conciencias para confessarse bien." See also Escobar y Mendoza, *Examen de confessores*, for which much of the text is geared toward guiding lay readers through their confessions.

22. Vitoria, *Confesionario util*, fols. 18v–19r.

23. Escobar y Mendoza, *Examen de confessores*, 224. See also Diaz de Luco, *Aviso de curas*, fol. 81v; Machado de Chávez, *Perfecto confesor*, 1:374; and Noydens, *Practica de curas*, 270.

24. Fernández de Córdoba, *Instrucion de confessores*, 449–50.

25. Coma, *Directorium curatorum*, fols. 143v–144r.

26. Azpilcueta, *Manual de confessores y penitentes*, 38–39.

27. Noydens, *Practica de curas*, 285–86.

28. Puente, *Vida del V.P. Baltasar Álvarez*, 24.

29. Ibid., 200.

30. Escobar y Mendoza, *Examen de confessores*, 6.

31. Gavarri, *Noticias singularissimas*, fol. 53v. For Gavarri's comments on the problem of bestiality, see fol. 35r–v. "Porque de no hazerlas, en las mas será en vano todo su trabajo de oirlas de confession, y fuera menos malo que no se confessaran, ni las oyera, si están comprehendidas en algunos pecados de las siete preguntas ya dichas."

32. *Constituciones synodales, del Obispado de Salamanca*, 164–65.

33. AHN, Inq., leg. 128, exp. 2, fol. 33v. "Llego a su casa un fraile moço que no sabe como se llamaba i que le pregunto si era de confesion que se queria confesar con el i que la respondio que era de confesion i entonces se puso a sus pies i la confeso de la mesma manera que se podia confesar con el teniente cura del dicho lugar o con otro confesor qualquiera exsaminado."

34. Ibid., fol. 33r. "I la dijo si era berdad que se abia confesado con dicho religioso i le respondio que si i la adbirtio que no podia comulgar porque era nula la confesion por no estar aprobado i no tener edad ni ordenes sacerdotal."

35. Relatively few inquisitorial cases against false confessors survive, but note the following: AHN, Inq., leg. 129, exp. 13 (1527), exp. 16 (1576–78), exp. 15 (1585–86), exp. 5 (1588), exp. 7 (1627), exp. 4 (1660–61); leg. 128, exp. 3 (1667–74), exp. 9 (1676–82). See also Sierra, *Procesos en la Inquisición de Toledo*, nos. 65, 66, 124, 319, 439, and 492.

36. Pérez de Heredia y Valle, *Concilio provincial de Granada*, 460.

37. Juan Mendez de Salvatierra, "Compendio de los capitulos cerca de la reformacion de lo tocante a la confession y decencia de las ymagines," 30 January 1582, Universidad de Granada, Biblioteca Hospital Real, caja A-031–168 (10).

38. *Constituciones Synodales, del Arcobispado de Sanctiago*, fol. 19v.

39. *Constituciones synodales del obispado de Cuenca*, 376.

40. Fernández Collado, *Concilio Provincial Toledano*, 142.

41. *Constituciones Synodales del Arçobispo de Toledo* (1601), fol. 88v, advocated a similar structure. "Mandamos que . . . los confessionarios sean abiertos, con cancel y rallo."

42. *Synodo diocesana del Arzobispado de Toledo*, 308. "Cerrados por todas partes, y con puertecilla por delante, como una vara de alto, por donde los Confessores puedan entrar, y ser vistos del Pueblo."

43. De Boer, *Conquest of the Soul*, 84–125.

44. AHN, Inq., leg. 233, exp. 6 (7 August 1576 and 12 February 1577); leg. 228, exp. 7, fols. 41v–42r.

45. AHN, Inq., leg. 233, exp. 3 (10 March 1602).

46. Ibid., exp. 9, fol. 15v. "Esta que declara se hincaba de rodillas p[ar]a confesarse con el suso d[ic]ho en un confisionario por la parte de adentro del d[ic]ho monesterio y el d[ic]ho fray p[edr]o de villa nueba se asentaba por la parte de afuera donde caye una bentanilla con un rallo de hiero y en el unos agujeros pequenos por donde no se puede entrar mano ni dedo que es el confisonario hordinario por donde todos se confiesan." On the development of confessional spaces in monasteries, see Cobianchi, "Practice of Confession."

47. AHN, Inq., leg. 231, exp. 16 (20 April 1605).

48. AHN, Clero, libro 19484, fol. 84v.

49. AHN, Inq., leg. 231, exp. 8 (2 July 1625).

50. AHN, Inq., leg. 230, exp. 7, fols. 63r, 65r.

51. *Constituciones Synodales del Arçobispo de Toledo*, fol. 88v.

52. AHN, Inq., leg. 227, exp. 8.

53. Quoted in Kamen, *Phoenix and the Flame*, 125.

54. Bilinkoff, *Related Lives*, 20–25.

55. *Constituciones synodales del obispado de Cuenca*, 282. "Mandamos, q[ue] el penitente este hincado de rodillas, en demostracion de su humildad, y del reconocimiento de sus culpas: y el confessor sentado como juez, que es en aquel acto."

56. *Constituciones promulgadas por . . . D. Fr. Francisco de Roys y Mendoza*, 235. "Mandamos, que assi los Sacerdotes, como los demas Fieles, q[ue] llegaren al Sacramento de la Penitencia se confiessen de rodilla, con la humildad que pide aquel respetoso acto, y no de otra manera; pues no es razon, ni puede dexar de ser de escandalo, que el que en aquel sagrado Tribunal se presenta como reo esté de otra posicion, ante aquel que mira como Iuez."

57. Fernández Collado, *Concilio Provincial Toledano*, 143.

58. *Synodo diocessana que su Señoria Don Fray Enrique Henriquez*, fol. 19v. "Mandamos, que los confessores . . . esten siempre sentados como juezes que son en aquel acto."

59. *Constituciones synodales, del Obispado de Salamanca*, 164–65. See also *Constituciones synodales del Obispado de Barbastro*, 71.

60. AHN, Inq., leg. 231, exp. 9, fol. 80r–v.

61. AHN, Inq., leg. 233, exp. 1 (22 April 1582). "[Mariana] se ynco de rrodillas a sus pies con proposito de confesarse y enpeçandose a persignar el d[ic]ho fray gregorio dixo no quiero confesarse porque soy escrupuloso un poco de la conçiençia porq[ue] me aveys pareçido bien y era yo pariente de v[uest]ro padre y peso me mucho de su muerte y quisiera estar emparte donde pudiera hazer algo por sus cosas." "Y el d[ic]ho fray Gregorio la dixo estad os queda q[ue] ay muy mala gente en este lugar."

62. Ibid. "La dixo si se benia a confesar y ella dixo q[ue] no y este dixo digo lo porque si es confesion no ay que burlar con el Sacramento y ella dixo que no se benia a confesar, y con esto este se empeço a burlar con ella diciendo las palabras de chocarrerias y algunas desonestas. . . . Y ella se levanto de alli y se fue sin confesarla ni tratar de confesion entonzes ni para siempre jamas y todo lo que este la dixo fue burlando chocarreando riyendose con ella."

63. *Constituciones Synodales del Arçobispo de Toledo,* fol. 7r.

64. *Constituciones y estatutos fechos y ordenados,* fol. aiiir. "Ordenamos y mandamos q[ue] . . . todos los confessores q[ue] tuvieren cargo de oyr penitencia sean diligentes en enseñar a sus parrochianos y a los q[ue] confessaren las cosas q[ue] han de saber y creer p[ar]a su salvacion especialmente q[ue] les enseñen como se han de santiguar y signar con la señal de la cruz diziendo selo en romance. porq[ue] mejor lo puedan entender y tomar."

65. *Constituciones sinodales del obispado de Cordova,* fol. 9v.

66. *Constituciones Synodales del Arçobispado de Toledo . . . Año de. 1566,* fol. 77v.

67. *Constituciones Synodales del Arçobispo de Toledo* (1601), fol. 84r.

68. In this context, "General Confession" refers to a specific prayer that acknowledged the penitents' sinfulness and sought intercession. See ibid., fols. 6v–7r, and *Synodo diocesana del Arzobispado de Toledo,* 298.

69. AHN, Inq., legs. 31–48 and 69–75. Nalle, in *God in La Mancha,* and Dedieu, in "'Christianization' in New Castile," reached similar conclusions.

70. AHN, Inq., leg. 47, exp. 12 (p.a.).

71. AHN, Inq., leg. 37, exp. 13 (p.a.).

72. AHN, Inq., leg. 33, exp. 32 (p.a.).

73. AHN, Inq., leg. 72, exp. 26 (p.a.).

74. AHN, Inq., leg. 36, exp. 21 (p.a.).

75. AHN, Inq., leg. 1706, exp. 15, fol. 7r. "Dixo que el confesor no se avia de cuidar si las penitentes eran hermosas o no sino que el no se havia de cuydar de aquellos quentos sino oyr los pecados, y no mas."

76. AHN, Inq., leg. 229, exp. 1, fol. 7r-v. "No se ha confessado mas con el porq[ue] tiene fama q[ue] diria algunas cosas en las confessiones."

77. ADC, Inq., leg. 786, exp. 3374, fol. 1r. "Pedro galindo clerigo presbitero dixo a esta que relata que maria ventera era libertina y vivia mal y riñendole la dicha juliana texera por que se atrebia a decir tal que ella conoçia a la dicha maria ventera i la tenia por doncella recogida y muger de bien, replico el dicho pedro galindo, que el sabia que no era doncella y antes sabia trataba con martin de albendea clerigo presbitero carnalmente a lo qual esta testigo dixo que mirase lo que deçia y a esto respondio que era una boba la dicha juliana texera, que el lo sabia por que los confesaba a ambos. Porque tal dice dixo la susodicha si es cosa de confision, y respondio el dicho pedro galindo, si que no lo digo yo sino a v[uestra] m[erce]d." Similarly, see ADC, Inq., leg. 781, exp. 2393, fols. 1r, 3v–4r.

78. AHN, Inq., libro 731, fol. 224v.

79. See, for example, AHN, Inq., leg. 1825, exp. 2, fol. 3r, and leg. 562, exp. 12, fol. 8r.

80. AHN, Inq., leg. 229, exp. 6, fol. 2r.

81. See, for example, Rojas y Sandoval, *Interrogatorios y preguntas.*

82. On confessing merchants, see Medina, *Breve instrucción,* fol. 219r-v; and Alcozer, *Confesionario breve,* 31.

83. Fernández de Córdoba, *Instrucion de confessores,* 397–99.

84. Morgado García, "Pecado y confesión en la España moderna," 131–38.

85. For example, AHN, Inq., leg. 1825, exp. 8 (2 March 1682) and leg. 232, exp. 17, fol. 28v describe laywomen confessing through the Ten Commandments. On the seven deadly sins, see Escobar y Mendoza, *Examen de confessores,* 214–22.

86. Gavarri, *Noticias singularissimas,* fol. 118r.

87. For example, AHN, Inq., leg. 229, exp. 11, fol. 5r, and leg. 1825, exp. 2, fol. 2r. The general confession provided penitents with a fresh start in contexts where traditional use of sacramental confession had proved ineffective. In 1633, for instance, Jesuits in Hospitalet and Sarrià (Barcelona) claimed that "over eight hundred general confessions were necessary, since people had in previous confessions hidden their sins out of shame for twenty, thirty, forty, fifty and

more years." Kamen, *Phoenix and the Flame,* 383. See Maher, "Confession and Consolation," 184–200.

88. Fernández de Córdoba, *Instrucion de confessores,* 98–100.

89. AHN, Inq., leg. 2042, fol. 5r.

90. Fernández de Córdoba, *Instrucion de confessores,* 100–101.

91. Gavarri, *Instrucciones predicables,* fol. 133v. "Y si luego que el penitente se arrodilla, se dize: Padre mio, vengo a hazer una Confession general, y assi vamos por los Mandamientos; respondale: Con mucho gusto; pero digame hija primero los pecados que ha callado por verguença, y despues hará la Confession general, y assi digame quales son? Porque los mas que dizen esto han callado pecados por verguença, y los traen embueltos con los que ya han confessado."

92. AHN, Inq., libro 731, fols. 322v–323r. "Le dixo que no jurase y continuando a hablar el Reo de pecados de carne le dixo que mirase que todo aquello lo avia de confessar, que el Reo respondio, que quando el avia dicho la confession general ya en ella havia dicho todos sus pecados y reprehendiendole disiendo que era neçessario espeçificar los pecados y quantos eran y las çircunstançias devidas." "Dixo que entendia que el hombre que desia la confession general, conbiena contricion ya havia dicho todos sus pecados."

93. See also the case of Josepe Balaguer of Cerevera (1619), who made a similar argument. AHN, Inq., libro 733, fols. 2r–3r.

94. AHN, Inq., leg. 129, exp. 5, fol. 23v.

95. Melvin, "Fathers as Brothers in Early Modern Catholicism," 20; MHSI, *Litterae quadrimestres,* 6:898.

96. Bilinkoff, *Avila of Saint Teresa,* 63–64. Confessors in Freising made similarly astonishing claims. See Myers "Poor Sinning Folk," 96.

97. AHN, Inq., leg. 232, exp. 9, fol. 20r. María later retracted this testimony and accused Fray Alonso of sexual solicitation.

98. Ibid., fol. 45v.

99. Diaz de Luco, *Aviso de curas,* fol. 81r. "No puede ser esto sin gran peligro de las consciencias de los parrochianos y suyas, pues confessando se de priessa, ni ellos pueden dezir todo lo que les conviene, ni el cura examinar sus consciencias como deve."

100. Teresa of Avila, *Life of Saint Teresa,* 29.

101. Azpilcueta, *Manual de confessores y penitentes,* 38. See also Ledesma, *Primera parte de la Summa,* 277; Corella, *Practica del confesionario,* introduction.

102. Henry E. Huntington Library, Pasadena, California, HM35109, fol. 4v. "Le pregunto (Habiendole Recordacion, de su conffession [sic]) que si auia hecho otros peccados, con algunas mugeres, delante alguna imagen de nuestra Señora, y Respondia auia y a dicho todos sus peccados, y conffesadosse, enteramente y que no tenia mas que dezir."

103. Ledesma, *Primera parte de la Summa,* 276.

104. Gavarri, *Noticias singularissimas,* fol. 39v. "Y mas vale con migo confessarlos que soy pecador como v[uestra] m[erced] que con el demonio en el infierno; y assi digamelos, que con esto se salvará."

105. Azpilcueta, *Manual de confessores y penitentes,* 41. "Y quando le oyere algun graue, o torpe peccado, no se maraville, ni haga señal de abominacion, o espanto, escupiendo, santiguandose, o commouiendose, antes dissimule, como si nada oyesse, hasta al fin dela confession y entonces al imponer de la penitencia, le declarara la grauedad de sus peccados, y quanto son ennormes, segun todos." Likewise, Fernández de Córdoba, *Instrucion de confessores,* 23–26.

106. Fernández, *Tratado de algunos documentos,* fol. 18v. "No conviene a todos una misma exortacion, porque no todos tienen unas mismas costumbres. Y muchas vezes lo que a unos aprovecha a otros daña, y muchas vezes la yerva que a unos animales engorda, a otros mata." Juan de Avila advocated a similar approach. See Coleman, "Moral Formation and Social Control."

107. Gavarri, *Noticias singularissimas,* fols. 39v–40r.

108. AHN, Inq., leg. 1931, exp. 8, fol. 8r. "Podia un lebantarse de los pies del confesor sin decir la verdad y que no peccaba."

109. Ibid., exp. 19, fol. 8v. "Respondio no pecava ni lo tenia por pecado ni entendia confesallo porque hera pecado benial y no mortal."

110. AHN, Inq., leg. 210, exp. 7 (p.a.). "Dixo q[ue] el es ignorante y q[ue] quando se confessava los confessores le preguntavan sy abia tenydo p[ar]te con alg[un]a muger casada o soltera y este respondia la verdad por q[ue] no le preguntava sy abia tenydo p[ar]te con alg[un]a de la mançeba."

111. Fernández de Córdoba, *Instrucion de confessores*, 37.

112. Noydens, *Practica de curas*, 286.

113. Machado de Chávez, *Perfecto confesor*, 2:607.

114. Baptista, at least, believed that native Mexicans could learn to make good confessions, but he blamed their ignorance on the clergy, who demonstrated less concern for the religious education of their charges than had the pagan priests of the pre-Conquest era. See his *Advertencia para confessores*, fols. 12v–13r, 59r.

115. Ibid., fols. 2v–4r, 7r.

116. Noydens, *Practica de curas*, 286–87.

117. Azpilcueta, *Manual de confessores y penitentes*, 40.

118. Tausiet, "Agua en los ojos."

119. Baptista, *Advertencia para confessores*, fols. 1r–2v.

120. López, *Historia legal de la bula llamada In coena Domini*.

121. *Constitvciones Sinodales hechas por . . . Don Gaspar de Quiroga*, fol. 20r–v.

122. Pedro Benito, for instance, went to the Inquisition after a friar refused to absolve him of lewdness. AHN, Inq., leg. 69, exp. 14.

123. O'Malley, *First Jesuits*, 144.

124. AHN, Inq., leg. 71, exp. 8, testimony of Juan de Zuniga (8 August 1634) and Juan García (5 September 1634).

125. Toledo, *Instruccion de sacerdotes*, fol. 179r.

126. Azpilcueta, *Manual de confessores y penitentes*, 32.

127. On medieval public penance, see Mansfield, *Humiliation of Sinners*.

128. AHN, Inq., leg. 31, exp. 25 (26 February 1617). "Ya se avia confesado con un frayle del colegio de atocha y que con un pater noster y una ave maria le avia absuelto."

129. Machado de Chávez disputed the wisdom of this practice but conceded that others, including Azpilcueta and Cajetan, endorsed it. *Perfecto confesor*, 1:376.

130. Ibid., 1:376–77.

131. Coma, *Directorium curatorum*, fol. 171v.

*Chapter 3*

1. Avila, "Memorial segundo para Trento," 129–32.

2. Chacón Jiménez, "Problema de la convivencia," 129.

3. Sánchez Herrero notes in his study of the dioceses of the Kingdom of León in the Middle Ages that he found not a single document referring to frequent confession or communion before the late fifteenth century. *Diocesis del reino de León*, 301, 303–4.

4. See Kamen, *Phoenix and the Flame*, 123–24.

5. Linehan, "Pedro de Albalat," 21–22.

6. Tejada y Ramiro, *Colección de cánones*, 3:564, 579.

7. García y García, *Synodicum hispanum VII*, 365. The 1346 synod reinforced the same statute. See Sánchez Herrero, *Concilios Provinciales y Sínodos Toledanos*, 305.

8. García y García, *Synodicon hispanum VII*, 386.

9. Hilgarth and Silano, "Compilation of the Diocesan Synods," 103.

10. *Constituziones del Arzobispado de Toledo*, fols. 172r–173r.

11. See Martínez Sanz, "Aproximación a la documentación," 172–74; Morena Almárcegui, "Fuente útil," 115–33; Alijo Hidalgo, "El cumplimiento pascual," 307–34; and Casanovas, "Las listas de cumplimiento pascual," 89–94.

12. Conceivably, *libros de matrícula* were widely kept during the early modern period but lost, destroyed, or removed from parish and diocesan archives at some later point. Nevertheless, the preponderance of parishes with books of baptism, confirmation, marriage, and death dating to the sixteenth century but *libros de matrícula* dating only to the eighteenth, nineteenth, or twentieth century is remarkable. To cite only two examples, Santa María in Elche has sixteenth-century books of baptism (1547), confirmation (1583), and marriage (1575), but of confession only from 1734. The Valencian parish of San Miguel de Enguera retains early books of baptism (1556), marriage (1537), and the dead (1744), but books of confession from 1850.

13. Moreno Almárcegui, "Fuente útil," 118–19.

14. Cf. AHN, Clero, libro 19484 (9 March 1593), "Ynventario de todos los vienes de la ygl[esi]a," and libro 19541, fols. 47r–50v.

15. *Constituciones synodales del Arçobispado de Toledo* (1536), fols. 18r, 24v, 37r–39r, 40r.

16. *Constituciones Synodales del Arçobispado de Toledo . . . Año de. 1566*, fols. 50r–v, 67v–68r, 88v. See Dedieu, "'Christianization' in New Castile," 2–8.

17. *Constituciones Synodales del Arçobispado de Toledo . . . Año de. 1566*, fols. 81v–82r.

18. Fernández Collado, *Concilio Provincial Toledano*, 140.

19. Quiroga did not explain his reason for doing so, but he emphasized the need to enforce old laws already on the books rather than implement new ones. *Constitvciones Sinodales hechas por . . . Don Gaspar de Quiroga*, fol. 1v.

20. Those who failed to comply were still to be denounced publicly and proceeded against judicially. See ibid., fol. 10r–v. All of these precepts were reinstituted at the next episcopal synod in 1601 under Bernardo Sandoval y Rojas.

21. Ibid., fols. 2v–6r, 10v. These were included in each of his successors' synodal constitutions.

22. *Constituciones Synodales del Arçobispo de Toledo* (1601), fols. 6v–7r, 83v–84r. Cf. *Constituciones Synodales del Arçobispado de Toledo . . . Año de. 1566*, fol. 77v.

23. *Constituciones Synodales del Arçobispo de Toledo* (1601), fol. 97v.

24. See the regular clergy's response to his policies in BNM, MS VE/34/21, which probably dates to just after March 1620, when the *cardenal infante* was named archbishop of Toledo.

25. *Constitvciones Sinodales del S^mo Señor Don Fernando*, fols. 14r–15r, 34v, 83v. At the 1682 synod, further restrictions were placed on granting licenses for extraparochial confessions. See *Synodo diocesana del Arzobispado de Toledo*, 294.

26. *Constitvciones Sinodales del S^mo Señor Don Fernando*, fol. 85r. In 1682 the *Confesión General* was added to the list. See *Synodo diocesana del Arzobispado de Toledo*, 298.

27. *Constitvciones Sinodales del S^mo Señor Don Fernando*, fols. 83v, 89v.

28. *Constitvciones synodales del Emin^mo y Rever^mo señor Don Baltasar de Moscoso y Sandoval*, 198.

29. *Synodo diocesana del Arzobispado de Toledo*, 78, 294–95.

30. Bilinkoff, *Related Lives*, 10, 13–16.

31. Brown, *Pastor and Laity*, 57–59.

32. Marshall, "Frequent and Daily Communion," 1–31; O'Malley, *First Jesuits*, 136–37.

33. MHSI, *Litterae quadrimestres*, 3:215.

34. Prosperi, "Missionary"; and Dompnier, "Missions et confession au XVIIe siècle."

35. With reference to the Jesuits, see Maryks, "Census of the Books."

36. Kamen, *Spanish Inquisition*, 258; and Rawlings, *Spanish Inquisition*, 13–14.

37. Similar trends hold for the other sacraments. Trials against bigamists, for example, were seen as protecting the sacrament of matrimony. Pérez, *Spanish Inquisition*, 90.

38. Since at least the fourteenth century, some inquisitors and churchmen (among them Nicholás Eymerich, whose *Directorium inquisitorum* had greatly influenced procedure in Spain) had made close connections between blasphemy and heresy. Flynn, "Blasphemy and the Play of Anger," 35–36. On the inquisitorial appropriation of the right to proceed against *proposiciones malsonantes* and blasphemy, see Schwartz, *All Can Be Saved,* 17–26.

39. The figure is based on the *relaciones de causas* in Sierra, *Procesos en la Inquisición de Toledo.*

40. Dedieu, *Administration de la foi,* 305.

41. Jiménez Monteserín, *Introducción a la Inquisición Española,* 206, 400.

42. AHN, Inq., legs. 31–48, 69–75, 199–211.

43. Flynn, "Blasphemy and the Play of Anger," 41–43.

44. AHN, Inq., leg. 72, exp. 30 (p.a.). See also the *primeras audiencias* of legs. 38, exp. 27; 199, exp. 8; and 203, exp. 24.

45. AHN, Inq., leg. 32, exp. 28; leg. 33, exps. 26, 32, 44; leg. 34, exp. 46; leg. 38, exp. 41; leg. 43, exp. 28; leg. 46, exp. 17; leg. 72, exps. 12, 26.

46. This was not always the case. Andrés González, who fell into a dispute with his *cura* over a testament, offers a counterexample. Their disagreement caused the priest to refuse Andrés absolution in 1558. Being barred (unjustly, as he saw it) from the sacraments, Andrés was absolved and received communion in the parish church of a neighboring village. AHN, Inq., leg. 203, exp. 23 (p.a.).

47. AHN, Inq., leg. 207, exp. 20 (p.a.).

48. AHN, Inq., leg. 72, exp. 27 (p.a.).

49. AHN, Inq., leg. 69, exp. 33 (p.a.).

50. Cf. Nalle, *God in La Mancha,* 130–31.

51. AHN, Inq., leg. 71, exp. 29 (p.a.).

52. AHN, Inq., leg. 45, exp. 9 (p.a.).

53. AHN, Inq., leg. 209, exp. 12 (6 November 1568).

54. AHN, Inq., leg. 72, exp. 35 (p.a.).

55. AHN, Inq., leg. 40, exp. 3; leg. 48, exp. 24; leg. 200, exp. 21; leg. 204, exp. 18; leg. 205, exp. 39.

56. AHN, Inq., leg., 48, exp. 24; leg. 70, exp. 17; leg. 75, exps. 12, 28; leg. 206, exp. 6; leg. 208, exp. 17.

57. The province of Guadalajara's population rose 55 percent between 1530 and 1597. During the same period, La Mancha's population skyrocketed by 86 percent. González Martínez, *Población española,* 37.

58. Rawlings, *Church, Religion, and Society,* 70; and González, *Censo de la población,* 391, 394–95.

59. Rawlings, "*Arbitrismo* and the Early Seventeenth-Century Spanish Church," 32–33.

60. Ibid., 31; Rawlings, *Church, Religion, and Society,* 75.

61. Diaz, *Quinze tratados,* 64–65.

62. Bennassar, "Clergé rural en Espagne à l'époque moderne," 115–28.

63. Dedieu, *Administration de la foi,* 54–55; Molinié-Bertrand, "Clergé dans le Royaume de Castille," 5–53; and Ruiz-Martín, "Demografía eclesiástica," esp. 2:684–85.

64. Toledo and Madrid appear far more frequently in the sample of 189 individuals than other locations, none of which is mentioned more than a handful of times. The samples are dispersed as follows: 1530–69: 32 examples; 1570s: 39 examples; 1580s: 42 examples; 1590–1619: 50 examples; 1620–1700: 26 examples.

65. As we have seen, later synods increased the fine to four *reales* (1601) and eventually imposed an additional fine of two *reales* for every week of noncompliance (1658).

66. Dedieu, "'Christianization' in New Castile," 14–18. In more remote areas of Spain, such as Galicia, efforts were less successful. See Poska, *Regulating the People,* 47–48.

67. María Tausiet has examined the phenomena of lay refusals to confess and of excommunication in "Conciencias insumisas" and "Excluded Souls."

68. Gómez, *Perfecto examen,* fol. 1v.

69. Alfonso de Madrigal's *Confesional o Breve forma de confesion* (1544), for example, suggested that a penitent could legitimately confess outside the parish (1) if the *cura* was simple and did not know how to confess; (2) when traveling; (3) when the penitent sinned in another parish; (4) in the case of students away at school; (5) in time of necessity or in danger of death; (6) if the confessant moved or (7) sincerely believed that his *cura* would permit him to confess elsewhere; (8) when at sea; and (9) when confessing to a Dominican or Franciscan—"con estos nos podemos confesar quando quisieremos, no demandando licencia a nuestro cura, porque estos tienen privilegio especial para ello." Sánchez Herrero, *Diócesis del reino de León,* 306.

70. ADC, leg. 783.

71. Ibid., exps. 2936 (9 July 1581) and 2948 (19 July 1581).

72. Kamen, *Phoenix and the Flame,* 381.

73. *Constituciones synodales del Arçobispado de Toledo* (1536), fol. 24v. On confession and the dangers of plague, see Kamen, *Phoenix and the Flame,* 39.

74. *Constituciones Synodales del Arçobispo de Toledo,* fol. 84v.

75. Martínez Gil, *Muerte y sociedad,* 547–48.


*Chapter 4*

1. AHN, Inq., leg. 231, exp. 7, fol. 67r. "Aviendo preguntado ysabel martinez . . . si por la bula de la cruçada podia escoger se confessor que quisiesse este t[estig]o la dixo que si con que fuese de los aprovados por el hordinario."

2. Ulloa, *Hacienda real de Castilla,* 571–95; Marcos Martín, "Tráfico de indulgencias"; Elliott, *Imperial Spain, 1469–1716,* 34, 193; France, *Crusades and the Expansion of Catholic Christendom,* 303; and Braudel, *Mediterranean and the Mediterranean World,* 2:1065, 1084, 1092.

3. See Goñi Gaztambide, *Historia de la bula de la cruzada;* O'Callaghan, *Reconquest and Crusade;* and Housley, *Later Crusades.*

4. See also Torres Gutiérrez, "Implicaciones económicas del miedo religioso." More recent evaluations of late medieval indulgences include Swanson, *Indulgences in Late Medieval England;* Edwards, "'España es diferente'?"; and Housley, "Indulgences for Crusading."

5. Portugal also enjoyed a bull of crusade, and southern Italy received the *cruzada* by virtue of its inclusion in the Spanish Empire. See Caldas, *História da origem e establecimento da bula da cruzada.*

6. Pérez de Lara, *Compendio de las tres gracias,* 21–23.

7. Phillips, "O Magnum Crucis Mysterium," 168–225.

8. O'Callaghan, *Reconquest and Crusade,* 24–38. On crusading ideology in medieval Spain, see Purkis, *Crusading Spirituality in the Holy Land;* and O'Banion, "What Has Jerusalem to Do with Iberia?"

9. See Goñi Gaztambide, "Holy See and the Reconquest."

10. O'Banion, "For the Defense of the Faith?" 177, 182; García Fernández, "De cara a la salvación," 57–58.

11. In 1494 the monastery secured the privilege of printing *cruzada* indulgences, although later in the sixteenth century it shared the privilege with Nuestra Señora del Prado in Valladolid. Gonzálvez Ruiz, "Bulas de la catedral de Toledo," 16, 113–17.

12. Guicciardini, *Opere inedite,* 6:296.

13. Goñi Gaztambide, *Historia de la bula de la cruzada*, 656–68.

14. Brundage, *Medieval Canon Law and the Crusader*, 145–157, 175, 187.

15. In 1581 the Franciscan Francisco de Peruela celebrated Mass in Fuentenovilla while it was under interdict but did so with the doors closed and allowed only those with *bulas de la cruzada* to enter the church. AHN, Inq., leg. 231, exp. 17, fol. 66.

16. See Benito Rodríguez, *Bula de la cruzada en Indias;* and Alonso Acero, *Cisneros y la conquista española.*

17. Elliott, *Imperial Spain, 1469–1716*, 42.

18. Ibid., 53.

19. For more on this theme, see O'Banion, "Crusading State."

20. Quoted in Parker, "Place of Tudor England," 174.

21. Papal brief *Propensa nostra* (12 April 1601), in Guerra, *Pontificiarum constitutionum*, 2:162.

22. Ruano, "Extranjeros a la guerra de Granada," 167–69, 196–204.

23. See O'Banion, "Defense of the Faith?"

24. For more on the *patronato,* see Shiels, *King and Church*, 1–43.

25. Kamen, "Spain," 211.

26. Elliott, *Imperial Spain, 1469–1716*, 9; and see Perrone, *Charles V and the Castilian Assembly.*

27. AGS, PRCS, leg. 20, doc. 54, fol. 325r.

28. See ibid., doc. 56, fols. 329r–330v, and doc. 106, fols. 569r–570v; and Goñi Gaztambide, *Historia de la bula de la cruzada,* 508–16. For a description of *echacuervos'* preaching, see BAV, Urbani latini, 834, fol. 79v. Also pertinent are Pérez de Lara, *Compendio de las tres gracias,* 39–46; and Ulloa, *Hacienda real,* 577–78.

29. AGS, PRCS, leg. 20, doc. 65, fol. 366v.

30. Vives y Cebría, ed., *Usajes y otros derechos de Cataluña*, 1:54–58.

31. Pérez de Lara, *Compendio de las tres gracias,* 16.

32. "Advertimientos sobre la expedición de la Cruzada" [1568?], AGS, PRCS, leg. 20, doc. 106, fol. 367v.

33. Pérez de Lara, *Compendio de las tres gracias,* 64, 234. Throughout the early modern period, commissioners-general retained authority to appoint "appropriate preachers" (*predicatores idoneos*), but these preachers were to have been examined by their superiors or ordinaries. See Marcos Martín, "Tráfico de indulgencias," 229.

34. Danvilla, *Cortes de los antiguos reinos*, 4:369, 408.

35. Danvilla, *Historia crítica y documentada*, 1:273–74.

36. Goñi Gaztambide, *Historia de la bula de la cruzada,* 516. Pedro Guerrero, archbishop of Granada, expressed his strong opposition to this practice: see AGS, PRCS, leg. 20, doc. 98, fols. 511v–512r. See Cereceda, "Episodio de la historia eclesiástica española," 121.

37. Guicciardini, *Opere inedite*, 6:296. "Dipoi è diminuita, perchè nelle città pochi la pigliano; nel contado assai, quasi sforzati per paura."

38. *Novísima recopilación*, 1:294–95.

39. Ulloa, *Hacienda real de Castilla*, 578.

40. *Novísima recopilación*, 1:295–300.

41. *Vida de Lazarillo de Tormes*, 205, 228.

42. AHN, Inq., leg. 213, exp. 14.

43. AHN, Inq., leg. 4972, no. 11, fol. 12v.

44. AHN, Inq., leg. 2042, no. 26, fol. 13r–v. Cf. leg. 2042, no. 25, fol. 3r.

45. AHN, Inq., leg. 1931, exp. 6, fol. 10v. "Se començo a tratar de la bulla de la cruzada, y diziendo uno que traya plenaria remision de todos los peccados, Respondio el d[ic]ho Ju[an] desguevillas, no preguntando sino negando, como puede de ser, que un honbre en la tierra pueda perdonar los peccados?"

46. AHN, Inq., leg. 202, exp. 24, fols. 2r–v, 3v. "Para que queria gastar dos Reales que que le avia de aprovechar y vino a dezir diziendo le este t[estig]o q[ue] lo q[ue] qualquier sumo pontifice otorga en la tierra lo otorga dios en el cielo y es fee catholica y dixo el d[ic]ho fran[cis]co antes q[ue] este t[estig]o se lo dixese que a st p[edr]o le avia dado dios aquella libertad lo qual dixo poniendo dudba en que los demas papas no tenian aquella facultad." "Quando otros años venian p[er]dones y jubileos era por maravilla y que agora vienen muchos y por esto lo dubdo. . . . [C]ada dia pregonavan p[er]dones."

47. Ulloa, *Hacienda real de Castilla*, 581–85.

48. See Dandalet, "Paying for the New St. Peter's."

49. Serrano, "Papa Pío IV y dos embajadores de Felipe II."

50. AGS, PRCS, leg. 20, doc. 65, fol. 365v.

51. Philip II to Juan de Zúñiga, Madrid, 15 December 1568, AGS, PRCS, leg. 20, doc. 66, fol. 369r. "Sera mas facil el suplir y acreçentar despues lo que falta que no litigar sobre todo."

52. Zúñiga to Philip II, Rome, 9 March 1568, AGS, PRCS, leg. 20, doc. 55, fol. 327v. "Yo tengo oppinion, que aunque en las bullas no se conçeda mas que la facultad de comer huebos y leche los dias vedados, y trayendo suspension de las passadas y no alterando la tassa de la limosna que no perderia V. M. ninguna cossa de interes."

53. AGS, PRCS, leg. 20, doc. 64, fol. 364r. See also Serrano, *Correspondencia diplomática*, 3:29–30.

54. Pius remained opposed to alms-based indulgences on principle and condemned episcopal attempts to promulgate them. *Quam plenam*, in Matthieu, *Septimus decretalium constitutionum apostolicarum*, 397–99. See Goñi Gaztambide, *Historia de la bula de la cruzada*, 586. On the episcopal indulgence known as the *bula de hermandad*, see Pérez de Lara, *Compendio de las tres gracias*, 99; and Ulloa, *Hacienda real de Castilla*, 586.

55. AGS, PRCS, leg. 20, docs. 79, 80. It became standard practice from this point to extend the *cruzada* for six years rather than three. Under Pius V three *predicationes* were granted for the sexennial period, one every other year, and the indulgences received during each *predicatio* lasted for two years. In a brief dated 4 February 1573, Gregory XIII amended this system by making *predicationes* and suspensions annual. See Pérez de Lara, *Compendio de las tres gracias*, 5–6.

56. Although Innocent XI refused to grant the *tres gracias* from 1679 to 1681, claiming that they were not being used for their intended purposes, the matter was smoothed over under Innocent XII. Goñi Gaztambide, *Historia de la bula de la cruzada*, 611, 630.

57. Ibid., 520–25.

58. Pedro González de Mendoza, "Lo sucedido en el concilio de Trento desde el año 1561 hasta que se acabó," BAV, Vaticani latini, codex 6963, fol. 32r–v.

59. Philip's conciliar ambassador, the Count de Luna, succeeded in altering the wording of the decree on indulgences to remove the prohibitions against set prices and suspensions, which would have substantially undermined the Spanish *cruzada*. See Paleotto, *Acta Concilii Tridentini*, 644–45; and O'Banion, "Crusading State."

60. Cereceda, "Un proyecto tridentino sobre las indulgenias."

61. *Canons and Decrees of the Council of Trent*, 253.

62. Philip continued to request permission from Pius's successors to pay *cruzada* preachers on commission. See Philip II to Juan de Zúñiga, 4 June 1573, *Colección de documentos inéditos*, 112:146.

63. Serrano, *Correspondencia diplomática*, 3:506–8.

64. AGS, PRCS, leg. 20, doc. 81; Goñi Gaztambide, *Historia de la bula de la cruzada*, 613–29.

65. Marcos Martín, "Tráfico de indulgencias," 229.

66. See Ojeda Nieto, "Población de Castilla y León"; Ojeda Nieto, "Población de España en el siglo XVII"; and Mejía Asensio, "La bula de la Santa Cruzada de 1618."

67. AGS, PRCS, leg. 20, doc. 106, fol. 570v.

68. In the 1620s, owing to the scarcity of silver, the Castilian Cortes petitioned that the alms might be paid in copper coins. The request was granted in 1623 but was quickly rescinded. In 1636, because many were unable to purchase the bull for lack of silver *reales*, allowances were again made briefly for payment in copper. See Domínguez Ortiz, *Política y hacienda de Felipe IV*, 242–43.

69. Pérez de Lara, *Compendio de las tres gracias*, 294.

70. Barrado, "Convento de San Pedro Mártir," 205.

71. AGS, CCC, leg. 451. See Ulloa, *Hacienda real de Castilla*, 591.

72. Goñi Gaztambide, *Historia de la bula de la cruzada*, 508.

73. AGS, CCC, leg. 453.

74. Lea, *History of Auricular Confession*, 3:429.

75. Ibid.

76. Ulloa, *Hacienda real de Castilla*, 592. See also Artola, *Hacienda del antiguo régimen*, 106, 142; Domínguez Ortiz, *Política y hacienda de Felipe IV*, 242; and Torres Gutiérrez, "Implicaciones económicas del miedo religioso."

77. AGS, CCC, legs. 456–58; Ulloa, *Hacienda real de Castilla*, 592.

78. AGS, CCC, leg. 458; Ulloa, *Hacienda real de Castilla*, 593. These figures include the *fábrica*. Kamen, *Philip of Spain*, 146.

79. Kamen, *Spain in the Later Seventeenth Century*, 359.

80. Marcos Martín, "Tráfico de indulgencias," 232–35. The figures that follow are drawn from this article.

81. Pérez de Lara, *Compendio de las tres gracias*, 70, 74–75, 94; Marcos Martín, "Tráfico de indulgencias," 235.

82. See O'Banion, "Defense of the Faith?"

83. AHN, Inq., libro 733, fol. 115v. "Probo q[ue] era tenido y reputado por buen xpiano catholico y que oya missa y daba limosnas y se le hulló la bula de la cruzada."

84. AGS, PRCS, leg. 20, doc. 65, fol. 365v. "La neçesidad de recivir a ministro y confessor çierto y de venir ante el perlado y superior para en lo de los casos reservados, a sido y es ocasion de que muchos se dexen de confessar, y lo que peor es que otros muchos por la misma ocasion, hazen confessiones fictas e imperfectas y resultan grandes inconvinientes y escrupulos para la conçiençia y en estos tiempos importa grandemente façilitar y disponer lo deste s[an]to sacramento y remover todos los obstaculos e impedimentos."

85. Escobar y Mendoza, *Liber theologiae moralis*, 743–44. "Ab homine denique illam habere solent Reges, aliisque Principes, & per Bullam Cruciatae Hispaniae & Siciliae populi."

86. To cite but two examples, see the remarkable number of references to the *bula de la cruzada* in the index of the first volume of Machado de Chávez, *Perfecto confesor*, and the inclusion of Vicente Antonio Ibañez de Aoyz's "Tratado de la bula de la sancta cruzada" in all Spanish printings of Herman Busenbaum's *Medula de la teologia moral*.

87. AHN, Inq., leg. 202, exp. 24 (13 May 1561). "Estaba obligado a confessarse en la perrocha nuestra (no tenia bulla para poder elegir confessor)."

88. AHN, Inq., leg. 230, exp. 5, fol. 8r–v. "Haviendo acavado la d[ic]ha confess[i]on dixo el d[ic]ho fr. Phelippe que no podia absolver a esta hasta ber la bulla de la cruçada."

89. AHN, Inq., leg. 231, exp. 7, fol. 77r. "El dicho ortega dixo no vale nada la bula para hesso sin licencia del Cura."

90. Ibid. "Que nunca a confesado esta t[estig]o con el d[ic]ho hortega xamas."

91. Alcozer, *Confessionario breve*, fol. 39v; Fernández de Córdoba, *Instrucion de confessores*, 88–90; Villalobos, *Manual de confessores*, 100–103.

92. Villaroel, *Gobierno eclesiástico pacifico*, 564–65.

93. Ibid.; Barbosa, *Summa apostolicarum decisionum*, 152; and Machado de Chávez, *Perfecto confesor*, 1:19.

94. Soto, *Commentarium in IV. sententiarum*, 808; Ledesma, *Primera parte de la Summa*, 258; Enríquez, *Questiones practicas de casos morales*, 415–16.

95. Machado de Chávez, *Perfecto confesor*, 1:19. "La Bula no pide mas requisito, sino que esté aprobado el Sacerdote a quien el penitente huviere de elegir por Confessor en virtud della."

96. Pérez de Lara, *Compendio de las tres gracias*, 34.

97. AGS, PRCS, leg. 20, doc. 98, fol. 511r. "Tan fáçil confession y tan frequente y de tantos años con la perpetuidad necesariamente engendra algun menos preçio o menor reverençia y devoçio[n] en los animos de los fieles y con esta una revocaçio[n] g[ene]ral çesaria el escandalo perpetuo de tantas revocaçiones."

*Chapter 5*

1. Diego de Yepes, *Relación de algunas particularidades que pasaron en los vecinos dias de la enfermedad de que murió nuestro Catolico Rey Don Phelipe II*, BNM, 1504 F154, fol. 56v.

2. Siguenza, *Fundación del monasterio de El Escorial*, 186.

3. Weissberger, "'Me atrevo a escribir así,'" 149.

4. Marshall, "Frequent and Daily Communion," 318–36.

5. Gallego de Vera, *Explicacion de la Bula de la Santa Cruzada*, fol. 19v. "Lo cierto es que la floxedad, y demasia de regalo, y pereza, ha introduzido tanto el dezir las Missas en casa, y tarde, que parece que las Iglesias solo son para ge[n]te ordinaria."

6. Quoted in Marshall, "Frequent and Daily Communion," 318–19.

7. Ibid., 329–31.

8. Puente, *Vida del V.P. Baltasar Álvarez*, 107.

9. Casey, *Early Modern Spain*, 232.

10. Casey, *Family and Community*, 242; Henríquez de Jorquera, *Anales de Granada*, 2:886.

11. *Constituciones Synodales, del Arcobispado de Sanctiago*, fol. 20r. See also *Constituciones synodales, del Obispado de Salamanca*, 149.

12. *Constituciones synodales, del Obispado de Salamanca*, 146. See also Pérez de Heredia y Valle, *Concilio provincial de Granada*, 461; *Constitvciones Sinodales hechas por . . . Don Gaspar de Quiroga*, fol. 12v; *Constituciones synodales del Obispado de Barbastro*, 73; *Constituciones synodales del obispado de Coria*, 248; *Constituciones Synodales del Obispado de Avila*, fol. 189r.

13. AHN, Inq., libro 730, fol. 159r.

14. Ibid., fols. 199r–200v.

15. AHN, Inq., libro 732, fol. 65r. "Se sentia pecador empero q[ue] la causa era porq[ue] era muy pobre."

16. *Constitvciones Sinodales hechas por . . . Don Gaspar de Quiroga*, fol. 53r. "Que oyan missa entera los domingos y fiestas de guardar, y que se confiessen cada año como estan obligadas, y muestren cedula de averse confessado al tiempo que lo manda nuestra madre sancta yglesia."

17. *Constitvciones synodales del Emin^{mo} y Rever^{mo} señor Don Baltasar de Moscoso y Sandoval*, 204.

18. AHN, Inq., leg. 40, exp. 3 (p.a.). "No comulgo por bivir esta en una casa donde entraban hombres a tratar con esta no la dieron licencia."

19. See, for example, AHN, Inq., leg. 44, exp. 22 (p.a.).

20. Perry, *Crime and Society*, 119. Perry offers no examples of these strategies in practice.

21. AHN, Inq., leg. 47, exp. 36 (p.a.).

22. AHN, Inq., leg. 74, exp. 6 (p.a.). "Lo qual hiço por hallarse alli en d[ic]ho t[ie]mpo porq[ue] este no tiene lugar fixo, por andar vendiendo de lugar en lugar."

23. *Constituciones Synodales del Obispado de Avila*, fol. 189r.

24. AHN, Inq., leg. 234, exp. 12 (22 September 1558). "Preguntado sy se a confesado esta curre[n]t[e] año. dixo que no. Preguntado que tanto a que no se confeso. dixo que veynte y seys

a[ñ]os. Preguntado sy oye mysa las fiestas y dias de domingos. dixo que sy. Preguntado que por q[ue] no se a confesado tanto tiempo a. dixo por floxedad y bellaqueria."

25. Ibid. (3 September 1558). "Preg[unta]do q[ue] pues este declarante sabia que ~~no~~ [sic] estavan obligados a confesarse cada año que porq[ue] lo a dexado de hazer la tantos años. dixo que por perdido. fue le d[ic]ho que quien le hyzo p[er]der en no confessarse. dixo q[ue] la ventura. fue le d[ic]ho q[ue] si alguien le preguntava q[ue] porq[ue] no se confesava. dixo que no."

26. See Ruiz, *Spanish Society, 1400–1600*, 85–90.

27. Carrera, *Teresa of Avila's Autobiography*, 89–118.

28. After a protracted battle, Carmelite abbesses finally lost this privilege in the seventeenth century. See Haliczer, *Sexuality in the Confessional*, 40.

29. Carrera, *Teresa of Avila's Autobiography*, 144–62.

30. Quoted in Ahlgren, "Negotiated Sanctity," 381.

31. Weber, *Teresa of Avila and the Rhetoric of Femininity*, 58. Similarly, note the case of the abbess of Las Huelgas, who claimed the power to hear confessions. Lehfeldt, *Religious Women in Golden Age Spain*, 5–6.

32. Ruiz, *Spanish Society, 1400–1600*, 88.

33. Panes, *Crónica de la Provincia de San Juan*, 2:668–92; Pons Fuster, "Francisca López." For additional examples, see Bilinkoff, "Confessors, Penitents, and the Construction of Identities," 86–87.

34. Marshall, "Frequent and Daily Communion," 171.

35. For more on this, see Bilinkoff, *Related Lives*, 76–95.

36. Fernández Valencia, *Historia y grandezas del insigne templo*, 144.

37. *Constitutions of the Society of Jesus*, 92–93.

38. Puente, *Vida del V.P. Baltasar Álvarez*, 106.

39. Ibid., 108–9.

40. Lamet, *Yo te absuelvo, Majestad*; Martínez Peñas, *El confesor del rey*; Bierley, *Jesuits and the Thirty Years' War*; and Reinhardt, "Spin-Doctor of Conscience?"

41. Lamet, *Yo te absuelvo, Majestad*, 86–87.

42. Haliczer, *Sexuality in the Confessional*, 30.

43. Bilinkoff, *Avila of Saint Teresa*, 45. See also the example of the Duchess of Medina Sidonia and her confessor at the beginning of the seventeenth century, in Taylor, *Structures of Reform*, 383–84.

44. Coleman, *Creating Christian Granada*, 101–2.

45. Eire, *From Madrid to Purgatory*, 178, 186.

46. Martínez Gil, *Muerte y sociedad*, 547–48; Nalle, *God in La Mancha*, 187–89; Coleman, *Creating Christian Granada*, 100–101.

47. Rawlings, *Church, Religion, and Society*, 89.

48. Caro Baroja, "Religion, World Views, Social Classes," 97.

49. AHN, Inq., leg. 231, exp. 9, fol. 80r–v.

50. E.g., Pérez Heredia y Valle, *Concilio provincial de Granada*, 460; *Constituciones Synodales, del Arcobispado de Sanctiago*, fol. 19v.

51. *Constitvciones Sinodales hechas por . . . Don Gaspar de Quiroga*, fol. 27r. Likewise, *Constituciones synodales del Obispado de Barbastro*, 72.

52. *Constituciones synodales del Arçobispado de Toledo* (1536), fol. 38r–v; *Constituciones Synodales del Obispado de Avila*, fol. 189v.

53. See Martínez de Vega, "Formas de vida del clero regular," 170.

54. Haliczer, *Sexuality in the Confessional*, 30.

55. AHN, Inq., leg. 129, exp. 15 (24 October 1585 and 4 November 1585).

56. AHN, Inq., leg. 232, exp. 11, fols. 155r, 158v, 169r. "Los quales siendo gente sensual y viciossa, an dado en fingir virtud, de muchos años a esta parte, para que tiniendolo, por gente

recogida, y virtuossa se fiasen de ellos, y con esta occassion tenerla, para grangear dinero, y cometer sus delictos, y lo peor, que esto pareze hazerlo por medio de los confessiones." "Con caja de confessar y predicar; y era para juntar muchos dineros, aves, trigo, y zevada, y otras cossas que pedia, para repartir entre pobres, vergonçantes, y se alzava conello." "Le regalo como se puede y debe con los confesores y no con ecseso y siempre con muy sana y buena yntension y sin q[ue] en ello hubiese ofenso."

57. AHN, Ordenes Militares, Santiago, leg. 59374, fol. 1r.

58. AHN, Inq., leg. 232, exp. 9, fol. 20r.–v. "No queria recibir limosna de dineros que le queria dar por hacer algun agradecimiento a su muncho trabaxo. Le dio unas guarniciones de camysa para q[ue] diese algunas sobrinas por q[ue] esta t[estig]o las hacia y no tenia otra cosa que enbialle."

59. Diaz de Luco, *Aviso de curas*, fol. 81r.

60. *Constituciones synodales del Arçobispado de Toledo* (1536), fol. 37v.

61. AHN, Inq., leg. 232, exp. 9, fols. 22v, 48r.

62. Marshall, "Frequent and Daily Communion," 345–46.

63. Molina, *Breve tratado de las virtudes*, fols. 51v–52r.

64. AHN, Inq., leg. 200, exp. 12 (20 June 1625).

65. Weber, *Teresa of Avila and the Rhetoric of Femininity*, 62.

66. Teresa of Avila, *Life of Saint Teresa*, 44.

67. Ranft, "A Key to Counter-Reformation Activism," 17.

68. Teresa de Jesús, *Libro de la vida*, 79.

69. AHN, Inq., leg. 69, exp. 34, fol. 48r. "Y quiriendose ella confessar para rescibir los sacramentos (porque estava mala en la cama) el d[ic]ho lic[encia]do la dixo, y persuadio (dos, o tres vezes) que no dixese la verdad, ni confessarse el peccado, que havia cometido, en haver tenido ordinariamente, todo el t[iem]po que estubo en su casa quenta carnal con el." "Le respondio, pues, como estando como estoy, no he de confessar verdad?"

70. Wiesner, *Women and Gender in Early Modern Europe*, 214.

71. See Elliott, *Proving Woman*, 264–303.

72. Quoted in Elliott, "Dominae or Dominatae?" 67.

73. See Bynum, *Holy Feast and Holy Fast*, 20–23; and Liebowitz, "Virgins in the Service of Christ."

74. Ranft, "Key to Counter-Reformation Women's Activism," 8.

75. Haliczer, *Between Exaltation and Infamy;* Keitt, *Inventing the Sacred;* and Cooper-Rompato, *Gift of Tongues.*

76. Ranft, "Key to Counter-Reformation Women's Activism"; Zarri, "From Prophecy to Discipline"; and Bilinkoff, *Related Lives*, 12–31.

77. Bilinkoff, *Related Lives*, 13–16.

78. Wiesner, *Women and Gender in Early Modern Europe*, 219.

79. Ranft, "Key to Counter-Reformation Women's Activism," 24.

80. See Haliczer, *Sexuality in the Confessional*, 4, 6.

81. Bilinkoff, *Related Lives*, 81–85, and "Confession, Gender, Life-Writing," 176–77.

82. Teresa of Avila, *Spiritual Testimonies*, 35 and 36, in *Collected Works of St. Teresa of Avila*, vol. 1. Gracián records Teresa receiving the vision in his *Peregrinación de Anastasio*, 260–63.

83. Ranft, "Key to Counter-Reformation Women's Activism," 8.

84. Lincoln, *Teresa, a Woman*, 75.

85. Lehfeldt, *Religious Women in Golden Age Spain*, 200. For what follows, see also Perry, *Gender and Disorder*, 68–69.

86. Vives, *Education of a Christian Woman*, 110.

87. Perry, *Gender and Disorder*, 53.

88. Leon, *Perfecta casada*, 94.

89. Dopico Black, *Perfect Wives, Other Women*, 62, 106.

90. Bergmann, "Exclusion of the Feminine," 128.

91. Lehfeldt, *Religious Women in Golden Age Spain*, 2.

92. See Poska, *Women and Authority*, 75–111 and 193–227.

93. Casey, *Family and Community*, 157.

94. Flynn, *Sacred Charity*, 23, 133.

95. MHSI, *Litterae quadrimestres*, 5:205–6; see also Marshall, "Frequent and Daily Communion," 30.

96. Marshall, "Frequent and Daily Communion," 127.

97. Granada, *Sermón contra los escándalos*, 37.

98. MHSI, *Litterae quadrimestres*, 2:513.

99. Quoted in Mir, *Historia interna*, 2:605. On Jesuits being called Theatines, see O'Malley, *First Jesuits*, 68–69.

100. Lamet, *Yo te absuelvo, Majestad*, 83.

101. Alcozer, *Confessionario breve*, fol. 129r. "Estos mismos pecados mortales pueden hazer las labranderas, y costureras."

102. Gavarri, *Noticias singularissimas*, fols. 189r–203v.

103. Fernández de Córdoba, *Instrucion de confessores*, 184–88, 432–35, 532–35.

104. Alvarez, *Escritos espirituales*, 151.

105. Vigil, *Vida de las mujeres*.

106. Casey, *Family and Community*, 126.

107. Quoted in ibid., 138.

108. Ibid.

109. Casey, *Early Modern Spain*, 192.

110. Bilinkoff, *Related Lives*, 101.

111. Poutrin, *Le voile et la plume*, 283–467.

112. Bilinkoff, *Related Lives*, 98–110.

113. Marshall, "Frequent and Daily Communion," 110.

114. Haliczer counts 1,131 cases of sexual solicitation in the confessional between 1560 and 1700, but this figure corresponds to a substantially higher number of solicited women, since multiple confessants often accused a single priest in a trial. *Sexuality in the Confessional*, 211.

115. AHN, Inq., leg 228, exp. 7, fol. 40r.

116. AHN, Inq., leg. 231, exp. 9, fol. 78r. "El quiso llegarla con la mano d[e]r[ech]o a sus pechos della la q[ua]l hizo un movimi[en]to azia tras dando a entender q[ue] no q[ue]ria que la pusiese la mano en parte ninguna."

117. Ibid., fol. 80v. "Por amor de dios a confesar no hagais escandalo que quien os vido a sentar y lebantar tan presto que dira."

118. AHN, Inq., leg. 563, exp. 14, fol. 15r.

119. AHN, Inq., leg. 229, exp. 1, fol. 11v.

120. AHN, Inq., libro 731, fol. 123r.

121. AHN, Inq., leg. 228, exp. 1 (Juan Baptista de Cabrera to Juan de Llano [11 March 1593] and the testimonies of the women [15 March 1593]).

122. AHN, Inq., leg. 231, exp. 3, fol. 44r. "Oya las rrazones que adelante dize, y las mire con ojos de Padre, porque yo soy solo, y ellas son poderosas."

123. AHN, Inq., leg. 232, exp. 9 (10 May 1575). "El dicho clerigo le dixo calla hija no digais eso ni saqueis tal por v[uest]ra boca ni lo digais a nadie." "Siempre a dicho q[ue] por que es ya viejo y no entiende bien las cosas."

124. AHN, Inq., leg. 231, exp. 9, fol. 80v.

125. AHN, Inq., leg. 1825, exp. 2, fol. 3r. "Dixo que porque avia muchas personas que se iban a confesar con otros confesores y hallar a este mas desembarazado y tambien porque le parece que no se acordo esta declarante."

126. Agapita waffled in her account of where the solicitation occurred. On 12 July 1687 she claimed that it was during confession. Ten years later (3 July 1697) she retracted that testimony and said that, while the substance of her testimony was correct, the solicitation had occurred outside the confessional.

127. AHN, Inq., leg. 562, exp. 12, fol. 8r. "Dixo que antes de conocer sus torpes intentos se confesaba con mas libertad con d[ic]ho P[adr]e Verde, pero despues con mas cautela mui raras veces, y solo en aquellas, que su confessor ord[inari]o . . . no la podia confesar por el mucho concurso de penitentes q[ue] tenia, y especialmente en aquella que veia desocupado en su silla al P[adr]e Verde."

128. See, for example, Dutton, *Domestic Assault of Women*, 189–217.

129. See Peristiany, *Honour and Shame;* and Pitt-Rivers, *Fate of Shechem.*

130. Ruiz, *Spanish Society, 1400–1600*, 239.

131. Twinam, *Public Lives, Private Secrets*, 33, and "Negotiation of Honor."

132. Poska, *Women and Authority*, 107. See also Cohen, "Honor and Gender."

133. AHN, Inq., leg 1706, exp. 15, fol. 6v.

134. Casey, *Family and Community*, 139.

135. AHN, Inq., leg. 232, exp. 9 (12 April 1575).

136. Ibid. (13 April 1575).

137. Ibid. "Ella le a respondida que por la honrra de anbos no cunplia hablar en la yglesia tan a menudo que sospecharian mal que si la queria ver que fue se a su casa."

138. Dyer, "Heresy and Dishonor," 133–36.

139. Poska, *Women and Authority*, 83.

140. AHN, Inq., leg. 225, exp. 2, fol. 17v.

141. Ibid., fols. 7v–18r. "No se a de confessar mas que una vez cada año."

142. Ibid., 26 January, 22 February, and 15 March 1631.

143. Ibid., fol. 58v.

144. Ibid., fol. 7v. "El dicho guillermo es lombardo frances de tierra de herejes."

145. Bilinkoff, "Confession, Gender, Life-Writing," 171.


## Chapter 6

1. On *convivencia* as an organizing concept for interfaith coexistence, see Castro, *España en su historia*, 200–209. In *Communities of Violence*, David Nirenberg emphasizes the undercurrent of religious violence.

2. Coleman, *Creating Christian Granada*, 44.

3. Graizbord, *Souls in Dispute*, 4.

4. Henry Kamen has suggested that of about eighty thousand unconverted Jews in 1492, perhaps forty to fifty thousand emigrated, but that many of them later returned and received baptism. See "Mediterranean and the Expulsion of Spanish Jews," 44. James Casey has more recently allowed that "up to 200,000 may have left." *Early Modern Spain*, 223.

5. On Talavera's urging *moriscos* to confess, see AGS, Diversos de Castilla, leg. 8, fol. 114. For general comments on these developments, see Bataillon, *Erasmo y España*, 58; and Harvey, *Muslims in Spain*, 16–17. Mark Myerson argues that the Catholic Monarchs intended to break the treaty made with the Muslims of Granada and force them to convert. *Muslims of Valencia*, 54.

6. Kriegel, "Edicto de expulsión," 144.

7. Harvey, *Muslims in Spain*, 101.

8. Between 1484 and 1530 the Tribunal of Valencia tried 2,354 individuals, more than 90 percent of them for Judaizing. The same crime made up 99 percent of the Toledan Tribunal's trials between 1483 and 1500. Zagorin, *Ways of Lying*, 45, 47.

9. AHN, Inq., leg. 1930, exp. 7, fol. 32r. "Si saben q[ue] el dicho p[edr]o bernal . . . se confesava e comulgava a lo menos una vez en el año como catholico e buen x[risti]ano deve hazer en el tiempo de la cuaresma con su cura o con su licencia con otros cl[er]igos i frayles."

10. Gitlitz, *Secrecy and Deceit*, 154.

11. Rábade Obradó, *Judeoconversos en la corte*, 383. See also Blázquez Miguel, *Huete y su tierra*, 48.

12. Carrete Parrondo, *Tribunal de la Inquisición*, 56. Cf. 72, 90.

13. Gracia Boix, *Autos de fe*, 133, 136.

14. AHN, Inq., leg. 4983, no. 12.9. See also leg. 4972, no. 1.9, fol. 14r, and leg. 4983, no. 12.18.

15. Gracia Boix, *Autos de fe*, 275; see also 268. The Tribunal of Granada charged a few *cristianos viejos* with making similar claims. AHN, Inq., leg. 1953 (25 March 1574 [nos. 41, 42, and 43] and 24 May 1575 [nos. 7 and 10]).

16. For more on the *alumbrados*, see Hamilton, *Heresy and Mysticism*.

17. Ibid., 27–29.

18. Ibid., 46.

19. Longhurst, "Alumbrados, erasmistas y luteranos," 105.

20. Bataillon, *Erasmo y España*, 26.

21. Hamilton, *Heresy and Mysticism*, 46.

22. Hamilton, *Proceso de Rodrigo de Bivar*, 24, 27, 43–44, 46, 53, 59–60, 77, 84, 88–89; Longhurst, "Alumbrados, erasmistas y luteranos," 141, 160–61; and Hamilton, *Heresy and Mysticism*, 28, 46.

23. Hamilton, *Proceso de Rodrigo de Bivar*, 84. On Lerma, see Bietenholz and Deutscher, *Contemporaries of Erasmus*, 325.

24. Hamilton, *Heresy and Mysticism*, 65–75.

25. AHN, libro 735, fol. 142v.

26. See, for example, "Algunos medios que podrian aprovechar para la conversion de los moriscos del Rey[n]o de Val[enci]a," in Boronat, *Moriscos españoles y su expulsión*, 2:493–99.

27. On the crisis of credibility over confession as a result of Protestant inroads in Italy, see de Boer, *Conquest of the Soul*, 13–18.

28. Mariana, *Historia general de España*, 31:202.

29. Baer, *History of the Jews*, 2:424; Beinart, "Records of the Inquisition," 215.

30. Roth, *Conversos, Inquisition, and the Expulsion of the Jews*, xii–xiii.

31. Starr-LeBeau, *In the Shadow of the Virgin*, 38.

32. Ibid., 2. Similarly, see Graizbord, *Souls in Dispute*, 171.

33. Quoted in Coleman, "Moral Formation and Social Control," 23.

34. For some early examples, see Roth, *Conversos, Inquisition, and the Expulsion of the Jews*, 134–39; and Rábade Obradó, *Elite de poder*.

35. Ruiz, *Spanish Society, 1400–1600*, 94.

36. Starr-LeBeau, *In the Shadow of the Virgin*, 38.

37. Casado Alonso, "De la judería a la Grandeza de España."

38. AHN, Inq., leg. 1953 (27 May 1593). "Niegan . . . que no ay potestad en los confesores para perdonar pecados y por esto no confesaban sino cosas lebes para hacer burla de la confesion y por miedo de la inquisicion."

39. The first *gitanos* (from the Castilian *Egicianos*, Egyptians) probably entered Iberia in the 1420s, when gypsy leaders ("dukes" or "counts" of "Egypt" or "Little Egypt") received safe conduct passes to make pilgrimages to Santiago de Compostela. *Gitano* communities eventually

included several waves of immigrants as well as indigenous Iberians who adopted the nomadic lifestyle. Pym, *Gypsies of Early Modern Spain*, 1–19.

40. *Actas de las Cortes de Castilla*, 13:220.

41. Salazar de Mendoza, *Memorial de el hecho de los Gitanos*, fol. 1v.

42. Huélamo, *Libro primero de la vida y milagros del glorioso Confessor Sant Ginés*, 3. "De la libertada vivienda de los sobredichos gitanos, sin tener cura inmediato ni dyocessano alguno (por estar oy aquí, mañana en Francia) se siguen mil inconvenientes. Porque como no está a cargo de alguno el preguntar cómo viven ni se han confesado, ni qué días ayan de guardar, ni quales sean de ayuno, viven como ethnicos y publicanos."

43. Sánchez Ortega, *Inquisición y los gitanos*, 70–71.

44. Pym, *Gypsies of Early Modern Spain*, 105.

45. *Constituciones synodales del obispado de Cuenca*, 58.

46. Huélamo, *Libro primero de la vida y milagros del glorioso Confessor Sant Ginés*, 3.

47. Pym, *Gypsies of Early Modern Spain*, 57; *Actas de las Cortes de Castilla*, 27:68–69.

48. Pym, *Gypsies of Early Modern Spain*, 118–27.

49. Ibid., 128.

50. Tueller, *Good and Faithful Christians*, 24.

51. See Cardaillac, *Moriscos y cristianos*, 21–31; Harvey, *Muslims in Spain*, 112–13; Tueller, *Good and Faithful Christians*, 206.

52. García-Arenal, *Inquisición y moriscos*, 10.

53. Tueller, *Good and Faithful Christians*, 67.

54. Ibid., 26.

55. Gallego y Burín and Gámir Sandoval, *Moriscos del reino de Granada*, 273–74.

56. Coleman, *Creating Christian Granada*, 150, 159. Inquisitorial opposition forced Guerrero to limit this privilege to Jesuits alone.

57. Ibid., 145–76, 178–79.

58. Pérez de Heredia y Valle, *Concilio provincial de Granada*, 459, 463.

59. Ibid., 459. Cf. Coleman, *Creating Christian Granada*, 128, for an earlier example of a similar strategy.

60. Pérez de Heredia y Valle, *Concilio provincial de Granada*, 459.

61. Harvey, *Muslims in Spain*, 210.

62. See, for example, the Conde de Fuentes's request in AHN, Inq., libro 961, fol. 221 (October 1553); Halavais, *Like Wheat to the Miller*, 133–34; and Monter, *Frontiers of Heresy*, 202–7.

63. Monter notes that in Aragon, of the 903 *morisco* prisoners of the Inquisition, only 28 percent were farmers, while nearly 40 percent were artisans. Roughly another hundred were shopkeepers or carters (192). On *morisco* assimilation in Aragon, see Boswell, *Royal Treasure*, 382; Monter, *Frontiers of Heresy*, 211–12; Halavais, *Like Wheat to the Miller*, 31–36; and Vincent, "Les Morisques et les prénoms chrétiens," 59–69.

64. Halavais, *Like Wheat to the Miller*, 82–93.

65. Ibid., 123–26.

66. Monter, *Frontiers of Heresy*, 196–99.

67. Of the 964 individuals tried for practicing Islam in Valencia, 68 percent were farmers, which indicates a proclivity for rural life. Ibid., 192. Most of the 450 *morisco* settlements in Valencia had fewer than 250 inhabitants; in only twenty-four settlements did Old Christian inhabitants also reside. Lapeyre, *Géographie de l'Espagne morisque*, 33–47.

68. Ehlers, *Between Christians and Moriscos*, 98–99.

69. Ibid., 80–105.

70. Rawlings, *Church, Religion, and Society*, 21.

71. Quoted in Casey, *Early Modern Spain*, 225.

72. Gallego y Burín and Gámir Sandoval, *Moriscos del reino de Granada*, 207.

73. Coleman, *Creating Christian Granada*, 179.

74. *Constituciones Synodales Fechas . . . Obispado de Valladolid*, fols. 152v–157r.

75. Ibid., fol. 155r. "Y como quiera que para conseguir nuestro intento, que es ganar las animas desta gente, sea el principal medio y reparo el del Sacramento de la Penitencia."

76. Ibid.

77. Ibid., fol. 155r–v.

78. Ibid., fol. 155v.

79. Tueller, *Good and Faithful Christians*, 32.

80. Coleman, *Creating Christian Granada*, 45; Cabanelas Rodríguez, "Moriscos," 505–6.

81. Harvey, *Muslims in Spain*, 240. See Maryks, *Jesuit Order as a Synagogue*.

82. Alvarez Rodríguez, "Casa de doctrina del Albaicín," 233–46.

83. Coleman, *Creating Christian Granada*, 45–49.

84. El Alaoui, "Ignacio de las Casas."

85. Quoted in Tueller, *Good and Faithful Christians*, 227.

86. "Algunos medios que podrian aprovechar para la conversion de los moriscos del Rey[n]o de Val[enci]a." Quoted in Boronat, *Moriscos españoles y su expulsión*, 2:493–99.

87. Tueller, *Good and Faithful Christians*, 229.

88. Ibid., 171.

89. For Pereda's report, see AGS, Estado, leg. 254 (30 April 1612). See also Tueller, *Good and Faithful Christians*, 180–83; and Flores Arroyuelo, *Ultimos moriscos*, 162–76.

90. Lapeyre, *Geógraphie de l'Espagne morisque*, 272–73.

91. Ibid., 273.

92. Tueller, *Good and Faithful Christians*, 185.

93. Perry, *Handless Maiden*, 87.

94. Resines, *Catecismo del sacromonte*, 163.

95. Quoted in Tueller, *Good and Faithful Christians*, 223.

96. ADC, Inq., leg. 269, no. 5214. "Abia cometido grande número de sacrilegios todas las veçes que abia comulgado y confesado para cumplir con la parrochia cada año, haçiendo las tales confesiones y comuniones por sólo cumplimiento exterior y paliar su apostasía con apariencia de cristiano."

97. "Instrucción dada por el arzobispo de Granada, don Gaspar de Avalos, al canónigo [Don Esteban] Núñez (c. 1530)," in Gallego y Burín and Gámir Sandoval, *Moriscos del reino de Granada*, 230–31.

98. Miguel de Torres to Ignatius Loyola, Lisbon, 4 November 1555, MHSI, *Epistolae mixtae*, 5:81.

99. Rawlings, *Church, Religion, and Society*, 21.

100. On the *plomos*, see Harris, *From Muslim to Christian Granada*.

101. Al-Hajari, *Kitab Nasir al-din 'ala 'l-qawm al-kafirin*, 81.

102. "El memorial que dio el marqués de Mondéjar sobre los nuevamente convertidos del reino de Granada," in Gallego y Burín and Gámir Sandoval, *Moriscos del reino de Granada*, 249.

103. Harvey, *Muslims in Spain*, 295.

104. Rawlings, *Church, Religion, and Society*, 22–23.

105. See Lapeyre, *Geógraphie de l'Espagne morisque*, 163.

106. Pym, *Gypsies of Early Modern Spain*, 130.

## Conclusion

1. AHN, Inq., leg. 2042, no. 1, fol. 7r.

2. *Constituciones Synodales del Arçobispo de Toledo*, fols. 6v–7r.

3. Fernández Terricabras, *Philippe II et le Contre-Réforme*, 183–217.

4. García Oro and Portela Silva, "Felipe II y las iglesias de Castilla," 26–27; Fernández Terricabras, "Primeros momentos de la Contrarreforma," 455–62. On Philip II's role in reforming religious orders, see Pujana, *Reforma de los Trinitarios*, 1–2.

5. Spanish support for confession crystalized after evangelical groups were discovered in Valladolid and Seville in the late 1550s. The result was "near-hysteria among the authorities and a well-orchestrated surge of popular hatred of *luteranos*, this animosity being so strong that when members of the Valladolid cell were arrested they had to be rescued from a furious mob by the Inquisition's own agents." Griffin, *Journey-Men Printers*, 4.

6. See Knipping, *Iconography of the Counter-Reformation*, 2:307–28; Arblaster, "Southern Netherlands Connection," 129; Lottin, *Lille*, 225–35.

7. De Boer, *Conquest of the Soul*, 328.

8. For more on this process in Italy, see Prosperi, *Tribunali della conscienza*, 316–35; Romeo, *Ricerche su confessione dei peccati*, 63–88.

9. Myers, *"Poor Sinning Folk,"* 116–21.

10. Ibid., 96, 188–89; Myers, "From Confession to Reconciliation," 253.

11. Myers, *"Poor Sinning Folk,"* 91–93.

12. Sorkin, *Religious Enlightenment*, 245–48.

13. Forster, *Counter-Reformation in the Villages*, 24–26, 111–12, 215–16.

14. Briggs, *Communities of Belief*, 312–13.

15. Ibid., 323–24.

16. Bergin, *Church, Society, and Religious Change in France*, 29.

17. McManners, *Church and Society*, 2:241–62.

18. Parker, *Faith on the Margins*, 129, 148, 239.

19. Quoted in McClain, *Lest We Be Damned*, 119–20.

20. Walsham, "Beads, Books, and Bare Ruined Choirs," 105.

21. Poska, *Regulating the People*, 159.

22. Pym, *Gypsies of Early Modern Spain*, 130.

23. AHN, Inq., leg. 225, exp. 2, fol. 7v.

24. McManners, *Church and Society*, 2:261.

25. Lee, "Condemnation of Fanaticism," 73–74.

26. McManners, *Church and Society*, 2:258, 260–61.

27. See Bethencourt, *Inquisition*, 364–415.

28. Doblado, "Letters from Spain," 31–32.

29. Dowling, *History of Romanism*, 334.

30. *Roman Catholicism in Spain*, 154, 156.

31. MacKray, *Essay on the Effect of the Reformation*, 196–97.

32. For example, see Foucault, *Abnormal*; Senior, *In the Grip of Minos*; Brooks, *Troubling Confessions*; Delumeau, *Sin and Fear*; Bossy, "Moral Arithmetic" and *Christianity in the West*; and Bernasconi, "Infinite Task of Confession," 75–92.

33. See, for example, Berggren, *Psychology of Confession*, 3–18.

34. Taylor, *Culture of Confession*, 9; see also Foucault, *Abnormal*, 213.

35. Myers, "From Confession to Reconciliation," 256.

36. Ammerman, *Everyday Religion*, 38–40.

37. Amelang, "Exchange Between Italy and Spain," 450. See also Coleman, "Moral Formation and Social Control," for Juan de Avila's long-term impact on moral formation.

38. On Fiesole, see Comerford, "What Did Early Modern Priests Read?" 210. On England, see Holmes, *Elizabethan Casuistry*, 1; and Questier, *Catholicism and Community*, 236.

39. Maryks, "Census of the Books," 467–68.

40. Schumacher, *Readings in Philippine Church History*, 17.

41. See ibid., 80–84; Rafael, "Confession, Conversion, and Reciprocity"; and Brewer, *Shamanism, Catholicism, and Gender Relations,* 63–80.

42. See Gruzinski, "Individualization and Acculturation"; Klor de Alva, "Colonizing Souls"; Vivas Moreno, "Los manuales de confesión para indígenas"; Harrison, "Confesando el pecado en los Andes"; Martínez Ferrer, *Penitencia en la primera evangelización;* and Pardo, *Origins of Mexican Catholicism.*

43. Kamen, *Phoenix and the Flame,* 84–85.

# BIBLIOGRAPHY

*Primary Sources*

ARCHIVES

Archivo Diocesano de Cuenca
    Inquisición, legajos 269, 783, 786.
Archivo General de Simancas
    Consejo y Comisaría de Cruzada, legajos 451, 453, 456–58
    Patronato Real, Concilios y Disciplina Eclésiastica, legajo 22
    Patronato Real, Cruzada y Subsidio, legajos 20–21
Archivo Histórico Nacional de España, Madrid
    Clero, legajos 3581, 4069; libros 3424, 4455, 8418, 8579, 8582, 10545, 11130, 19371, 19425–26,
        19481–85, 19540–41
    Consejos (Cruzada), legajos 7413–14; libro 2605
    Inquisición, legajos 28, 31–48, 69–76, 99–101, 109–10, 128–29, 199–211, 225–33, 321, 503,
        546, 561–64, 1570, 1625, 1679, 1705–6, 1713–14, 1786, 1825–26, 1856, 1930–31, 1951–53,
        2022, 2042, 2135, 2353, 4972, 4983, 5312, 5323; libros 101, 167, 730–35, 934, 940
    Ordenes Militares, legajo 59374
Biblioteca Apostolica Vaticana, Rome
    Ottoboni latini, codex 495
    Urbani latini, codex 834
    Vaticani latini, codex 6963
Biblioteca Nacional de España, Madrid
    Sala de Cervantes, 13033, 3/13076, VE/18/30, VE/34/21, VE/196/102
Henry E. Huntington Library, Pasadena, California
    HM35109
Real Academia de la Historia, Madrid
    Papeles de Jesuitas
Universidad de Granada, Granada
    Biblioteca Hospital Real, cajas A-031–168 (10), A-044–112 (16–1), A-044–124 (27)

PRINTED SOURCES

*Actas de las Cortes de Castilla.* 57 vols. Madrid: Imprenta Nacional, 1861–1956.
Alcozer, Francisco de. *Confesionario breve y provechoso para los penitentes.* Alcalá de Henares, 1619.
Al-Hajari, Ahmad Ibn Qasim. *Kitab Nasir al-din 'ala'l-qawn al-kafirin (The Supporters of Religion
    Against the Infidel).* Edited by P. Sj. van Koningsveld, Q. al-Sammarai, and G. A. Wiegers.
    Madrid: CSIC, 1997.
Alva, Bartolomé de. *Confessionario mayor y menor en lengua mexicana y platicas contra las supres-
    ticiones [sic] de idolatria, que el dia de oy an quedado a los naturales desta Nueva España, è
    instruccion de los Santos Sacramentos &c.* Mexico City, 1634.
Álvarez, Baltasar. *Escritos espirituales.* Edited by Camilo M. Abad and Faustino Boado. Barce-
    lona: Juan Flors, 1961.

Ambrosio de Filguera, Manuel. *Summa de casos de conciencia que se disputan en la teologia moral.* Madrid, 1671.

Arias, Francisco de. "Del buen uso de los Sacramentos." In Arias, *Aprovechamiento espiritual,* 802–63. León, 1603.

———. *Vida del V.Y.R. Fray Simón de Rojas.* 2 vols. Madrid, 1670.

Avila, Juan de. "Memorial Segundo para Trento, 1561." In Camilo M. Abad, "Dos memoriales ineditos para el Concilio de Trento," *Miscelánea Comillas* 3 (1945): 129–32.

Azpilcueta, Martín de. *Manual de confessores y penitentes.* Coimbra, 1552.

Baptista, Joan. *Advertencia para confessores de los naturales.* Mexico City, 1600.

Barbosa, Aghostinho. *Summa apostolicarum decisionum.* Lyon, 1680.

Boronat, Pascual. *Los moriscos españoles y su expulsión: Estudio histórico-crítico.* 2 vols. Valencia: Imprenta de Francisco Vives y Mora, 1901.

Calvin, Jean. *Institutes of the Christian Religion.* Edited by John T. McNeill. Translated by Ford Lewis Battles. 2 vols. Louisville, Ky.: Westminster Press, 1960.

Camargo y Salgado, Hernando de. *Luz clara de la noche obscura: Vnico exemplar de confessores y penitentes.* Madrid, 1650.

*The Canons and Decrees of the Council of Trent.* Edited by Theodore Alois Buckley. London: George Routledge, 1851.

Carrasco, Francisco de. *Manual de escrupulosos y de los confesores que los goviernan.* Valladolid, 1686.

*Colección de documentos inéditos para la historia de España.* 112 vols. Madrid: Rafael Marcos y Viñas, 1842–95.

Coma, Pedro Martír. *Directorium curatorum, o instrucion de cura, util y provechoso para los que tienen cargo de almas.* Burgos, 1577.

*Constituciones promulgadas por . . . D. Fr. Francisco de Roys y Mendoza . . . Opispo de Badajoz . . . En la santa Synodo . . . de 1671 años.* Madrid, 1673.

*Constituciones sinodales del obispado de Cordova por el illustre y muy manifico señor el señor don Alonso manrique . . . de mil y quinientos y. xx. años.* N.p., 1521.

*Constituciones sinodales del Obispado de Orense . . . [de 1619].* Madrid, 1622.

*Constituciones Synodales, del Arcobispado de Sanctiago . . . Año de 1576.* Santiago, 1601.

*Constituciones Synodales del Arçobispo de Toledo. . . .* Toledo, 1601.

*Constituciones synodales del Arçobispado de Toledo: Hechas por el Illustrissimo y Reverendissimo señor don Juan Tavera. . . .* N.p., 1536.

*Constituciones Synodales del Arçobispado de Toledo: Hechas por los Prelados passados. Y agora nueva-mente copiladas, y añadidas, por el muy illustre señor don Gomez Tello Giron . . . Año de. 1566.* Toledo, 1568.

*Constituciones Synodales del Obispado de Avila.* Madrid, 1617.

*Constituciones synodales del Obispado de Barbastro . . . de 1605.* Zaragoza, 1605.

*Constituciones synodales del obispado de Coria . . . de M.DC.VI.* Salamanca, 1608.

*Constituciones synodales del obispado de Cuenca . . . de mil y seyscientos y dos años.* Cuenca, 1603.

*Constituciones synodales, del Obispado de Salamanca, Copiladas hechas y ordenadas, por el Illustrissimo Señor don Geronymo Manrique Obispo de Salamanca . . . de M.D.LXXXIII. Años.* Salamanca, 1584.

*Constituciones Synodales Fechas y promulgadas en la primera Synodo q[ue] se celebró en la Ciudad y Obispado de Valladolid. . . .* Valladolid, 1607.

*Constituciones y estatutos fechos y ordenados por el muy reverendo y muy magnifico señor don Alonso manrrique por la gracia de dios y de la sancta yglesia de Roma obispo de Badajoz.* N.p., [1501].

*The Constitutions of the Society of Jesus.* Translated by George E. Ganss. St. Louis, Mo.: Institute of Jesuit Sources, 1970.

*Constituziones del Arzobispado de Toledo.* N.p., [1498].

*Constitvciones Sinodales del S<sup>mo</sup> Señor Don Fernando Cardenal Infante. . . .* Madrid, 1622.

*Constitvciones Sinodales hechas por . . . Don Gaspar de Quiroga . . . Arçobispo de Toledo. . . .* Madrid, 1583.

*Constitvciones synodales del Emin^{mo} y Rever^{mo} señor Don Baltasar de Moscoso y Sandoval. . . .* Toledo, 1660.

Corella, Jaime de. *Practica del confesionario y explicación de los sesenta y cinco proposiciones condenadas por la santidad de N.S.P. Inocencio XI.* Pamplona, 1686.

Cruz, Felipe de la. *Norte de confesores y penitentes.* Valladolid, 1629.

Danvilla, Manuel, ed. *Cortes de los antiguos reinos de León y de Castilla.* 5 vols. Madrid: M. Rivadeneyra, 1882.

Daza y Berrio, Juan. *Tesoro de confesores y perla de conciencia para todos estados.* Madrid, 1648.

Diaz, Felipe. *Quinze tratados en los quales se contienen muchas y muy excelentes consideraciones para los actos generales que se celebran en la Sancta Iglesia de Dios. . . .* Salamanca, 1602.

Diaz de Luco, Juan Bernal. *Aviso de curas muy provechoso para todos.* Alcalá de Henares, 1543.

Doblado, Leucadio. "Letters from Spain." *New Monthly Magazine and Literary Journal* 2 (1821): 25–35.

Dowling, John. *The History of Romanism: From the Earliest Corruptions of Christianity to the Present Time.* New York: Edward Walker, 1845.

Enríquez, Juan. *Questiones practicas de casos morales.* Valencia, 1657.

Escobar y Mendoza, Antonio. *Examen de confessores y práctica de penitentes.* Pamplona, 1630.

——— . *Liber theologiae moralis.* Lyon, 1644.

Fernández, Alonso. *Tratado de algunos documentos y avisos, a cerca de la prudencia que el confessor deve guardar, en la administracion del sacramento de la confession, con su Penitente.* Cordoba, 1588.

Fernández Collado, Angel, ed. *El Concilio Provincial Toledano de 1582.* Rome: Iglesia Nacional Española, 1995.

Fernández de Córdoba, Antonio. *Instrucion de confessores: como se han de administrar el sacramento de la penitencia y de los penitentes: como se han de examinar segun su estado y oficio y ultimamente como se harà bien una confesion general y otras de veniales.* Valencia, 1633.

Fernández Valencia, Bartolomé. *Historia y grandezas del insigne templo, fundación milagrosa, basílica sagrada y célebre santuario de los santos mártires hermanos San Vicente, Santa Sabina y Santa Cristeta.* Avila: Institución "Gran Duque de Alba," 1992.

Gabino, Carta. *Gvia de confessores, y practica de administrar los sacramentos, en especial el de la penitencia.* Sacer, 1681.

Gallego de Vera, Bernabé. *Explicacion de la Bula de la Santa Cruzada.* Madrid, 1652.

Gallego y Burín, Antonio, and Alfonso Gámir Sandoval. *Los moriscos del reino de Granada según el Sínodo de Guadix de 1554.* Granada: Universidad de Granada, 1968.

García y García, Antonio, ed. *Synodicum hispanum VII: Burgos y Palencia.* Madrid: BAC, 1997.

Gavarri, José. *Instrucciones predicables y morales que deben saber los padres predicadores y confesores.* Malaga, 1674.

——— . *Noticias singularissimas.* Granada, 1676.

Gómez, Alonso. *El perfecto examen de confessores matritense.* Madrid, 1676.

Gracia Boix, Rafael. *Autos de fe y causas de la Inquisición de Córdoba.* Cordoba: Excma. Diputación Provincial, 1983.

Gracián, Jerónimo. *Peregrinación de Anastasio.* Edited by Giovanni Maria Betini. Barcelona: Juan Flors, 1966.

Granada, Luis de. *Guia de pecadores.* Badajoz, 1555.

——— . *Sermón contra los escándalos en las caídas públicas.* Barcelona: Red-Ediciones, 2005.

Guerra, Aloysius. *Pontificiarum constitutionum in Bullariis Magno et Romano contentarum et aliunde desumptarum epitome.* 4 vols. Venice, 1772.

Guicciardini, Francesco. *Opere inedite di Francesco Guicciardini.* Edited by Giuseppe Canestrini. 10 vols. Florence: Bianchi, 1857–67.

Henriquez, Enrique. *Summa theologiæ moralis*. Salamanca, 1593.

Henríquez de Jorquera, Francisco. *Anales de Granada: Descripción del reino y ciudad de Granada, crónica de la reconquista (1482–1492), sucesos de los años 1588 a 1646*. 2 vols. Granada: Facultad de Letras, 1934.

Hilgarth, J. N., and Giulio Silano. "A Compilation of the Diocesan Synods of Barcelona (1354): Critical Edition and Analysis." *Medieval Studies* 46 (1984): 78–157.

Huélamo, Melchor de. *Libro primero de la vida y milagros del glorioso Confessor Sant Ginés de la Xara*. Murcia, 1607.

Jiménez Monteserín, Miguel. *Introduccion a la Inquisición Española*. Madrid: Editora Nacional, 1980.

Ledesma, Pedro de. *Primera parte de la Summa: En la qual va cifrado todo lo que pertenece a los siete sacramentos*. Salamanca, 1621.

León, Luys de. *La perfecta casada*. Edited by Elizabeth Wallace. Chicago: University of Chicago Press, 1903.

Luther, Martin. "Exhortation to All Clergy Assembled at Augsburg, 1530." In *Selected Writings of Martin Luther: 1529–1546*, ed. Theodore G. Tapper, 55–114. Minneapolis: Fortress Press, 1967.

Machado de Chávez, Juan. *Perfecto confesor y cura de almas*. 2 vols. Barcelona, 1641.

MacKray, William. *Essay on the Effect of the Reformation on Civil Society in Europe*. Edinburgh: William Blackwell, 1859.

Madrid, Francisco de. *Bullarium fratrum ordinis minorum Sancti Francisci strictioris observantiae Discalceatorum*. 5 vols. Madrid: Emmanuel Fernández, 1744–49.

Madrigal, Alfonso de. *Confesional o Breve forma de confesion*. Medina del Campo, 1544.

Mariana, Juan de. *Historia general de España*. Biblioteca de Autores Españoles, vols. 30–31. Madrid: Ediciones Altas, 1950.

Matthieu, Pierre, ed. *Septimus decretalium constitutionum apostolicarum*. Frankfurt, 1590.

Medina, Bartolomé de. *Breve instrucción de como se ha de administrar el sacramento de la penitencia*. Salamanca, 1557.

———. *Expositiones in primam secundae divi Thomae*. Salamanca, 1577.

Menses, Felipe de. *Luz del alma christiana*. Valencia, 1554.

Mir, Miguel. *Historia interna documentada de la Compañía de Jesús*. 8 vols. Madrid: Jaime Ratés Martín, 1913.

Molina, Bartolomé de. *Breve tratado de las virtudes de don Iuan Garcia Alvarez de Toledo*. Madrid, 1621.

Monumenta Historica Societatis Iesu (MHSI). *Epistolae mixtae ex variis europae locis ab anno 1537 ad 1556 scriptae*. 5 vols. Madrid: Editorial Ibérica, 1898–1901.

———. *Litterae quadrimestres ex universis praeter Indiam et Brasiliam locis, in quibus aliqui de Societate Jesu versabantur, Romam missae.* . . . 7 vols. Madrid: Augustinus Avrial, 1894–1932.

*Novísima recopilación de las leyes de España*. 6 vols. Madrid, 1805.

Noydens, Benito Remigio. *Practica de curas, y confessores y doctrina para penitentes*. Valencia, 1652.

Paleotto, Gabriele. *Acta Concilii Tridentini anno MDLXII et MDLXIII usque in finem concilii*. Edited by Joseph Mendham. London: Jacobum Duncan, 1842.

Panes, Antonio. *Crónica de la Provincia de San Juan Bautista de religiosos menores de la regular observancia de nuestro padre seráphico S. Francisco*. 2 vols. Valencia, 1665–66.

Pascal, Blaise. *The Provincial Letters of Blaise Pascal*. Translated by Thomas M'Crie. New York: Robert Carter and Brothers, 1850.

Pérez de Heredia y Valle, Ignacio, ed. *El concilio provincial de Granada en 1565: Edicion critica del malogrado concilio del Arzobispo Guerrero*. Rome: Iglesia Nacional Española, 1990.

Pérez de Lara, Alfonso. *Compendio de las tres gracias de la Santa Cruzada, Subsidio, y Escusado*. Madrid, 1610.

Puente, Luis de la. *Vida del V.P. Baltasar Álvarez de la Compañía de Jesús.* Madrid: Apostolado de la Prensa, 1943.

Resines, Luis, ed. *Catecismo del sacromonte y doctrina christiana de Fr. Pedro de Feria: Conversión y evangelización de moriscos e indios.* Madrid: CSIC, 2002.

Rojas y Sandoval, Christoval de. *Interrogatorios y preguntas que mando hazer . . . don Christoual de Rojas y Sandoual, Obispo de Cordoua . . . por los quales examinaran los confessores deste obispado los officiales del que confessaren.* Cordoba, 1567.

*Roman Catholicism in Spain.* Edinburgh: Johnstone and Hunter, 1855.

Román, Gaspar. *Tratado historial y moral del Iubileo de Nuestra Senora de los Angeles de Porciuncula.* Granada, 1668.

Salazar de Mendoza, Pedro. *Memorial de el hecho de los Gitanos, para informar el ánimo de el Rey nuestro señor, de lo mucho que conviene al servicio de Dios, y bien de estos Reynos desterrallos de España.* Madrid, [1618?].

Sánchez Herrero, José, ed. *Concilios Provinciales y Sínodos Toledanos de los siglos XIV y XV: La religiosidad cristiana del clero y pueblo.* Laguna: Universidad de Laguna, 1976.

Serrano, Luciano. *Correspondencia diplomática entre España y la Santa Sede durante el pontificado de Pío V.* 4 vols. Madrid: Imprenta del Pío IX, 1924.

Sierra, Julio, ed. *Procesos en la Inquisición de Toledo (1575–1610): Manuscrito de Halle.* Madrid: Editorial Trotta, 2005.

Soto, Domingo de. *Commentarium in IV. sententiarum.* Salamanca, 1581.

*Synodo diocesana del Arzobispado de Toledo, celebrado por el eminentissimo y reverendissimo señor D. Luis Manuel, del titulo de Santa Sabina presbytero cerdenal Portocarrero Protector de España, Arzobispo de Toledo . . . de M.DC.LXXXII.* Madrid, n.d.

*Synodo diocessana que su Señoria Don Fray Enrique Henriquez, Obispo de Osma . . . celebró . . . de 1607 años.* Madrid, 1609.

Tejada y Ramiro, Juan, ed. *Colección de cánones y de todos los concilios de la Iglesia de España y de América.* 6 vols. Madrid: Pedro Montero, 1859–62.

Teresa de Jesús. *Libro de la vida.* Edited by María de los Hitos Hurtados. Madrid: ALGABA, 2007.

Teresa of Avila. *The Collected Works of St. Teresa of Avila.* Translated by Kieran Kavanaugh and Otilio Rodríguez. 3 vols. Washington, D.C.: Institute of Carmelite Studies, 1976–1980.

———. *The Life of Saint Teresa of Ávila by Herself.* Translated by J. M. Cohen. London: Penguin, 1957.

Toledo, Francisco de. *Instruccion de sacerdotes y suma de casos de conciencia.* Valladolid, 1650.

Valencia, Pedro de. *Obras completas.* Edited by Gaspar Morocho Gayo. 12 vols. to date. León: Universidad de León, 1993–.

Valtanás, Domingo de. *Confessionario muy cumplido.* Seville, 1555.

*La Vida de Lazarillo de Tormes.* Madrid: Espasa-Calpe, 1962.

Villalobos, Enrique de. *Manual de confessores.* Madrid, 1664.

Villaroel, Gaspar de. *Gobierno eclesiástico pacifico.* Madrid, 1656.

Villegas, Bernardino de. *La esposa de Christo instruida con la vida de Santa Lutgarda, virgen, monja de S. Bernardo.* Murcia, 1635.

Vitoria, Francisco de. *Confesionario util.* Salamanca, 1568.

Vives, Juan Luis. *The Education of a Christian Woman.* Edited and translated by Charles Fantazzi. Chicago: University of Chicago Press, 2000.

Vives y Cebría, Pedro Nolasco, ed. *Usajes y otros derechos de Cataluña conocidos en general con el nombre de constituciones.* 5 vols. Barcelona: J. Verdaguer, 1832–38.

SECONDARY SOURCES

Ahlgren, Gillian T. W. "Negotiated Sanctity: Holy Women in Sixteenth-Century Spain." *Church History* 64 (1995): 378–88.

Alejandre, Juan Antonio. *El veneno de Dios: La Inquisición de Sevilla ante el delito de solicitación en confesión.* Madrid: Siglo XXI, 1994.

Alijo Hidalgo, Francisco. "El cumplimiento pascual en la parroquia de San Salvedor de Antequera, año 1517: Mentalidad religiosa y datos para un estudio demografica." *Baetica* 17 (1995): 307–34.

Alonso Acero, Beatriz. *Cisneros y la conquista española del norte de África: Cruzada, política y arte de la guerra.* Madrid: Ministerio de Defensa, 2006.

Alvarez Rodríguez, J. Rosaura. "La casa de doctrina del Albaicín: Labor apostólica de la Compañía de Jesús con los moriscos." *Cuadernos de la Alhambra* 19–20 (1983–84): 233–46.

Amelang, James S. "Exchange Between Italy and Spain: Culture and Religion." In *Spain in Italy: Politics, Society, and Religion, 1500–1700,* ed. Thomas James Dandalet and John A. Marino, 433–56. Leiden: Brill, 2007.

Ammerman, Nancy Tatom. *Everyday Religion: Observing Modern Religious Lives.* Oxford: Oxford University Press, 2007.

Arblaster, Paul. "The Southern Netherlands Connection: Networks of Support and Patronage." In *Catholic Communities in Protestant States: Britain and the Netherlands, c. 1570–1720,* ed. Benjamin Kaplan, Bob Moore, and Henk van Nierop, 122–38. Manchester: Manchester University Press, 2009.

Artola, Miguel. *La hacienda del antiguo régimen.* Madrid: Alianza Editorial, 1982.

Baer, Yitzhak. *A History of the Jews in Christian Spain.* 2 vols. Philadelphia: Jewish Publication Society, 1961.

Barnes, Andrew. "The Social Transformation of the French Parish Clergy, 1500–1800." In *Culture and Identity in Early Modern Europe (1500–1800): Essays in Honor of Natalie Zemon Davis,* ed. Barbara B. Diefendorf and Carla Hesse, 139–57. Ann Arbor: University of Michigan Press, 1993.

Barrado, José. "El convento de San Pedro Mártir: Notas históricas en el V centenario de su imprenta (1483–1983)." *Toletum* 18 (1985): 181–211.

Bataillon, Marcel. *Erasmo y España: Estudios sobre la historia espiritual del siglo XVI.* Mexico City: Fondo de Cultura Económica, 1950.

Beinart, Haim. "The Records of the Inquisition, a Source of Jewish and Converso History." *Proceedings of the American Academy for Jewish Research* 2 (1986): 211–27.

Benito Rodríguez, Juan Antonio. *La bula de la cruzada en Indias.* Madrid: Fundación Universitaria Española, 2002.

Bennassar, Bartolomoé. "Le clergé rural en Espagne à l'époque moderne." In *Le clergé rural dans l'Europe médiévale et moderne:* Actes des XIIIèmes Journées Internationales d'Histoire de l'Abbaye de Flaran, 6–8 septembre 1991, ed. Pierre Bonnassie, 15–28. Toulouse: Presses Universitaires du Mirail, 1991.

Berggren, Erik. *The Psychology of Confession.* Leiden: Brill, 1975.

Bergin, Joseph. *Church, Society, and Religious Change in France, 1580–1730.* New Haven: Yale University Press, 2009.

Bergmann, Emilie. "The Exclusion of the Feminine in the Cultural Discourse of the Golden Age: Juan Luis Vives and Fray Luis de León." In *Religion, Body, and Gender in Early Modern Spain,* ed. Alain Saint Saëns, 124–36. San Francisco: Mellen Research University Press, 1991.

Bernasconi, Robert. "The Infinite Task of Confession: A Contribution to the History of Ethics." *Acta Institutiones Philosophiae et Aestheticae* 6 (1988): 75–92.

Bethencourt, Francisco. *The Inquisition: A Global History, 1478–1834.* Translated by Jean Birrell. Cambridge: Cambridge University Press, 2009.

Bierley, Robert. *The Jesuits and the Thirty Years' War: Kings, Courts, and Confessors.* Cambridge: Cambridge University Press, 2003.

Bietenholz, Peter G., and Thomas B. Deutscher, eds. *Contemporaries of Erasmus: A Biographical Register of the Renaissance and Reformation.* Toronto: University of Toronto Press, 2003.

Bilinkoff, Jodi. *The Avila of Saint Teresa: Religious Reform in a Sixteenth-Century City.* Ithaca: Cornell University Press, 1989.

———. "Confession, Gender, Life-Writing: Some Cases (Mainly) from Spain." In *Penitence in the Age of the Reformations,* ed. Katharine Jackson Lualdi and Anne T. Thayer, 169–83. Aldershot: Ashgate, 2000.

———. "Confessors, Penitents, and the Construction of Identities in Early Modern Avila." In *Culture and Identity in Early Modern Europe (1500–1800): Essays in Honor of Natalie Zemon Davis,* ed. Barbara B. Diefendorf and Carla Hesse, 83–100. Ann Arbor: University of Michigan Press, 1993.

———. *Related Lives: Confessors and Their Female Penitents, 1450–1750.* Ithaca: Cornell University Press, 2005.

Blanco, Arturo. *Historia del confesionario.* Madrid: Rialp, 2000.

Blanco Sánchez, Antonio. "Inventario de Juan de Ayala, gran impresor toledano (1556)." *Boletin de la Real Academia Española* 67 (1987): 207–50.

Blázquez Miguel, Juan. *Huete y su tierra: Un enclave inquisitorial conquense.* Huete: Ayuntamiento, 1987.

Bossy, John. *Christianity in the West, 1400–1700.* Oxford: Oxford University Press, 1987.

———. "Moral Arithmetic: Seven Sins into Ten Commandments." In *Conscience and Casuistry in Early Modern Europe,* ed. Edmund Leites, 214–34. Cambridge: Cambridge University Press, 1988.

———. "The Social History of Confession in the Age of the Reformation." *Transactions of the Royal Historical Society* 25 (1975): 21–38.

Boswell, John. *The Royal Treasure: Muslim Communities Under the Crown of Aragon in the Fourteenth Century.* New Haven: Yale University Press, 1977.

Braudel, Fernand. *The Mediterranean and the Mediterranean World in the Age of Philip II.* 2 vols. London: Harper Collins, 1975–77.

Brewer, Carolyn. *Shamanism, Catholicism, and Gender Relations in Colonial Philippines, 1521–1685.* Aldershot: Ashgate, 2004.

Briggs, Robin. *Communities of Belief: Cultural and Social Tension in Early Modern France.* Oxford: Clarendon Press, 1995.

Brooks, Peter. *Troubling Confessions: Speaking Guilt in Law and Literature.* Chicago: University of Chicago Press, 2001.

Brown, D. Catherine. *Pastor and Laity in the Theology of Jean Gerson.* Cambridge: Cambridge University Press, 1987.

Brundage, James A. *Medieval Canon Law and the Crusader.* Madison: University of Wisconsin Press, 1969.

Burke, Peter. "How to Become a Counter-Reformation Saint." In *Religion and Society in Early Modern Europe, 1500–1800,* ed. Kaspar von Greyerz, 45–55. London: Routledge, 1984.

Bynum, Caroline Walker. *Holy Feast and Holy Fast: The Religious Significance of Food to Medieval Women.* Berkeley and Los Angeles: University of California Press, 1987.

Cabanelas Rodríguez, Darío. "Los moriscos: Vida religiosa y evangelización." In *La incorporación de Granada a la Corona de Castilla,* ed. Miguel Ángel Ladero Quesada, 497–511. Granada: Diputación Provincial, 1993.

Caldas, José. *História da origem e establecimento da bula da cruzada em Portugal: Desda a sua introdução no reino, em 1197 até à data de última reforma do seu estatuto organico en 20 de Setembro de 1851.* Coimbra: Coimbra Editora, 1923.

Carbajo Isla, María F. *La población de la villa de Madrid: Desde finales del siglo XVI hasta mediados del siglo XIX.* Madrid: Siglo XXI, 1987.

Cardaillac, Louis. *Moriscos y cristianos: Un enfrentamiento polémico.* Madrid: Fondo de Cultura Económica, 1979.

Caro Baroja, Julio. "Religion, World Views, Social Classes, and Honor During the Sixteenth and Seventeenth Centuries in Spain." In *Honor and Grace in Anthropology,* ed. Jean G. Peristiany and Julian Pitt-Rivers, 91–102. Cambridge: Cambridge University Press, 1992.

Carrera, Elena. *Teresa of Avila's Autobiography: Authority, Power, and the Self in Mid-Sixteenth-Century Spain.* London: Legenda, 2005.

Carrete Parrondo, Carlos. *El Tribunal de la Inquisición en el Obispado de Soria (1486–1502).* Salamanca: Universidad Pontificia de Salamanca, 1985.

Casado Alonso, Hilario. "De la judería a la grandeza de España: La trayectoria de la familia de mercaderes de los Bernuy, siglos XIV–XIX." *Bulletin of the Society for Spanish and Portuguese Historical Studies* 22 (1997): 9–27.

Casanovas, Miguel Angel. "Las listas de cumplimiento pascual: Una fuente para la demografía histórica." *Memoria Ecclesiae* 9 (1996): 89–94.

Casey, James. *Early Modern Spain: A Social History.* London: Routledge, 1999.

———. *Family and Community in Early Modern Spain: The Citizens of Granada, 1570–1739.* Cambridge: Cambridge University Press, 2007.

Castro, Américo. *España en su historia: Cristianos, moros y judíos.* 2nd ed. Barcelona: Editorial Crítica, 1983.

Cereceda, Feliciano. "Un episodio de la historia eclesiástica española: La conceción de la cruzada el año 1567." *Separata de Miscelánea Comillas* 5 (1946): 109–48.

———. "Un proyecto tridentino sobre las indulgencias." *Estudios Eclesiásticos* 20 (1946): 245–56.

Chacón Jiménez, Francisco. "El problema de la convivencia: Granadinos, mudéjares y cristianos viejos en el Reino de Murcia, 1609–1614." *Mélange de la Casa de Velásquez* 18 (1965): 103–34.

Christian, William A., Jr. *Local Religion in Sixteenth-Century Spain.* Princeton: Princeton University Press, 1981.

Cobianchi, Roberto. "The Practice of Confession and Franciscan Observant Churches: New Architectural Arrangements in Early Renaissance Italy." *Zeitschrift für Kunstgeschichte* 69 (2006): 289–304.

Cohen, Elizabeth S. "Honor and Gender in the Streets of Early Modern Rome." *Journal of Interdisciplinary History* 22 (1992): 597–625.

Coleman, David. *Creating Christian Granada: Society and Religious Culture in an Old-World Frontier City, 1492–1600.* Ithaca: Cornell University Press, 2003.

———. "Moral Formation and Social Control in the Catholic Reformation: The Case of San Juan de Avila." *Sixteenth Century Journal* 26 (1995): 17–30.

Comerford, Kathleen M. "'The care of souls is a very grave burden for [the pastor]': Professionalization of Clergy in Early Modern Florence, Lucca, and Arezzo." *Nederlands Archief voor Kerkgescheidenis* 85 (2005): 349–68.

———. "Clerical Education, Catechesis, and Catholic Confessionalism: Teaching Religion in the Sixteenth and Seventeenth Centuries." In *Early Modern Catholicism: Essays in Honour of John W. O'Malley, S.J.,* ed. Kathleen M. Comerford and Hilmar M. Pabel, 241–64. Toronto: University of Toronto Press, 2001.

———. *Ordaining the Catholic Reformation: Priests and Seminary Pedagogy in Fiesole, 1575–1675.* Florence: Leo S. Olschki, 2001.

———. *Reforming Priests and Parishes: Tuscan Diocesan Seminaries to 1700.* Leiden: Brill, 2006.

———. "What Did Early Modern Priests Read? The Library of the Seminary of Fiesole, 1646–1721." *Libraries and Culture* 34 (1999): 203–21.

Contreras, Jaime. "Aldermen and Judaizers: Crypto-Judaism, Counter-Reformation, and Local Power." In *Culture and Control in Counter-Reformation Spain,* ed. Anne J. Cruz and Mary Elizabeth Perry, 93–123. Minneapolis: University of Minnesota Press, 1992.

Cooper-Rompato, Christine F. *Gift of Tongues: Women's Xenoglossia in the Later Middle Ages.* University Park: Pennsylvania State University Press, 2010.

Daddson, Trevor J. "Literacy and Education in Early Modern Rural Spain: The Case of Villar-rubia de los Ojos." *Bulletin of Spanish Studies* 81 (2004): 1011–38.

Dandalet, Thomas James. "Paying for the New St. Peter's: Contributions to the Construction of the New Basilica from the Spanish Lands, 1506–1620." In *Spain in Italy: Politics, Society, and Religion, 1500–1700,* ed. Thomas James Dandalet and John A. Marino, 181–94. Leiden: Brill, 2007.

Danvilla, Manuel. *Historia crítica y documentada de las comunidades de Castilla.* 5 vols. Madrid: Viuda e Hijos de M. Tello, 1897.

de Boer, Wietse. *The Conquest of the Soul: Confession, Discipline, and Public Order in Counter-Reformation Milan.* Leiden: Brill, 2001.

Dedieu, Jean Pierre. *L'administration de la foi: L'Inquisition de Tolède (XVIe–XVIIIe siècle).* Madrid: Casa de Velázquez, 1989.

———. "The Archives of the Holy Office of Toledo as a Source for Historical Anthropology." In *The Inquisition in Early Modern Europe: Studies on Sources and Methods,* ed. Gustav Henningsen and John Tedeschi, 158–89. De Kalb: Northern Illinois University Press, 1986.

———. "'Christianization' in New Castile: Catechism, Communion, Mass, and Confirmation in the Toledo Archbishopric, 1540–1650." In *Culture and Control in Counter-Reformation Spain,* ed. Anne J. Cruz and Mary Elizabeth Perry, 1–24. Minneapolis: University of Minnesota Press, 1992.

Delumeau, Jean. *La confesión y el perdón: Las dificultades de la confesión, siglos XIII a XVIII.* Barcelona: Altaya, 1990.

———. *Sin and Fear: The Emergence of a Western Guilt Culture, Thirteenth–Eighteenth Centuries.* New York: St. Martin's Press, 1991.

Domínguez Ortiz, Antonio. *Política y hacienda de Felipe IV.* Madrid: Editorial de Derecho Financiero, 1960.

Dompnier, Bernard. "Missions et confession au XVIIe siècle." In *Pratiques de la confession: Des pères du désert à Vatican II,* ed. Groupe de la Bussiere, 201–22. Paris: Cerf, 1983.

Dopico Black, Georgina. *Perfect Wives, Other Women: Adultery and Inquisition in Early Modern Spain.* Durham: Duke University Press, 2001.

Doran, Susan, and Christopher Durstan. *Princes, Pastors, and People: The Church and Religion in England, 1500–1700.* 2nd ed. London: Routledge, 2003.

Dunoyer, Emilio. *L'enchiridion confessariorum de Navarro.* Pamplona: Gurrea, 1957.

Dutton, Donald G. *The Domestic Assault of Women: Psychological and Criminal Justice Perspectives.* Vancouver: University of British Columbia Press, 2001.

Dyer, Abigail. "Heresy and Dishonor: Sexual Crimes Before the Courts of Early Modern Spain." PhD diss., Columbia University, 2000.

Eamon, William. *Science and the Secrets of Nature: Books of Secrets in Medieval and Early Modern Culture.* Princeton: Princeton University Press, 1994.

Edwards, John. "'España es diferente'? Indulgences and the Spiritual Economy in Late Medieval Spain." In *Promissory Notes on the Treasury of Merits: Indulgences in Late Medieval Europe,* ed. Robert N. Swanson, 147–68. Leiden: Brill, 2006.

Ehlers, Benjamin. *Between Christians and Moriscos: Juan de Ribera and Religious Reform in Valencia, 1568–1614.* Baltimore: Johns Hopkins University Press, 2006.

Eire, Carlos M. N. *From Madrid to Purgatory: The Art and Craft of Dying in Sixteenth-Century Spain.* Cambridge: Cambridge University Press, 1995.

El Alaoui, Youssef. "Ignacio de las Casas, jesuita y morisco." *Sharq al-Andalus* 14–15 (1997–98): 317–39.

Elliott, Dyan. "Dominae or Dominatae? Female Mysticism and the Trauma of Textuality." In *Women, Marriage, and Family in Medieval Christendom: Essays in Memory of Michael M. Sheehan, CSB,* ed. Constance M. Rousseau and Joel D. Rosenthal, 44–77. Kalamazoo: Medieval Institute Publications, 1998.

————. *Proving Woman: Female Spirituality and Inquisitorial Culture in the Later Middle Ages.* Princeton: Princeton University Press, 2004.

Elliott, J. H. *Imperial Spain, 1469–1716.* New York: St. Martin's Press, 1963.

Fernández Terricabras, Ignasi. *Felipe II y el clero secular: La aplicación del Concilio de Trento.* Madrid: Sociedad Estatal para la Conmemoración de los Centenarios de Felipe II y Carlos V, 2000.

————. *Philippe II et la Contre-Réforme: L'église espagnole à l'heure du Concile de Trente.* Paris: Publisud, 2001.

————. "Primeros momentos de la Contrarreforma en la monarquía hispánica: Recepción y aplicación del Concilio de Trento por Felipe II (1564–65)." In *Felipe II y su tiempo,* ed. Pereira Iglesias, José Luis, and Jesús Manuel González Beltrán, 455–62. Cadiz: Universidad de Cádiz, 1999.

Firey, Abigail, ed. *A New History of Penance.* Leiden: Brill, 2008.

Flores Arroyuelo, Francisco José. *Los ultimos moriscos (valle de Ricote, 1614).* Murcia: Academia Alfonso X El Sabio, 1989.

Flynn, Maureen. "Blasphemy and the Play of Anger in Sixteenth-Century Spain." *Past and Present* 149 (1995): 29–56.

————. *Sacred Charity: Confraternities and Social Welfare in Spain, 1400–1700.* Ithaca: Cornell University Press, 1989.

Fonseca Montes, Josué. *El clero en Cantabria en la edad moderna: Un estudio sobre la implantación de la Contrarreforma en el norte de España.* Santander: Universidad de Cantabria, 1996.

Forster, Marc R. *Catholic Revival in the Age of the Baroque: Religious Identity in Southwest Germany, 1550–1750.* Cambridge: Cambridge University Press, 2001.

————. *The Counter-Reformation in the Villages: Religion and Reform in the Bishopric of Speyer, 1560–1720.* Ithaca: Cornell University Press, 1992.

Foucault, Michel. *Abnormal: Lectures at the College de France, 1974–1975.* Translated by Graham Burchell. New York: Picador, 2003.

————. *Discipline and Punish: The Birth of the Prison.* Translated by Alan Sheridan. New York: Vintage Books, 1977.

————. *The History of Sexuality.* Vol. 1, *An Introduction.* Translated by Robert Hurley. New York: Random House, 1978.

France, John. *The Crusades and the Expansion of Catholic Christendom, 1000–1714.* London: Routledge, 2005.

García-Arenal, Mercedes. *Inquisición y moriscos: Los procesos del Tribunal de Cuenca.* Madrid: Siglo XXI, 1983.

García Fernández, Máximo. "De cara a la salvación en la España del antiguo régimen: 'La solución de los problemas temporales y de conciencia.'" In *La religiosidad popular y Almería,* ed. José Ruiz Fernández and Valeriano Sánchez Ramos, 41–67. Almería: IEA, 2004.

García Oro, José, and María José Portela Silva. "Felipe II y las iglesias de Castilla a la hora de la reforma Tridentina (preguntas y respuestas sobre la vida religiosa castellana)." *Cuadernos de Historia Moderna* 20 (1998): 9–32.

García-Villoslada, Ricardo. "Felipe II y la Contrarreforma Catolica." In *Historia de la iglesia en España,* ed. Ricardo García-Villoslada, 5 vols., 3.2:3–106. Madrid: BAC, 1980.

Gitlitz, David. *Secrecy and Deceit: The Religion of the Crypto-Jews.* Philadelphia: Jewish Publication Society, 1996.

Goñi Gaztambide, José. *Historia de la bula de cruzada en España.* Vitoria: Editorial del Seminario, 1958.

————. "The Holy See and the Reconquest of the Kingdom of Granada (1479–1492)." In *Spain in the Fifteenth Century, 1369–1516,* ed. Roger Highfield, 354–79. New York: Harper and Row, 1972.

González, Tomás. *Censo de la población de las provincias y partidos de la Corona de Castilla en el siglo xvi*. Madrid: Instituto Nacional de Estadística, 1829.

González Martínez, Rosa María. *La población española (siglos XVI, XVII y XVIII)*. Madrid: Actas, 2002.

González Povillo, Antonio. *El gobierno de los otros: Confesión y control de la conciencia en la España moderna*. Seville: Universidad de Sevilla, 2010.

Gonzálvez Ruiz, Ramón. "Las bulas de la catedral de Toledo y la imprenta incunable castellana." *Toletum* 18 (1985): 11–165.

Graizbord, David L. *Souls in Dispute: Converso Identities in Iberia and the Jewish Diaspora, 1580–1700*. Philadelphia: University of Pennsylvania Press, 2004.

Griffin, Clive. *Journey-Men Printers, Heresy, and the Inquisition in Sixteenth-Century Spain*. Oxford: Oxford University Press, 2005.

Gruzinski, Serge. "Individualization and Acculturation: Confession Among the Nahuas of Mexico from the Sixteenth to the Eighteenth Century." In *Sexuality and Marriage in Colonial Latin America*, ed. Asunción Lavrin, 96–115. Lincoln: University of Nebraska Press, 1989.

Halavais, Mary. *Like Wheat to the Miller: Community, Convivencia, and the Construction of Morisco Identity in Sixteenth-Century Aragon*. New York: Columbia University Press, 2005.

Haliczer, Stephen. *Between Exaltation and Infamy: Female Mystics in the Golden Age of Spain*. Oxford: Oxford University Press, 2002.

———. *Sexuality in the Confessional: A Sacrament Profaned*. Oxford: Oxford University Press, 1996.

Hamilton, Alistair. *Heresy and Mysticism in Sixteenth-Century Spain: The Alumbrados*. Toronto: University of Toronto Press, 1992.

———. *El proceso de Rodrigo de Bivar (1539)*. Madrid: Fundación Universitaria Española, 1979.

Harris, A. Katie. *From Muslim to Christian Granada: Inventing a City's Past in Early Modern Spain*. Baltimore: Johns Hopkins University Press, 2007.

Harrison, Regina. "Confesando el pecado en los Andes: Del siglo xvi hacia nuestros días." *Revista de Crítica Literaria Latinoamericana* 37 (1993): 169–84.

Harvey, L. P. *Muslims in Spain, 1500–1614*. Chicago: University of Chicago Press, 2005.

Hathaway, Janet. "'Music charms the senses . . .': Devotional Music in the *Triunfos festivos* of San Ginés, Madrid, 1656." In *Devotional Music in the Iberian World, 1450–1800*, ed. Tess Knighton and Álvaro Torrente, 219–30. Aldershot: Ashgate, 2007.

Hepworth, Mike, and Bryan S. Turner. *Confession: Studies in Deviance and Religion*. London: Routledge, 1982.

Hoffman, Philip T. *Church and Community in the Diocese of Lyon, 1500–1789*. New Haven: Yale University Press, 1984.

Holmes, Peter J. *Elizabethan Casuistry*. London: Catholic Record Society, 1981.

Homza, LuAnn. *Religious Authority in the Spanish Renaissance*. Baltimore: Johns Hopkins University Press, 2000.

Housley, Norman. *The Avignon Papacy and the Crusades, 1305–1378*. Oxford: Oxford University Press, 1986.

———. "Indulgences for Crusading, 1417–1517." In *Promissory Notes on the Treasury of Merits: Indulgences in Late Medieval Europe*, ed. Robert N. Swanson, 277–307. Leiden: Brill, 2006.

———. *The Later Crusades: From Lyon to Alcazar, 1274–1580*. Oxford: Oxford University Press, 1992.

Hsia, Ronnie Po-Chia. *Social Discipline in the Reformation: Central Europe, 1550–1750*. London: Routledge, 1989.

Kagan, Richard L. *Students and Society in Early Modern Spain*. Baltimore: Johns Hopkins University Press, 1974.

Kallendorf, Hilaire. *Conscience on Stage: The Comedia as Casuistry in Early Modern Spain*. Toronto: University of Toronto Press, 2007.

Kamen, Henry. "The Mediterranean and the Expulsion of Spanish Jews in 1492." *Past and Present* 119 (1988): 30–55.

———. *Philip of Spain.* New Haven: Yale University Press, 1997.

———. *The Phoenix and the Flame: Catalonia and the Counter-Reformation.* New Haven: Yale University Press, 1993.

———. "Spain." In *The Reformation in National Context,* ed. Bob Scribner, Ray Porter, and Mikuláš Teich, 202–14. Cambridge: Cambridge University Press, 1994.

———. *Spain in the Later Seventeenth Century, 1665–1700.* London: Longman, 1980.

———. *The Spanish Inquisition: A Historical Revision.* New Haven: Yale University Press, 1989.

Keitt, Andrew W. *Inventing the Sacred: Imposture, Inquisition, and the Boundaries of the Supernatural in Golden Age Spain.* Leiden: Brill, 2005.

Kidder, Annemarie S. *Making Confession, Hearing Confessions: A History of the Cure of Souls.* Collegeville, Minn.: Liturgical Press, 2010.

Kizenko, Nadieszda. "Written Confession and the Construction of Sacred Narrative." In *Sacred Stories: Religion and Spirituality in Modern Russia,* ed. Mark D. Steinberg and Heather J. Coleman, 93–118. Bloomington: Indiana University Press, 2007.

Klor de Alva, J. Jorge. "Colonizing Souls: The Failure of the Indian Inquisition and the Rise of Penitential Discipline." In *Cultural Encounters: The Impact of the Inquisition in Spain and the New World,* ed. Mary Elizabeth Perry and Anne J. Cruz, 3–22. Berkeley and Los Angeles: University of California Press, 1991.

Knipping, John P. *Iconography of the Counter-Reformation in the Netherlands: Heaven on Earth.* 2 vols. Nieuwkoop: B. de Graaf, 1974.

Kriegel, Maurice. "El edicto de expulsión: Motivos, fines, contexto." In *Judíos, sefarditas, conversos: La expulsión de 1492 y sus consecuencias,* ed. Angel Alcalá, 134–49. Valladolid: Ambito, 1995.

Lamet, Pedro Miguel. *Yo te absuelvo, Majestad: Confesores de reyes y reinas de España.* Madrid: Temas de Hoy, 1991.

Lapeyre, Henri. *Geógraphie de l'Espagne morisque.* Paris: SEVPEN, 1959.

Lea, Henry Charles. *History of Auricular Confession and Indulgences in the Latin Church.* 3 vols. Philadelphia: Lea Brothers, 1896.

Lee, J. Patrick. "The Condemnation of Fanaticism in Voltaire's *Sermon du rabbin Akib.*" In *Rousseau and l'Infâme: Religion, Toleration, and Fanaticism in the Age of Enlightenment,* ed. Oureida Moustefai and John T. Scott, 67–76. Amsterdam: Rodopi, 2009.

Lehfeldt, Elizabeth. *Religious Women in Golden Age Spain: The Permeable Cloister.* Aldershot: Ashgate, 2005.

Leonard, Amy. *Nails in the Wall: Catholic Nuns in Reformation Germany.* Chicago: University of Chicago Press, 2005.

Leonard, Irving A. "Best-Sellers of the Lima Book Trade, 1583." *Hispanic American Historical Review* 22 (1942): 5–33.

———. "On the Mexican Book Trade, 1576." *Hispanic Review* 17 (1949): 18–34.

Liebowitz, Ruth P. "Virgins in the Service of Christ: The Dispute over an Active Apostolate for Women During the Counter-Reformation." In *Women of Spirit: Female Leadership in the Jewish and Christian Traditions,* ed. Rosemary Radford Ruether and Eleanor McLaughlin, 131–52. New York: Simon and Schuster, 1979.

Lincoln, Victoria. *Teresa, a Woman: A Biography of Teresa of Avila.* Albany: SUNY Press, 1984.

Linehan, Peter. "Pedro de Albalat, Arzobispo de Tarragona, y su 'Summa septem sacramentorum.'" *Hispania Sacra* 22 (1969): 9–30.

Longhurst, John E. "Alumbrados, erasmistas y luteranos en el proceso de Juan de Vergara." *Cuadernos de Historia de España* 27 (1958): 99–163.

López, Juan Luis. *Historia legal de la bula llamada In coena Domini.* Madrid: Gabriel Ramírez, 1768.

Lottin, Alain. *Lille: Citadelle de la Contre-Réforme? (1598–1668)*. Pas-de-Calais: Westhoek-Editions, 1984.

Lualdi, Katherine Jackson, and Anne T. Thayer, eds. *Penitence in the Age of the Reformations*. Aldershot: Ashgate, 2000.

Maher, Michael. "Confession and Consolation: The Society of Jesus and Its Promotion of the General Confession." In *Penitence in the Age of the Reformations*, ed. Katherine Jackson Lualdi and Anne T. Thayer, 184–200. Aldershot: Ashgate, 2000.

Mancino, Michelle. *Licentia confitendi: Selezione e controllo dei confessori a Napoli in età moderna*. Rome: Edizioni di Storia e Letteratura, 2000.

Mansfield, Mary C. *The Humiliation of Sinners: Public Penance in Thirteenth-Century France*. Ithaca: Cornell University Press, 1995.

Marcos Martín, Antonio. "Tráfico de indulgencias, guerra contra infieles y finanzas regias: La bula de cruzada durante la primera mitad del siglo XVII." In *Historia y perspectivas de investigación: Estudios en memoria del professor Angel Rodriguez Sanchez*, ed. Miguel Rodríguez Cancho, 227–36. Badajoz: Editoria Regional de Extremadura, 2002.

Marshall, Donald H. "Frequent and Daily Communion in the Catholic Church of Spain in the Sixteenth and Seventeenth Centuries." PhD diss., Harvard University, 1952.

Martínez de Vega, María Elisa. "Formas de vida del clero regular en la época de la Contrarreforma: Los franciscanos descalzos a la luz de la legislación provincial." *Cuadernos de Historia Moderna* 25 (2000): 125–87.

Martínez Ferrer, Luis. *La penitencia en la primera evangelización de México (1523–1585)*. Mexico City: Universidad Pontificia de México, 1998.

Martínez Gil, Fernando. *Muerte y sociedad en la España de los Austrias*. Madrid: Siglo XXI, 1993.

Martínez Peñas, Leandro. *El confesor del rey en el antiguo régimen*. Madrid: Editorial Complutense, 2007.

Martínez Sanz, José Luis. "Una aproximación a la documentación de los Archivos Parroquiales de España." *Hispania: Revista Española de Historia* 46 (1986): 169–93.

Maryks, Robert A. "Census of the Books Written by Jesuits on Sacramental Confession (1554–1650)." *Annali de Storia Moderna e Contemporanea* 10 (2004): 415–519.

———. *The Jesuit Order as a Synagogue of Jews: Jesuits of Jewish Ancestry and Purity-of-Blood Laws in the Early Society of Jesus*. Leiden: Brill, 2009.

———. *Saint Cicero and the Jesuits: The Influence of the Liberal Arts on the Adoption of Moral Probabilism*. Aldershot: Ashgate, 2008.

Mathers, Constance Jones. "Early Spanish Qualms About Loyola and the Society of Jesus." *Historian* 53 (1991): 676–90.

McClain, Lisa. *Lest We Be Damned: Practical Innovation and Lived Experience Among Catholics in Protestant England, 1559–1642*. London: Routledge, 2004.

McManners, John. *Church and Society in Eighteenth-Century France*. 2 vols. Oxford: Clarendon Press, 1998–99.

McNeill, John Thomas. *A History of the Cure of Souls*. New York: Harper, 1951.

Mejía Asensio, Ángel. "La bula de la Santa Cruzada de 1618: Aproximación a la estructura socioeconómica de la ciudad de Guadalajara a principios del siglo XVII." In *Iglesia y religiosidad en España: Historia y archivos; Actas de las V jornadas de Castilla–La Mancha sobre investigación en archivos, Guadalajara, 8–11 de mayo 2001*, 73–108. Guadalajara: Archivo Histórico Provincial de Guadalajara, 2002.

Melvin, James. "Fathers as Brothers in Early Modern Catholicism: Priestly Life in Avila, 1560–1636." PhD diss., University of Pennsylvania, 2009.

Molinié-Bertrand, A. "Le clergé dans le Royaume de Castille à la fin du XVIe siècle: Approche cartographique." *Revue d'Histoire Économique et Sociale* 51 (1973): 5–53.

Monter, William. *Frontiers of Heresy: The Spanish Inquisition from the Basque Lands to Sicily*. Cambridge: Cambridge University Press, 1989.

Moore, R. I. *The Formation of a Persecuting Society: Power and Deviance in Western Europe, 950–1250.* Oxford: Basil Blackwell, 1987.

Morán, Manuel, and José Andrés-Gallego. "The Preacher." In *Baroque Personae,* ed. Rosario Villari, 126–59. Chicago: University of Chicago Press, 1995.

Morena Almárcegui, Antonio. "Una fuente útil para el conocimiento de las estructuras familiares: Las listas de cumplimiento pascual." In *Prácticas de Historia Moderna,* ed. F. Sánchez Marcos, 115–33. Barcelona: PPU, 1990.

Morgado García, Arturo. "Pecado y confesión en la España moderna: Los manuales de confesores." *Trocadero* 8–9 (1996–97): 119–48.

Mullett, Michael. *The Catholic Reformation.* New York: Routledge, 1999.

Myers, W. David. "From Confession to Reconciliation and Back: Sacramental Penance." In *From Trent to Vatican II: Historical and Theological Investigations,* ed. Raymond F. Bulman and Frederick J. Parrella, 241–66. Oxford: Oxford University Press, 2006.

———. *"Poor Sinning Folk": Confession and Conscience in Counter-Reformation Germany.* Ithaca: Cornell University Press, 1996.

Myerson, Mark. *The Muslims of Valencia in the Age of Fernando and Isabel: Between Coexistence and Crusade.* Berkeley and Los Angeles: University of California Press, 1991.

Nalle, Sara T. *God in La Mancha: Religious Reform and the People of Cuenca, 1500–1650.* Baltimore: Johns Hopkins University Press, 1992.

———. "Literacy and Culture in Early Modern Castile." *Past and Present* 125 (1989): 65–96.

Nirenberg, David. *Communities of Violence: Persecution of Minorities in the Middle Ages.* Princeton: Princeton University Press, 1996.

O'Banion, Patrick J. "The Crusading State: The Expedition for the *Cruzada* Indulgence from Trent to Lepanto." *Sixteenth Century Journal* 44 (forthcoming).

———. "For the Defense of the Faith? The Crusading Indulgence in Early Modern Spain." *Archiv für Reformationsgeschichte* 101 (2010): 164–85.

———. "What Has Iberia to Do with Jerusalem? Crusading and the Spanish Route to the Holy Land in the Twelfth Century." *Journal of Medieval History* 34 (2008): 383–95.

O'Callaghan, Joseph F. *Reconquest and Crusade in Medieval Spain.* Philadelphia: University of Pennsylvania Press, 2003.

Oestereich, Gerhard. *Neostoicism and the Early Modern State.* Cambridge: Cambridge University Press, 1982.

Ojeda Nieto, José. "La población de Castilla y León en el siglo XVII: Un intento de la aproximación demográfica a través de la bula de la Santa Cruzada." *Studia Histórica: Historia Moderna* 22 (2000): 109–44.

———. "La población de España en el siglo XVII: Tratamiento demográfico de la bula de la Santa Cruzada." *Revista d'Història Moderna i Contemporània* 2 (2004): 77–113.

O'Malley, John W. *The First Jesuits.* Cambridge: Harvard University Press, 1993.

Ozment, Stephen. *When Fathers Ruled: Family Life in Reformation Europe.* Cambridge: Harvard University Press, 1983.

Pardo, Osvaldo F. *The Origins of Mexican Catholicism: Nahua Rituals and Christian Sacraments in Sixteenth-Century Mexico.* Ann Arbor: University of Michigan Press, 2004.

Parker, Charles H. *Faith on the Margins: Catholic Identity in the Dutch Golden Age.* Cambridge: Harvard University Press, 2008.

———. "Pilgrims' Progress: Narratives of Penitence and Reconciliation in the Dutch Reformed Church." *Journal of Early Modern History* 5 (2001): 222–40.

Parker, Geoffrey. "The Place of Tudor England in the Messianic Vision of Philip II of Spain." *Transactions of the Royal Historical Society* 12 (2002): 167–221.

Pérez, Joseph. *The Spanish Inquisition: A History.* New Haven: Yale University Press, 2004.

Peristiany, Jean G., ed. *Honour and Shame: The Values of Mediterranean Society.* Chicago: University of Chicago Press, 1966.

Perrone, Sean T. *Charles V and the Castilian Assembly of the Clergy*. Leiden: Brill, 2008.

Perry, Mary Elizabeth. *Crime and Society in Early Modern Seville*. Hanover: University Press of New England, 1979.

———. *Gender and Disorder in Early Modern Seville*. Princeton: Princeton University Press, 2005.

———. *The Handless Maiden: Moriscos and the Politics of Religion in Early Modern Spain*. Princeton: Princeton University Press, 2005.

Phillips, C. Matthew. "O Magnum Crucis Mysterium: Devotion to the Cross, Crusading, and the Imitation of Christ in the High Middle Ages, c. 1050–c. 1315." PhD diss., Saint Louis University, 2006.

Pitt-Rivers, Julian. *The Fate of Shechem or the Politics of Sex: Essays in the Anthropology of the Mediterranean*. Cambridge: Cambridge University Press, 1977.

Pons Fuster, Francisco. "Francisca López: Una beata valenciana en la 'Guía espiritual' de Miguel Molinos." *Estudis: Revista de Historia Moderna* 18 (1992): 77–96.

Poska, Allyson M. "Confessionalization and Social Discipline in Early Modern Spain." *Archiv für Reformationsgeschichte* 94 (2003): 308–19.

———. *Regulating the People: The Catholic Reformation in Seventeenth-Century Spain*. Leiden: Brill, 1998.

———. *Women and Authority in Early Modern Spain: The Peasants of Galicia*. Oxford: Oxford University Press, 2005.

Poutrin, Isabelle. *Le voile et la plume: Autobiographie et sainteté féminine dans l'Espagne moderne*. Madrid: Casa de Velázquez, 1995.

Prosperi, Adriano. "El inquisidor como confesor." *Studia Historica: Historia Moderna* 13 (1995): 61–85.

———. "The Missionary." In *Baroque Personae*, ed. Rosario Villari, 160–94. Chicago: University of Chicago Press, 1995.

———. *Tribunali della conscienza: Inquisitori, confessori, missionari*. Turin: Giulio Einaudi, 1996.

Pujana, Juan. *La reforma de los Trinitarios durante el reino de Felipe II*. Salamanca: Secretariado Trinitario, 2006.

Purkis, William J. *Crusading Spirituality in the Holy Land and Iberia, c. 1095–c. 1187*. Woodbridge: Boydell and Brewer, 2008.

Pym, Richard J. *The Gypsies of Early Modern Spain*. New York: Palgrave Macmillan, 2007.

Questier, Michael C. *Catholicism and Community in Early Modern England: Politics, Aristocratic Patronage, and Religion, c. 1550–1640*. Cambridge: Cambridge University Press, 2006.

Rábade Obradó, María del Pilar. *Una elite de poder en la corte de los reyes católicos: Los judeoconversos*. Madrid: Sigilo, 1993.

———. *Los judeoconversos en la corte y en la época de los reyes católicos*. Madrid: Universidad Complutense, 1990.

Rafael, Vicente L. "Confession, Conversion, and Reciprocity in Early Tagalog Colonial Society." *Comparative Studies in Society and History* 29 (1987): 320–39.

Ranft, Patricia. "A Key to Counter-Reformation Women's Activism: The Confessor–Spiritual Director." *Journal of Feminist Studies in Religion* 10 (1994): 7–26.

Rawlings, Helen. "*Arbitrismo* and the Early Seventeenth-Century Spanish Church: The Theory and Practice of Anti-Clericalist Philosophy." In *Rhetoric and Reality in Early Modern Spain*, ed. Richard J. Pym, 25–40. London: Tamesis, 2006.

———. *Church, Religion, and Society in Early Modern Spain*. Basingstoke: Palgrave, 2002.

———. *The Spanish Inquisition*. Malden, Mass.: Blackwell, 2006.

Reinhard, Wolfgang. "Reformation, Counter-Reformation, and the Early Modern State: A Reassessment." *Catholic Historical Review* 75 (1989): 383–404.

Reinhardt, Nicole. "Spin-Doctor of Conscience? The Royal Confessor and the Christian Prince." *Renaissance Studies* 23 (2009): 568–90.

Rittgers, Ronald K. *The Reformation of the Keys: Confession, Conscience, and Authority in Sixteenth-Century Germany.* Cambridge: Harvard University Press, 2004.

Romeo, Giovanni. *Ricerche su confessione dei peccati e Inquisizione nell'Italia del cinquecento.* Naples: Città del Sole, 1997.

Roper, Lyndal. *The Holy Household: Women and Morals in Reformation Augsburg.* Oxford: Oxford University Press, 1991.

Roth, Norman. *Conversos, Inquisition, and the Expulsion of the Jews from Spain.* Madison: University of Wisconsin Press, 1995.

Rouillard, Philippe. *Historia de la penitencia desde los orígenes a nuestros días.* Bilbao: Ediciones Mensajeros, 1999.

Ruano, Eloy Benito. "Extranjeros a la guerra de Granada." In *Gente del siglo XV,* ed. Eloy Benito Ruano, 167–204. Madrid: Real Academia de la Historia, 1998.

Ruiz, Teófilo F. *Spanish Society, 1400–1600.* Harlow: Longman, 2001.

Ruiz-Martín, Felipe. "Demografía eclesiástica." In *Diccionario de historia eclesiástica de España,* ed. Quintín Aldea Vaquero, Tomás Marín Martínez, and José Vives Gatell, 5 vols., 2:682–733. Madrid: CSIC, 1972.

Sánchez Herrero, José. *Las diocesis del reino de León, siglos XIV y XV.* Léon: Centro de Estudios e Investigación "San Isidoro," 1978.

Sánchez Ortega, Helena. *La Inquisición y los gitanos.* Madrid: Taurus, 1988.

Sarrión Mora, Adelina. *Sexualidad y confesión: La solicitación ante el Tribunal del Santo Oficio (siglos XVI–XIX).* Madrid: Alianza, 1994.

Schilling, Heinz. *Religion, Political Culture, and the Emergence of Early Modern Society: Essays in German and Dutch History.* Leiden: Brill, 1992.

Schumacher, John N. *Readings in Philippine Church History.* Quezon City: Ateneo de Manila University, 1979.

Schwartz, Stuart B. *All Can Be Saved: Religions, Tolerance, and Salvation in the Iberian Atlantic World.* New Haven: Yale University Press, 2008.

Scott, James C. *Weapons of the Weak: Everyday Forms of Peasant Resistance.* New Haven: Yale University Press, 1985.

Segura, Florencio. "El teatro en los colegios de los jesuitas." *Mescelánea Comillas* 43 (1985): 299–327.

Senior, Matthew. *In the Grip of Minos: Confessional Discourse in Dante, Corneille, and Racine.* Columbus: Ohio State University Press, 1994.

Sensi, Mario. *Il perdono di Assisi.* Assisi: Edizioni Porziuncula, 2002.

Serrano, Luciano. "El papa Pío IV y dos embajadores de Felipe II." *Cuadernos de Trabajo de la Escuela Española de Arqueología e Historia en Roma* 5 (1924): 1–65.

Shiels, William Eugene. *King and Church: The Rise and Fall of the Patronato Real.* Chicago: Loyola University Press, 1961.

Siguenza, José de. *Fundación del monasterio de El Escorial.* Madrid: Aguilar, 1963.

Simplicio, Oscar di. *Peccato, penitenza, perdono, Siena, 1575–1800: La formazione della coscienza nell'Italia moderna.* Milan: FrancoAngeli Storia, 1994.

Sorkin, David Jan. *The Religious Enlightenment: Protestants, Jews, and Catholics from London to Vienna.* Princeton: Princeton University Press, 2008.

Standaert, Nicolas, and Ad Dudink, eds. *Forgive Us Our Sins: Confession in Late Ming and Early Qing China.* Sankt Augustin: Styler Verlag, 2006.

Starr-LeBeau, Gretchen D. *In the Shadow of the Virgin: Inquisitors, Friars, and Conversos in Guadalupe, Spain.* Princeton: Princeton University Press, 2003.

Stone, M. W. F. "Scrupulosity and Conscience: Probabilism in Early Modern Scholastic Ethics." In *Contexts of Conscience in the Early Modern World, 1500–1700,* ed. Harald Braun and Edward Vallance, 1–16. Basingstoke: Palgrave Macmillan, 2004.

Swanson, Robert N. *Indulgences in Late Medieval England: Passports to Paradise?* Cambridge: Cambridge University Press, 2007.

———, ed. *Promissory Notes on the Treasury of Merits: Indulgences in Late Medieval Europe.* Leiden: Brill, 2006.

Tausiet, María. "Agua en los ojos: El don de lágrimas en la España moderna." In *Accidentes del alma: Las emociones en la edad moderna,* ed. María Tausiet and James S. Amelang, 167–202. Madrid: Abada, 2009.

———. "Conciencias insumisas: La resistencia a la confesión en el arzobispado de Zaragoza a finales del siglo XVI." In *Felipe II y su tiempo,* ed. Pereira Iglesias, José Luis, and Jesús Manuel González Beltrán, 589–96. Cadiz: Universidad de Cádiz, 1999.

———. "Excluded Souls: The Wayward and Excommunicated in Counter-Reformation Spain." *History* 88 (2003): 437–50.

Taylor, Bruce. *Structures of Reform: The Mercedarian Order in the Spanish Golden Age.* Leiden: Brill, 2000.

Taylor, Chloë. *The Culture of Confession from Augustine to Foucault: A Genealogy of the "Confessing Animal."* New York: Routledge, 2009.

Tejero, Eloy. "Los escritos sobre el Doctor Navarro." In *Estudios sobre el Doctor Navarro: En el IV centenario de la muerte de Martín de Azpilcueta,* ed. Institución Principe de Viana, 21–44. Pamplona: Ediciones Universidad de Navarra, 1988.

Tentler, Thomas. *Sin and Confession on the Eve of the Reformation.* Princeton: Princeton University Press, 1977.

———. "The Summa of Confessors as an Instrument of Social Control." In *The Pursuit of Holiness in Late Medieval and Renaissance Religion,* ed. Charles Trinkaus, 103–25. Leiden: Brill, 1974.

Theiner, Johann. *Die Entwicklung der Moraltheologie zur eigenständingen Disziplin.* Regensburg: F. Pustet, 1970.

Thomas, Keith. *Religion and the Decline of Magic: Studies in Popular Beliefs in Sixteenth- and Seventeenth-Century England.* London: Weidenfeld and Nicolson, 1971.

Torres Gutiérrez, Alejandro. "Implicaciones económicas del miedo religioso en dos instituciones del antiguo régimen: La Inquisición y la bula de cruzada." Paper presented at the Simposio Internacional de la Sociedad Española de Ciencias de las Religiones, Tenerife, Spain, February 2000. http://www.ull.es/congresos/conmirel/torres1.html (accessed 9 September 2011).

Tueller, James B. *Good and Faithful Christians: Moriscos and Catholicism in Early Modern Spain.* New Orleans: University Press of the South, 2002.

Twinam, Ann. "The Negotiation of Honor." In *The Faces of Honor: Sex, Shame, and Violence in Colonial Latin America,* ed. Lyman L. Johnson and Sonya Lipsett-Rivera, 68–102. Albuquerque: University of New Mexico Press, 1998.

———. *Public Lives, Private Secrets: Gender, Honor, Sexuality, and Illegitimacy in Colonial South America.* Stanford: Stanford University Press, 1999.

Ulloa, Modesto. *La hacienda real de Castilla en el reinado de Felipe II.* Madrid: Fundación Universitaria Española, 1977.

Vázquez, Isaac. "Las controversias doctrinales postridentinas hasta finales del siglo XVII." In *Historia de la iglesia en España,* ed. R. G. Villoslada, 5 vols., 4:419–77. Madrid: BAC, 1979.

Vigil, Mariló. *La vida de las mujeres en los siglos XVI y XVII.* Madrid: Siglo XXI, 1986.

Vincent, Bernard. "Les morisques et les prénoms chrétiens." In *Les morisques et leur temps,* ed. Louis Cardaillac, 59–69. Paris: Centre National de la Recherche Scientifique, 1983.

Vivas Moreno, Agustín. "Los manuales de confesión para indígenas del siglo XVI: Hacia un nuevo modelo de formación de la conciencia." *Estudios de Historia Moderna* 10–11 (1992–93): 245–59.

Walsham, Alexandra. "Beads, Books, and Bare Ruined Choirs: Transmutations of Catholic Rit-
    ual Life in Protestant England." In *Catholic Communities in Protestant States: Britain and
    the Netherlands, c. 1570–1720,* ed. Benjamin Kaplan, Bob Moore, Henk van Nierop, and
    Judith Pollmann, 103–22. Manchester: Manchester University Press, 2009.
Waugh, Evelyn. *Brideshead Revisited: The Sacred and Profane Memories of Captain Charles Ryder.*
    London: Chapman and Hall, 1960.
Weber, Alison. *Teresa of Avila and the Rhetoric of Femininity.* Princeton: Princeton University
    Press, 1990.
Weissberger, Barbara. "'Me atrevo a escribir así': Confessional Politics in the Letters of Isabel I
    and Hernando de Talavera." In *Women at Work in Spain: From the Middle Ages to Early
    Modern Times,* ed. Marilyn Stone and Carmen Benito Vessels, 147–69. New York: Peter
    Lang, 1998.
Whinnom, Keith. "The Problem of the 'Best-Seller' in Spanish Golden-Age Literature." *Bulletin
    of Hispanic Studies* 57 (1980): 189–98.
Wiesner, Merry E. *Women and Gender in Early Modern Europe.* 2nd ed. Cambridge: Cambridge
    University Press, 2000.
Zagorin, Perez. *Ways of Lying: Dissimulation, Persecution, and Conformity in Early Modern Europe.*
    Cambridge: Harvard University Press, 1990.
Zarri, Gabrilla. "From Prophecy to Discipline, 1450–1650." In *Women and Faith: Catholic Reli-
    gious Life in Italy from Late Antiquity to the Present,* ed. Lucretta Scaraffia and Gabrilla Zarri,
    83–122. Cambridge: Harvard University Press, 1999.